Ghost Towns of Oklahoma

University of Oklahoma Press : Norman and London

Ghost Towns of Oklahoma

By John W. Morris

Oklahoma Geography (Oklahoma City, 1952, 1962)

An Analysis of the Tourist Industry in Selected Counties of the Ozark Area (Washington, D.C., 1953)

Boreal Fringe Areas of Marsh and Swampland: A General Background Study (Washington, D.C., 1954)

World Geography (with Otis Freeman) (New York, 1958, 1965, 1972)

Historical Atlas of Oklahoma (with Charles R. Goins and Edwin C. McReynolds) (Norman, 1965, 1976, 1986)

Methods of Geographic Instruction (editor and coauthor) (Boston, 1968)

The Southwestern United States (New York, 1970)

Geography of Oklahoma (editor and coauthor) (Oklahoma City, 1977)

Cities of Oklahoma (editor and coauthor) (Oklahoma City, 1979)

Oklahoma Boundaries (editor and coauthor) (Oklahoma City, 1980)

Oklahoma Homes: Past and Present (with Charles R. Goins) (Norman, 1980)

History of the Greater Seminole Oil Field (with Louise Welsh) (Oklahoma City, 1981)

Development of Minerals in Oklahoma (editor and coauthor) (Oklahoma City, 1982)

Library of Congress Cataloging-in-Publication Data

Morris, John Wesley, 1907–
   Ghost towns of Oklahoma.

   Bibliography: p. 221
   Includes index.
   1. Cities and towns, Ruined, extinct, etc.—Oklahoma. 2. Oklahoma—History, Local. I. Title.
F694.M8195   976.6   77-22439
ISBN: 0-8061-1420-7 (paperback)

To four colleagues who, in years
past, roamed some of the highways
and byways of Oklahoma with me:

ARTHUR H. DOERR

HARRY E. HOY

RALPH E. OLSON

STEPHEN M. SUTHERLAND

Acknowledgments

During the development of this project many people have made helpful suggestions and valuable criticisms. The author alone, however, is responsible for any misinterpretations or errors that may follow. In the past three years uncounted numbers of individuals have been interviewed, numerous librarians have searched for materials, and any number of persons have willingly lent old photographs. To all of these the author gives his heartfelt thanks.

Special gratitude, however, must be expressed for the assistance of Mrs. Manon Atkins, Research Librarian, Oklahoma Historical Society, for aid in finding photographs and other materials, and to Jack Haley, Assistant Curator, and John Windolph, Western History Collections, University of Oklahoma, for aid in securing both photographs and archive materials. A very special thank you goes to Mrs. Alice Timmons for her interest, suggestions, and encouragement throughout the length of the project.

Jack Wettengel, Executive Director of the Oklahoma Historical Society, granted permission to use the maps of Boggy Depot, Eagletown Area, Ingalls, and Silver City which have appeared in various issues of the *Chronicles of Oklahoma*. The map of Mayes was based on a map printed in the *Stilwell Democrat Journal*, October 10, 1974. Other town maps are based upon the Sanborn map of that town for the year indicated.

Finally, I should like to acknowledge my debt, as always, to the calm assessment of all items by the one who is always my helper, researcher, and critic reader on all projects.

Contents

ix

Ghost Towns of Oklahoma

Introduction

This is a story about some of the ghost towns of Oklahoma—towns that are dead or dying—and some of the individuals who built them. This story is representative of the hundreds of Oklahoma towns which have bloomed, boomed, and busted during the past century and a half. Some have returned to their original dust in the forests and on the plains, their locations often marked only by the sites of nearby cemeteries. In many instances rockpiles, mine dumps, heaps of rubble, and acres of oil-soaked, ruined soil form reminders of their heyday. In other areas, especially western Oklahoma, a few buildings of rock or wood stand sandblasted into sharp relief by the ever-blowing winds. Even so, there are numerous never-say-die, once busy and populated centers still clinging stubbornly to life as their tempo diminishes and they shrivel to old age.

What is a *ghost town*? Frankly, there is no definite answer to this question. Each writer sets his own limits, depending largely upon the type and location of the places in which he is interested. Some ghost-town materials deal largely with places formerly important as mining centers, some study the remains along specific historic trails, others select places noted for their picturesque or sensational backgrounds, and a few confine their work to state boundaries. Many persons make the assumption that a ghost town must be a place in which no one lives. Numerous writers, however, do not consider this point at all. A large number of ghost towns that have been written about still have several hundred inhabitants. Also, the place called a ghost town may never have been a town at all; rather, it may have been a camp, hamlet, or village, or, as in a few instances, the place may be the remains of a city in which several thousand persons have lived.

In this book dealing with the Ghost Towns of Oklahoma the term *ghost town* will be applied to hamlets, villages, towns, and cities (1) that are no longer in existence, all buildings and indications of existence having been either destroyed or covered by water; (2) where the remains of business and/or residential structures still stand but are largely unused; and (3) where, in the case of larger places, the population has decreased at least 80 percent from its maximum. Using these three criteria, Oklahoma has approximately two thousand ghost towns. They all developed for varying lengths of time and then languished or died as agricultural technology changed, transportation lines developed and shifted, mineral resources became depleted, and a new life style, especially in Indian Territory, came into existence. The towns ranged in size from ten or fifteen inhabitants to modern cities with populations in the thousands.

HISTORICAL DEVELOPMENT

The very history of Oklahoma helps account for a large number of ghost towns within the state. Most of the territory that now makes up the state of Oklahoma was added to the United States within the nondefined boundaries of the Louisiana Purchase in 1803. The southern boundary along Red River and the western boundary along the 100th Meridian were determined by the Adams-Onís Treaty with Spain in 1819. The eastern boundary with Arkansas was defined in 1825 and 1828 by treaties between the United States and the Choctaw and Cherokee nations, respectively. The northern boundary, 37° North Latitude, was used to set the limits between the Osage Indians, a Plains Tribe, and the Cherokee Nation. The limits of the area which now forms the Panhandle were not finalized until 1850, when Texas was admitted to the Union as a state.

In the early 1820s, when the federal government started moving the inhabitants of the Five Civilized Nations into the area then designated as Indian Territory, there were no permanent settlements. Much of the future state had not been explored; thus, the location of good townsites was not known. Every state in the Union with the exception of Oklahoma was settled by a gradual infiltration, with a corresponding need for gradual readjustments to changing situations and increasing population. The movement of thousands of persons into the mountainous eastern part of Indian Territory resulted in the selection of and settlement on numerous unsatisfactory sites, many of which were soon abandoned. Since most of the members of the Five Civilized Tribes were agriculturalists, most settlements (towns) grew very slowly. The inhabitants of a settlement were usually limited to a blacksmith and a grocer. A typical example is Scalesville in the Choctaw Nation. The village started with a general merchandise store in a log cabin built alongside the Texas Trail. There was a blacksmith nearby and a house or two within a hundred yards of the store. Since mail was often left at the store, even though it was not an official post office, this tiny community was given the title and prestige of a town.

Although progress throughout the Five Nations was slow, the fifteen-year period preceding the Civil War was one of quiet and peaceful development and considerable advancement. The Civil War had a devastating effect on Indian Territory. All of the Five Nations officially joined the Confederacy, but large numbers of Cherokees, Creeks, and Seminoles, as well as smaller groups of Choctaws and Chickasaws, remained loyal to the Union. As a result, armies led by both Indians and whites roamed back and forth across the territory, causing much destruction and suffering. Villages and towns were looted and burned, and many were never rebuilt. Following the war, each of the Five Nations was penalized by being forced to relinquish claims to their western lands. These western lands were then set apart to be used as reservations for various Plains Tribes.

The first reservation carved out of the ceded lands was for the Sac and Fox in 1867. During the following twelve years large reservations were assigned to the Cheyennes and Arapahoes, the Kiowas, Comanches and Apaches, the Wichitas and Caddoes, and smaller reservations to other groups. There remained, however, such large areas as the Unassigned Lands and the Cherokee Outlet, on which no tribes had been settled. The number of Indians per square mile on each reservation was small. Only a few of the Indians became farmers, and most of the reservation land was leased to cattlemen for grazing. The Cherokee Nation, which controlled the Cherokee Outlet, except that small part controlled by the army at Fort Supply, had leased the entire area for grazing.

Many people throughout the United States soon demanded that the Indians living on the reservations be allotted farms and that the remaining land, along with the Unassigned Lands and the Cherokee Outlet, be opened to settlement. Thus, the Indians living on these western reservations were allocated certain lands of their choice, and the remaining lands were opened for settlement by a series of "runs," lottery, and sealed bids. As a result of such events there was, within a day's time in a specific area, an increase in population from nothing to many thousand. The situation entailed a necessity for rapid readjustments to rapidly changing situations. Towns were formed and populated over night. Tents and makeshift homes were erected and business put into operation within a few hours. In most areas there had been no planning for townsites. Often towns were formed within a mile or so of each other. In some instances the town founder learned the hard way that the site selected was destined to be a sparsely populated area, or that topography or streams hindered accessibility, or that after a brief period the settlers themselves became dissatisfied and moved on to "greener pastures." Many such towns lasted for a few months; others became ghosts only after a long and bitter struggle.

It must be noted that the Five Nations, Old Greer County, and the Panhandle were not involved in these openings. After the Civil War, town building in the Five Nations followed the more normal patterns of the eastern states. During this period Greer County was being settled slowly by those who claimed that area was a part of Texas and thereby public domain. The Panhandle, known as No Man's Land or the Public Land Strip, was not a part of any state or territory, nor was it under the jurisdiction of any law, even federal. Into this narrow strip of land came the flotsam and jetsam of humanity, men and women with unsavory records, evading the law and restless under its restraints, with no thought of helping to locate a permanent home. When the act of Congress creating Oklahoma Territory was passed on May 2, 1890, No Man's Land was included by the clause, "That portion of the United States known as the Public Land Strip."

NO MAN'S LAND

Added to Oklahoma Territory by Organic Act May 2, 1890

CHEROKEE OUTLET

Opened by Run
September 16, 1893

CHEROKEE NATION

CHEROKEE NATION

OSAGE
RESERVATION

Lands by Allotment
1906

KAW 6

5

2

5

PAWNEE 3

CREEK NATION

IOWA
1

SAC
AND
FOX
1

KICKAPOO
4

SEMINOLE NATION

SHAWNEE

AND

POTTAWATOMIE 1

CHOCTAW NATION

CHICKASAW NATION

UNASSIGNED LANDS

Opened by Run
April 22, 1889

CHEYENNE AND ARAPAHO

Opened by Run
April 19, 1892

WICHITA
AND CADDO
Opened by Lottery
June 9 to
August 6, 1901

GREER
COUNTY

Attached to Oklahoma
following decision of
United States Supreme
Court March 16, 1896

COMANCHE KIOWA
AND APACHE

Opened by Lottery
July 9 to August 6, 1901

BIG PASTURE
Opened by
Sealed Bids
December 1906

1. Opened by Run, September 22, 1891
2. Tonkawa Lands by Allotment, 1891
3. Pawnee Lands by Allotment, 1892
4. Opened by Run, May 23, 1895
5. Ponca and Oto-Missouri Lands by Allotment, 1904
6. Kaw Lands by Allotment, 1906

0   10   20   30   40   50

Land Openings

© 1986 by the University of Oklahoma Press

CAUSES OF GHOST TOWNS

The last of the great land openings was held in December, 1906. Eleven months later, on November 16, 1907, Oklahoma Territory and Indian Territory (the land occupied by the Five Nations) were joined to form the state of Oklahoma. The formation of the state neither stopped new town development nor prevented further town decay. The chief causes for both development and decay, however, changed from primarily historical chance in location to chiefly political and economic factors. It must be remembered that most ghost towns are not the result of a single factor but the product of a combination of factors.

POLITICAL FACTORS

County seats. Soon after the various reservations and unassigned lands were opened to settlement, it was necessary to establish a system of counties for government purposes. With the designation of county boundaries came the naming of a county seat. In most cases as soon as a town was designated a county seat its selection was challenged by other places. After much hard campaigning, both legal and illegal, a vote was taken and sometimes the seat of government was changed. For example, Cloud Chief was designated as the county seat for H County and Ioland as the county seat for E County. Elections resulted in a change from Cloud Chief to Cordell and Ioland to Grand. When the state constitution for Oklahoma was written, county boundaries were drawn, some different from those previously identified, and county seats were named. As before, there were many challenges to the places selected. Voters again made changes—Grand to Arnett, Kenton to Boise City, Lehigh to Coalgate, and others. The loss of political prestige in each case contributed significantly to making the original county seat a ghost town.

Liquor laws. Before statehood it was illegal to sell, distribute, make, or possess alcoholic liquor in Indian Territory. In Oklahoma Territory, on the other hand, such was not the case. As a result, a series of "liquor towns" developed on the Oklahoma Territory side of the boundary—Keokuk Falls, Appalachia, Violet Springs, and others. These towns flourished as Indians, cowboys, and various other inhabitants came to them to buy their "firewater." The Oklahoma Constitution, as adopted, contained a "blue law" section which made alcohol illegal throughout the state; thus, another group of towns became ghosts as they lost their chief source of income.

Lakes. Since the 1940s the United States Army, Corps of Engineers and the Bureau of Reclamation as well as a few cities have constructed dams that have caused the formation of large lakes. Most of the lakes are located in the eastern part of the state in the Ouachita Mountains and Ozark Plateau regions. In some instances it has been necessary to move towns, cemeteries, and transportation and communication lines— Woodville (Lake Texoma), Aylesworth (Lake Texoma), Hochatown (Broken Bow Reservoir), Keystone (Keystone Reservoir), Kaw City (Kaw Reservoir), and Lugert (Altus-Lugert Lake) are examples. In a few instances the old towns tried to reestablish themselves on nearby higher ground. None have been really successful, most becoming drowned ghost towns.

City expansion. Since the 1960s some of the larger cities and towns of Oklahoma have added many square miles of territory to their incorporated limits. Sometimes the annexation has included an area previously occupied by a place that had become a ghost town before annexation. For example, Cross was settled prior to the settlement of Ponca City a short distance away. Ponca City, however, developed, and Cross ceased to exist. Today the land that was Cross is within the city limits of Ponca City and is largely a residential district. Such current occupation, nevertheless, does not negate the fact that Cross is still a ghost town. Other examples of places no longer in existence as well as dying towns that have been absorbed into Oklahoma City, Tulsa, Norman, and other expanding urban communities could be listed.

ECONOMIC FACTORS

Timber. When first settled, eastern Oklahoma was a densely forested land. Rough topography, heavy rainfall, and a long growing season were ideal for numerous species of trees, especially pines and oaks. Sawmills were established soon after the first Indians were settled, and some wood was shipped from the area prior to the

Civil War. In the late 1800s and prior to World War II the felling of trees and the sawing of lumber became a prime economic activity. Cutting, at first, was not done on a selective basis, resulting in numerous sawmill towns that existed for only brief periods or until the prime trees had been cut. In a few cases the towns established were company towns. Kosoma, Big Cedar, Pine Valley, and other former sawmill towns are today only names on old maps.

Agriculture. Technological advances have brought about many, many changes in agricultural settlement patterns. The development of moving irrigation equipment, mechanical cotton pickers, combines, and the automobile, plus the extension of electric lines into rural areas, have made it possible for one person to do the work formerly done by two or more workers. Also, because of road improvement it has become easier for farmers to travel to larger markets for both selling and buying. The consolidation of former 80- or 160-acre farms into larger holdings, and in rural counties the change from crop production to animal raising, requires fewer persons and less intensive land use than was previously needed. Accordingly, many small towns that served agricultural needs were no longer able to support themselves. The remains of such places are found in all parts of the state. In fact, there are more agricultural ghost towns than any other kind.

Weather and climate. Dust storms and tornadoes have both been factors in town decay. During the Dust Bowl era of the 1930s many small agricultural settlements in western Oklahoma ceased to exist. The years of subnormal rainfall caused the land to be so dry that crops could not grow. The dry topsoils that had been plowed in anticipation of moisture blew away. With these conditions most farmers had no choice but to move from the area, thereby decreasing income for the towns. In such situations the merchants, if possible, sold their goods and moved. Some merchants simply closed their doors and left, leaving small stocks on the shelves. Tornadoes, the most destructive of all storms, have destroyed large sections of some towns in a matter of minutes. Even though some small places have tried to rebuild, they have had great difficulty in attaining their former economic status.

Transportation. Most of the railroads, when first extended into what is now Oklahoma, tried to locate stations along their tracks about every ten miles. As a result, numerous small railroad towns developed. They consisted of a depot, one or two general stores, a hotel-restaurant, a post office, a blacksmith shop, a school-church building, and possibly a doctor who also had a small drugstore, as well as a few homes. Over a period of years these places served primarily as shipping centers for agricultural products and livestock. With the development of the automobile and better highways, however, they began to decline. Eventually, the railroads themselves also declined in importance, and the towns were abandoned. By following the former route of the Fort Smith and Western Railroad eastward from Oklahoma City through central Oklahoma, one finds the sites of several nonexistent former towns. The same is also true along the former right-of-way of the Missouri-Kansas-Texas Railroad northward from Altus to the Panhandle and then westward across that part of the state.

The building of state and national highways across Oklahoma has also caused ghost towns. Formerly the principal routes of travel extended through the small settlements along the route. With the increase in speed and the demand for more direct routes, several towns were bypassed by a mile or more, and business suffered. Sometimes, especially during the past twenty-five years, attempts have been made to move the town to the highway. Almost all such efforts have failed.

Minerals. Oklahoma has been an exceedingly wealthy state as far as mineral wealth is concerned. The discovery of such minerals as petroleum, zinc, gold, coal, and others caused boom towns which almost always eventually became ghost towns. Petroleum has been found in many parts of the state. During the first half of the twentieth century oil boom towns were common; thus, during the last half of the century oil ghost towns are just as common. Such places as Pershing, Carter Nine, Ramsey, Sabo, Pooleville, Watchorn, Empire, and Roxana, along with countless others, were well known for various activities. One oil boom town, Wamego, boomed and died within a sixty-day period, even though it is said to have attained a maximum population of over one thousand.

7

Ottawa County, in the northeastern corner of the state, is dotted with ghost towns that resulted from declining zinc mining activities. The remains of short-lived gold mining towns can be seen in the Wichita Mountains west of Lawton. A few small places where granite was quarried in the Arbuckle or Wichita mountains can be found. The sites of former gypsum mill operations are scattered throughout the Gypsum Hills region of western Oklahoma. Even the mining of asphalt has left its mark in Pushmataha and Murray counties.

Coal mining has been important in east central Oklahoma for a hundred years. The first railroads built from Fort Smith westward into the Choctaw Nation were for the purpose of hauling out coal. Large numbers of Polish and Italian laborers were brought into the Choctaw Nation as coal miners. Some of the coal towns were company-owned and as such were usually built to last for relatively short periods. Where the remains of old coal tipples or slag piles can be seen, one often finds the remains of what was once a town. Midway and Phillips in Coal County, Gowen and Lutie in Latimer County, and Dow and Alderson in Pittsburgh County are just a few examples.

Cultural changes. During the past thirty years there has been an almost continuous movement from rural and small-town units to large-town units. This movement has been so great that many small towns have seen their schools, medical facilities, some of their churches, lodges, recreation centers, post offices, and leading stores close. Their young people, desiring more social contacts as well as greater job opportunities, were forced to leave the small towns. Under some conditions a place may still have a school to which the townspeople point with pride, but usually such a school remains largely because the physical plant was better than that of other places with which the school district consolidated. Many of the older people remaining in the smaller places are eventually transferred to nursing centers where doctors and hospitals are available. If the smaller town is near enough to a growing and expanding city, it may eventually be incorporated by annexation into the city and thus lose its identity.

In most of the small, isolated towns usually 60 percent or more of the inhabitants are past fifty years of age. A large majority are living on social security or retirement incomes. Most will live out their lives in the town because it is "home" and they can live cheaper there than in a city or larger town. They look forward to a non-changing life style and the nearby cemetery. With each death the town moves nearer to extinction.

OKLAHOMA PLACE NAMES

Before statehood town names were sometimes duplicated. It was not unusual for a newly established post office in Oklahoma Territory to select a name already in use in Indian Territory, Greer County, or the Public Land Strip. In some cases the same name was used three times (Harrison, Fairview, Kiamichi, for example) or four times (Golden, Jackson, for example). Thus, at the time of statehood it was necessary for the Post Office Department to change the names of places already in existence—for example, Cimarron to Boise City, Francis to Vinson, and Virgel to Sterling to Capron. As a result, numerous towns have had at least two names, and some as many as three or four.

Several Oklahoma towns were named after a first settler. Frequently the first postmaster would put his name or, as was often the case, the first name of his wife or daughter on the place. Some places were named after Indian tribes, Indian chiefs, or railroad men. A few town names were anagrams. A postmaster in Washita County wanted to name his office Porter but learned that there was already a Porter in Wagoner County. The new office was then named Retrop. In another case a group wishing to honor their home state of Alabama spelled the name of their new town Amabala. Four men founding a new town in Love County called it Jimtown, since each of the four had the first name of James. Several communities were named after authors, books, characters, or places in books—Shakespeare, Ruskin, Ramona, Ivanhoe, Zenda, Lynn.

Jenkin Lloyd Jones, in an article "The Folklore of Oklahoma's Fascinating Place Names" (*Tulsa Tribune*, October 26, 1965), wrote:

Out in Kingfisher County Alpha was five miles east of Omega. In Pottawatomie County Romulus was five miles northeast of Remus. Romulus, it will

8

be remembered, slew Remus, and the Romulus post office lasted a few years longer.

Many crossroad communities adopted grandiose names in the hope of attracting more settlers. Olympus (Delaware County) was to be the dwelling place of the gods, and perhaps it is for no human beings now live there. Optima (Texas County) was Latin for "best possible." Mirabile (Woods) was Latin "remarkable," and remarkably it has vanished. Moral (Pottawatomie) got its name because saloons were forbidden, but in that case virtue gained no reward. Shinewell (McCurtain) has flickered out.

Other settlers were not so bullish. Sleeper (Cherokee) was well-christened. Sunset (Beaver) has set. Titanic (Adair) has gone down. And Mirage (Tillman) proved to be just that. Needmore (Delaware) attested to the frank belief of its earliest citizens that they didn't have much. Under its new name, Bernice, they had to move up the hill to keep from drowning.

TO THE READER

The ghost towns discussed on the following pages have been selected because they were considered more or less representative of the ghost towns that have come into existence since 1825. Much has been written about some because of their historical or economic importance or because of some person or group of people that lived in them. Several of the towns discussed, however, have little written history. The story presented about each is largely the result of conversations with a few remaining old-timers who continue to live in the village or area or discussions with descendants of the original settlers. The towns selected for writeup are considered typical for their periods of time, geographical locations, or functions. Such places as Ferdinandina in Kay County, believed to be an early French trading post, and San Bernardo in Jefferson County, an early Spanish trading post, as well as such sites as the Spiro Mound in Le-

Flore County were omitted because of the early dates of their existence. None of the Indian villages as exemplified by Clermont's Town (Rogers County), Comanche Indian Village (Comanche County), or Keechi Village (Caddo County) have been included because of the brief period of time they existed at one location. Bethsheba, probably the most peculiar of all ghost towns in Oklahoma, was not written about because its specific location between Enid and Perry is not known. (Bethsheba was settled by women and exclusively for women. No males of any species—roosters, bulls, male horses, or men—were admitted to the settlement. It is said to have had a population of thirty-three, but twelve deserted after the first week. The remaining members disappeared one night and Bethsheba became a female ghost.)

Should you want to visit the remains of some of these old towns or old townsites, and the writer hopes you will, it is suggested that caution be used. Almost half of the ghost town sites are in plowed fields or pastures. Most farmers and ranchers will gladly grant permission for a visit to these sites, but they do object to people tramping across fields and pastures without permission. There are numerous examples in which a visitor has unintentionally started a pasture fire by throwing away a lighted cigarette, been involved with a cow or bull, not heeded the signal of a rattlesnake, become lost in a riverbed or gully, or had problems with an electric fence. Also, there is always danger in walking around or through old abandoned buildings. Rusty nails, splinters, cracking floorboards, and sagging staircases are all reasons that considerable care must be taken.

Be careful—and have fun.

Academy, *ca.* 1915. Armstrong Male Academy building, students, and teachers. *(Courtesy James D. Morrison)*

Academy

(ARMSTRONG ACADEMY,
CHAHTA TAMAHA)

COUNTY:	*Bryan*
LOCATION:	*(a) Sec. 12, T 6 S, R 11 E*
	(b) 15 miles east, 3 miles north of Durant; 1 mile east, 2 miles north of Bokchito.
MAP:	*Page 220*
POST OFFICE:	*April 22, 1898–March 15, 1920*

Academy, founded in 1844 as a school for Choctaw Indian boys, was known to government agents as Armstrong Academy and later to the Choctaw Indians as Chahta Tamaha (Choctaw Town). The site was selected for the school because there was a good spring of fresh water, a stream with a current strong enough to run a gristmill, and a large supply of wood available.

The first classroom buildings and dormitories were built of logs. As was the custom, the school was placed under the direction of a group of missionaries from eastern states. The Baptist Missionary Society of Louisville, Kentucky, directed activities until 1855, when operation of the school was transferred to the Cumberland Presbyterians. During the late 1850s a brick building replaced the log structure. Later, a two-story brick addition was added. As the school developed, so did the community about it. A trading post, a blacksmith shop, and a church were among the first establishments.

During the Civil War the Choctaw Nation sided with the Confederacy, and the academy was closed. In 1862 the Choctaw Council adopted a constitutional amendment providing that "in the fall of 1863 the Council should meet at Armstrong Academy, which should be the permanent capital of the Nation with the name of Chahta Tamaha." The large brick school building became the office building—the capitol—of

Academy, 1914. Diploma given by Armstrong Male Academy to Homer Michael Freeny. *(Courtesy James D. Morrison)*

Academy, 1974. Remains of the old cistern across the stream from the school building site. *(Courtesy Bryan County Star)*

the Choctaw Nation. A part of the building was also used as a Confederate hospital. Chahta Tamaha remained the capital until 1883, when the move was made to Tuskahoma. During that period the commercial activities in the vicinity increased.

Upon the movement of the seat of government, the school was reestablished, but admission was limited to Choctaw orphan boys. Again, the direction of the school was placed with the Presbyterians, and they continued in charge until the federal government took control. Life for the students followed a fairly rigid schedule. The boys were up at 7:00 A.M., had breakfast, and then milked the cows. From 8:00 to 8:30 they had military drill. Class or work activities started at 9:00 A.M. Classroom studies rotated with work details. For example, the boys would work Monday morning and go to class Monday afternoon, have classes Tuesday morning and work Tuesday afternoon. Discipline was strict.

A former principal wrote that "it was not unusual for him to whip ten to fifteen boys per day." The school continued to operate until February, 1921, when everything connected with the academy was destroyed by fire. The federal government refused to rebuild; thus, the operation of Armstrong Academy ceased.

With the closing of the school, the changing and improving of roads in the area, and the growing importance of nearby railroad towns, the community became deserted. Today, the site of the academy is in a pasture, posted to keep out visitors. Steps to the old building, bits of sidewalk, some foundations, and the concrete part of the cistern can be seen. The cemetery encloses the burial plots of some noted Choctaws. Pioneers have also been buried there, along with several Confederate soldiers. As Dr. W. B. Morrison expressed it, "Chahta Tamaha has returned to the virgin wilderness from which it emerged in 1844."

Academy, 1974. Steps and traces of sidewalks leading to where the main building stood. *(Courtesy Bryan County Star)*

Acme

COUNTY: *Grady*
LOCATION: *(a) Sec. 23, T 4 N, R 8 E*
     (b) 17 miles south, 4 miles west of Chickasha; 1 mile north, 3 miles west of Rush Springs
MAP: *Page 219*
POST OFFICE: *April 8, 1913–May 29, 1931*
RAILROAD: *Chicago, Rock Island and Pacific Railroad, abandoned 1930*

Acme developed when the Acme Cement and Plaster Company built a large mill and power plant at the site in 1911. The Rock Island extended a spur into the area to haul out the manufactured product. The machines used in the mill were of such size that they had to be put in place before the walls of the building could be completed. The mill employed 100 to 125 men and manufactured six to eight freight carloads of plaster per twenty-four-hour day. Near where the gypsum was being mined large stables were built to house the thirty teams of horses and mules that pulled the slip scrapers moving gypsum to the loading chutes.

Since roads were bad and transportation poor, many of the workers leased land and built homes near the factory. Single workers, or those who did not have families with them, lived in one of the two boarding houses located across the street from the mill or near the stables. The company built a home for the plant superintendent and the team boss, both across the street from the mill. A privately owned general store, also across the street from the mill, supplied groceries and other necessary items. The post office was located in one corner of the store. Since agriculture around Acme was important, two cotton gins and a blacksmith shop served the farm community. Eventually a large brick school and a gymnasium were constructed.

During the early 1920s the gypsum beds in the vicinity of Acme were worked out. The company built a narrow-gauge railroad to other beds near the Little Washita River. In 1927 floodwaters covered these beds with several feet of sand. The beds were worked with some difficulty until 1930, when exploitation became unprofitable. The mill in Acme was then closed. It was necessary to destroy the building in order to get the machinery out so that it could be moved. With the closing of the mill, people moved from the community.

Very little of Acme exists today. The school was sold and torn down. The rooming houses, stables, and store are gone. A few houses and some of the concrete ruins of the mill and power plant remain.

Adamson

COUNTY: *Pittsburgh*
LOCATION: *(a) Sec. 7, T 5 N, R 17 E*
     (b) 10 miles east of McAlester; 6 miles north of Hartshorne
MAP: *Page 220*
POST OFFICE: *March 1, 1906–*
RAILROADS: *Missouri, Kansas and Texas Railroad (Katy), abandoned 1950; Choctaw, Oklahoma and Gulf Railroad (Rock Island), abandoned 1902*

Adamson developed first as a coal mining camp then later in the early 1900s as a town. Within the four-square-mile area which it served as the trading center were fifteen mines, four of which were considered major producers. The town reached its peak during World War I, when coal formed the chief source of energy for railroads, electricity generating, and general manufacturing activities. At that time the population in the area was estimated in excess of 5,500 persons, including the 700 who lived in Adamson. The Rock Island and Katy railroads both built tracks into the community to serve the mines.

From 1913 to 1919 Adamson was known as a "live town." There was fighting and dancing, Choc beer drinking, and loving and marriage among the conglomerate of peoples who had moved in from various parts of the world. The mines were working twenty-four hours a day, the four major mines using about two hundred men each. Railroads carried out trainloads of coal daily. Money flowed freely. Holidays of a dozen different European countries were celebrated. One merchant of the time recorded:

"We had a busy city then. It was gay and happy and something happened all of the time."

All of the mines in the Adamson area were slope mines, and most had a dip of about 35° northward. Coal was taken from both the Mc-Alester and Hartshorne outcrops. The deepest bed was the Hartshorne, which was workable throughout most of the area. It averaged about four feet in thickness. The McAlester bed, approximately one thousand feet above the Hartshorne, varied in thickness from three feet to in a few places five feet. On September 4, 1914, one of the major mine disasters in Oklahoma occurred at Mine No. 1, one-fourth mile south of the principal business district of Adamson.

Adamson, *ca. 1915.* Most of the coal mined in the Adamson area was used as fuel by locomotives. All coal mined was moved from the area by train. *(Courtesy Oklahoma Publishing Company)*

Adamson, 1975. Monument erected to the fourteen men killed in the mine disaster of September 4, 1914. Joe Wayne Sirmans, standing next to the monument, is the great-grandson of the last miner to escape.

At about 3:30 P.M. a miner reported that he had heard a cracking noise in the mine. All men were ordered out of the mine at once. The trips carried the men up the sixteen-hundred-foot incline, set on a 45° angle, to the tenth level about

eight hundred feet below the surface. All were up to this level except fourteen from the bottom room. The underground tunnels and rooms of the mine, almost without warning, began to "squeeze" and collapse. "Increasing cracking noises, a groan from the earth, and a splintering of supports foretold the carnage." Several stated there was one great noise like an explosion far beneath the ground. On the surface the earth dropped about eight to ten feet. The fourteen men were buried alive. Rescue or even recovery of the bodies was impossible.

Today about ten small homes, largely occupied by retired individuals, remain north of the old main street. Two small grocery stores re-

Adamson, *ca.* 1916. Coal mine near Ardmore Junction in the Adamson mining area. *(Courtesy Western History Collections, University of Oklahoma)*

main, but much of their business comes from visitors to nearby Lake Eufaula. All the mines are now closed and filled with water. About one-quarter mile south of the former business area the land between the mine pillars continues to settle gradually, and a series of somewhat elongated ponds is forming. Water flowing from the old mines now presents a problem to the conservationists of the area. The water is highly mineralized, thereby contaminating the streams into which it flows and killing large numbers of fish.

One person now living in the area stated that Adamson was a ghost town with fourteen ghosts watching over it.

Addington, *ca.* 1910. City Drug Store was a popular meeting place for children because it had an ice cream making machine. *(Courtesy Marvin Huffer)*

Addington

COUNTY:	*Jefferson*
LOCATION:	*(a) Sec. 6, T 4 S, R 7 W*
	(b) 6 miles north, 2 miles east of Waurika
MAP:	*Page 219*
POST OFFICE:	*January 8, 1896–*
NEWSPAPERS:	*Addington Free Lance; Addington Advertiser; Addington Journal; Addington Herald*
RAILROAD:	*Chicago, Rock Island and Pacific Railroad*

Addington had its start in the 1890s after the Rock Island extended its tracks southward from Minco to the Red River. Located in an area of fertile soil and good grassland, the town developed as an agricultural trade center from which corn, cotton, and cattle were shipped. In 1908 Addington had three cotton gins and two livestock sales pens. The corn crop was so great that much had to be stored in long ricks on the ground.

The town was incorporated in 1901. The *Addington Herald* in December stated: "It is six months old and has more substantial buildings and more permanent business men than any other town of its age and size in either territory." Advertisements in the 1901 and early 1902 editions listed doctors, lawyers, paper hangers, real estate dealers, and building contractors in addition to the usual retail business notices. There was a brickyard manufacturing pressed brick. The Bank of Addington had been organized by a young woman who served as cashier. The paper stated she was the only woman bank officer in Oklahoma Territory. (See Lenora.)

Population in 1902 was estimated at about 350 people. Addington continued to increase in size until about 1915, when the population was about 1,000 persons. At that time there were fourteen stores, two cotton gins, a cottonseed oil mill, three livestock dealers, the bank, the brick plant,

Addington, 1912. The windows were broken during an August hailstorm. *(Courtesy Marvin Huffer)*

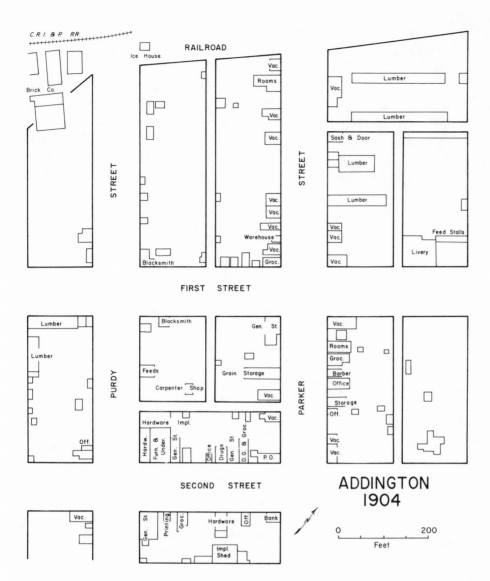

Addington, 1904

a hotel, a telephone exchange, and four real estate offices. The town added a "new addition making room for 1,500 families." Schools and churches had been developed, and the future looked bright—then came World War I.

During much of the 1920s Addington stood still. Most of the excitement centered around bank robberies. Twice within a short period of time the bank was held up and the robbers escaped. Two peace officers had been killed from ambush while on duty. The county sheriff then appointed "Two Gun" Bill Fowler as deputy sheriff and assigned him to Addington. Fowler was on duty when the third attempt was made

on October 26, 1928. One robber went inside the bank to get the money, and the second stood guard at the entrance. They left the motor of their car running. The robber in the bank found it necessary to fire a shot, which was heard by Fowler. The lookout stood behind a support column and fired at Fowler as he approached. After exchanging shots, the outside man exposed his arm to shoot again. Fowler's shot broke the man's arm, causing him to drop his gun. The inside man came out with the money, and both ran for their car. "Two Gun" was carrying only one gun at the time, and it was empty. He ran to his car, got his rifle, and shot at the fleeing car.

Addington, 1975. This former bank building remains standing at the corner of Second and Parker streets.

The shot cut the ignition wires and stopped the flight. Both robbers jumped and ran. Fowler immediately shot one, the fellow he had previously wounded. Leaving him under guard, the deputy went after the second and killed him. When the shooting was over, the banker stated: "I am tired of being shot at and robbed. This bank is going out of business." He immediately closed the bank and paid off all accounts in full.

The bank closing, the Depression of the 1930s, World War II, and other factors caused many people to move from the town and area. A barber shop, a pecan shelling plant, a filling station, and sometimes a cafe–grocery store are now in operation. Empty, ramshackle buildings, including the old bank structure, line U.S. Highway 81. In the northeastern part of town stand the blackened walls of the former school building, which was being used for the storage of hay when it burned. Fewer than one hundred people now live in Addington.

Alluwe

(LIGHTNING CREEK)

COUNTY: *Nowata*
LOCATION: *(a) Sec. 30, T 25 N, R 17 W*
           (b) 5½ miles south, 5½ miles east of Nowata
MAP: *Page 217*
POST OFFICE: *Lightning Creek, October 23, 1872–June 27, 1883;*
           Alluwe, June 27, 1883–July 31, 1909

Alluwe, previously known as Lightning Creek, was settled as a community by Delaware Indians. At first the settlement had but one store—a store that sold everything from harness to groceries to dry goods to hardware. In the 1880s the settlement became a somewhat compact village. Other stores were started, good homes were built, and a church and a school were organized. Chief Charles Journeycake, a noted chief of the Delawares, lived near the church. He preached to his people and used an interpreter for whites who might attend.

In 1905 oil was discovered, and Alluwe found itself in the midst of a boom. Tents and houses soon appeared in all parts of town. There was a constant movement of people and a constant flow of wagons hauling freight. Stores were built, a hotel was erected, saloons and livery stables appeared, doctors came, drugstores opened, and a new school was erected. The large oil companies built gasoline plants nearby as well as camps for their employees. Many natives of the area became rich as they invested in wildcat wells that became producers. This period of prosperity lasted for about ten years.

In the mid-1920s highways in the area were improved and good bridges crossed the Verdigris River and Lightning and Salt creeks. Garages replaced livery stables, and filling stations were doing a good business. Oil production, however, was decreasing, and jobs were be-

Alluwe, 1900. Home of Chief Charles Journeycake. *(Courtesy Nowata County Historical Museum)*

Alluwe, 1896. Annuity payment to the Delaware Indians. The hatless old gentleman on the porch is Chief Charles Journeycake. *(Courtesy Oklahoma Historical Society)*

coming fewer. Eventually the gasoline plants were closed, and the oil field camps were moved or abandoned. Many who had made their fortunes retired to larger towns, and others seeking jobs moved away. Alluwe again became a small and somewhat dilapidated place.

During the 1950s the Oologah Dam was built across the Verdigris River, forming Oologah Reservoir. The land on which Alluwe was lo-cated was close to the Verdigris and of such elevation that the Corps of Engineers included the townsite in its purchase of property. The town either had to move or be destroyed. Some residents moved a short distance eastward and established the new Alluwe. *Alluwe* is the Delaware word for "something better." The people living in the new town of Alluwe say they hope the future is *alluwe*.

Alluwe, 1946. Remains of the principal business area. *(Courtesy Oklahoma Publishing Company)*

America, 1942. Attaching a sack with mail so that the next passenger train could make the pickup without stopping. *(Courtesy Oklahoma Publishing Company)*

America

COUNTY:	*McCurtain*
LOCATION:	*(a) Sec. 36, T 8 S, R 26 E*
	(b) 5½ miles south, 16 miles east of Idabel
MAP:	*Page 220*
POST OFFICE:	*July 24, 1903–February 15, 1944*
RAILROAD:	*Arkansas and Choctaw Railway (Frisco)*

America, located in the pine forests of southeastern Oklahoma, was largely a one-family town. In 1907 William Spencer, with the help of three brothers, built a sawmill and about forty

houses, which were rented to lumber workers. By 1910 approximately two hundred persons lived in the town. In the brief period of four years practically all of the best timber was cut. Thus, in 1911 Spencer closed the sawmill, built a general store and a cotton gin, and encouraged those remaining in the area to grow cotton. Spencer then became a cotton buyer. He also bought cross-ties. These two products were shipped out by rail. During the late 1920s cotton production declined, and many people moved away. The cotton gin was closed in 1933 and the general stores in 1945. The village never had a church or a police force. A one-teacher school did operate for a few years.

America today is again in the middle of a pine forest, with the area being a part of the Ouachita National Forest. The store, cotton gin, and lumber mill have long since been removed. Two old houses, both dilapidated, remain, and a marker next to the railroad identifies the former townsite.

America, 1975. Identification marker where the depot and mail pickup stand formerly stood.

America, 1942. The general store. Logs stacked at the right of the store were used to make crossties. Mules were the chief source of power on the small farms in the area. *(Courtesy Oklahoma Publishing Company)*

19
A

Autwine

(VIRGINIA CITY)

COUNTY:	*Kay*
LOCATION:	*(a) Sec. 20, T 26 N, R 1 E*
	(b) 10 miles west, 11 miles south of Newkirk; 8 miles west, 1 mile north of Ponca City
MAP:	*Page 216*
POST OFFICE:	*Pierceton, May 26, 1894–March 5, 1903;*
	Autwine, March 5, 1903–June 30, 1922
RAILROAD:	*Hutchinson and Southern Railway (Santa Fe)*

Autwine, first called Virginia City, was platted on June 17, 1899. The post office which served the town of Virginia City was named Pierceton, and the railroad identified its station as Arta. Soon after the town was started, a meeting of the residents was called to decide upon a single name for the town, post office, and railroad station. The name agreed upon was Antwine, in honor of Antwine Roy, a Ponca Indian chief.

There are two different stories telling why the name became Autwine instead of Antwine. One is that the Santa Fe agent spelled the name incorrectly, had the sign for the station painted accordingly, and refused to change the spelling. The second story is that the town clerk who sent the name change to Washington to get it recorded was a poor penman. When the name came back from Washington it was spelled Autwine.

The town grew rapidly as an agricultural center, since roads were poorly developed and transportation methods were slow. At the turn of the century the town boasted of having two elevators, a stockyard, an implement yard, a bank, ten other business establishments, and a "good" doctor. The Modern Woodmen, Royal Neighbors, and the Anti Horsethief Association were active town boosters. There were about twenty-five homes in the town proper as well as surrounding farm homes. Autwine was a regular shipping point for cattle and hogs, as well as wheat during the harvest season. The 101 Ranch, Little V, and Big V ranches were regular livestock shippers.

Autwine, *ca.* 1905. Following an important town meeting, most of the citizens gathered in front of the bank for a community picture. *(Courtesy Gary Gallagher)*

A school for grades one through eight was soon organized. High school students attended classes in Blackwell, some six miles away. They rode the train to Blackwell, as the schedule was right to carry them both ways. Round trips between Ponca City and Blackwell, through Autwine, were made four times each day by mail and passenger trains. The first church and Sunday School activities were held in a grove of trees. Later, services were moved to the school.

In the early 1900s the importance of Autwine as a trading center started to decline as roads were improved, the first automobiles and trucks made their appearance, and people began to trade in the larger centers. In 1904 the bank closed, and in 1905 a fire devastated the business section, destroying the grocery and dry-goods stores, the depot, the blacksmith shop, the general merchandise store, the hardware store, and a part of the lumberyard. The only business building left standing was an empty one. Most merchants did not rebuild. In 1910 only one general store, a blacksmith shop, and an elevator remained in operation. In 1912 the local school was wrecked by a tornado. The last stores closed in 1930, and shortly thereafter the elevator also closed.

Today there is no physical evidence that Autwine ever existed. All land of the former platted area is now used for agricultural purposes.

Avard

COUNTY: *Woods*
LOCATION: *(a) Secs. 26/35, T 26 N, R 15 W*
(b) 7 miles south, 6 miles west of Alva
MAP: *Page 215*
POST OFFICE: *June 1, 1895–November 22, 1963*
NEWSPAPER: *Avard Tribune*
RAILROAD: *Southern Kansas Railway (Santa Fe); Arkansas Valley and Western Railway (Frisco)*

Avard was incorporated in 1904 when the Frisco tracks were extended westward from Enid to tie in with the transcontinental line of the Santa Fe. From the beginning the town was well supplied with mercantile establishments as well as two hotels, a bank, a livestock exchange, an elevator, and a weekly newspaper. Stock pens were adjacent to the tracks, and the town was the cattle shipping point for a large area. By 1909 some 250 people were reported living in Avard.

Since the town was both a railroad town and a cow town, it was a rough and tough place. Many exciting events were reported to have happened in Avard during the Gay Nineties. The town was wide open, and the saloons kept going all night. It was not uncommon for dead men to be found in the street after a gun battle.

Avard, 1975. Entrance to the large tornado cave.

Avard, 1975. Santa Fe and Frisco tracks interlock a short distance from the elevator.

Avard, 1921. Elementary school group and teachers in March, 1921. The house types are characteristic of western Oklahoma. The elevator in the background indicates the importance of wheat farming. *(Courtesy Mrs. Marie Ralston)*

During the years from 1910 to 1930 Avard became an important agricultural center and rail transfer point for both passengers and freight. The Santa Fe passenger trains through Avard made direct runs from Chicago to Los Angeles. Frisco passenger lines from the east connected with the Santa Fe time schedule. Both lines kept agents and full crews stationed in Avard. In addition to the livestock market the town had a large broomcorn warehouse, elevators for wheat storage and shipping, and a cotton gin. During this period the town built a community building where plays and concerts were given and public meetings held, churches were active, and an accredited school was developed. For a brief time there was a dance hall in operation, but after one brawl it was closed.

Avard continued to grow until the mid-1930s. Like many other Oklahoma agricultural towns, however, it became a victim of the economic depression, dust storms, farm consolidation, and changing methods of travel. In 1943 and 1944 the town was struck by tornadoes, each time on a different site. Soon thereafter a tornado-conscious community got busy and, with donated materials and labor, completed a ten-by twenty-foot underground shelter. It was made of solid concrete and was big enough to hold the entire population.

In 1973 the Frisco upgraded its line from Tulsa to Avard, at a cost of some four million dollars, so that it could interlock with the main line of the Santa Fe. There are now five or six transcontinental freight trains a day highballing through Avard. This change, however, had little effect on the town. A few unused store buildings remain, but the only services offered are those of a cafe and an elevator. One church continues to function, but the school has been closed.

Avery

COUNTY: *Lincoln*
LOCATION: *(a) Sec. 11, T 16 N, R 5 E*
(b) 12 miles north, 7 miles east of Chandler; 7 miles south, 1 mile east of Cushing
MAP: *Page 216*
POST OFFICE: *September 16, 1902–August 26, 1957*
RAILROAD: *Eastern Oklahoma Railway (Santa Fe)*

Avery, established in 1902, became one of the most important agricultural growing and shipping centers in central Oklahoma before World War I. The soils of the area were fertile, the

Avery, *ca.* 1916. Four passenger trains served Avery each day. *(Courtesy Oklahoma Historical Society)*

growing season long enough for crops such as cotton and fruits to mature, and the pastures suitable for cattle grazing. Roads were poor, and there were no large towns in the immediate vicinity until Cushing developed as an oil collecting and refining center. Also, the railroad through Avery made connections with the main line of the Santa Fe at Newkirk and Pauls Valley as well as connections with the Rock Island at Shawnee.

As agriculture developed, the railroad became the source of life for Avery. Reports indicate that more animals were shipped from the town during certain years than from any other place

Avery, 1974. Remaining abandoned buildings and foundations of former buildings located in the heart of the old business district.

between Pauls Valley and Arkansas City, Kansas. Herds of hogs and cattle were driven to the stockyards by men on foot. There was one day in 1907 when 125 cattle cars were loaded and shipped to Kansas City. About twice a year notice would be sent to farmers that a poultry car would arrive on a certain date. Farmers would then bring in chickens, ducks, and turkeys to sell. During the cotton picking season the gins would run twenty-four hours a day. One man stated that he "had counted 125 wagon loads of cotton and forty loads of grain on the streets of Avery in a single day." In addition to shipping out, the railroad was responsible for bringing in the feed, seed, coal, and machinery sold and used.

Avery was also the cultural and social center for the area. In addition to the saloons, which had to be closed at the time of statehood, the village had the usual stores, livery stables, blacksmith shops, and restaurants. There were two hotels, which tried to outdo each other. The price of a hotel room for one night plus breakfast was fifty cents. One could get an entire home-cooked dinner for twenty-five cents. Each Saturday night a dance was held in the hall above the drugstore. "The single boys came on horse back; those dating came in buggies; and those married came in wagons with plenty of hay and straw in the bottom so the youngsters could sleep while mamma and papa were at the dance." There was also a magic lantern show which operated on Saturday nights.

With the opportunity to make "big money" working in the oil fields near Cushing, Drumright, or Shamrock, many young men left the farms. World War I also took others away. The Model T Ford and better roads made it easier to buy and sell in the larger towns. The soils of the area, not having been fertilized, declined in production. Gradually, farms were consolidated and much land returned to pasture.

The old main street of Avery is now overgrown with weeds, and trees stand where buildings formerly stood. The remaining business buildings are unused, some half torn down, others rotting and falling down. The depot has long since been removed. Although the tracks remain, they are seldom used. The large school, built during WPA days, stands vacant and neglected. A few homes are still occupied.

Beer City, 1888. The Elephant Saloon and some of the residents of "The Sodom and Gomorrah of the Plains." (Reprinted from *Fifty Years on the Owl Hoot Trail*, © 1969 by Harry E. Chrisman, with permission of the Swallow Press, Inc., Chicago)

Beer City
(WHITE CITY)

COUNTY: *Texas*
LOCATION: *(a) Secs. 10/15, T 6 N, R 19 E, Cimarron Meridian*
(b) 21½ miles north, 27½ miles east of Guymon; 9 miles north, 10 miles east of Hooker
MAP: *Page 214*

In 1888 the Santa Fe railway extended its tracks through western Kansas to a place now known as Tyrone in Texas County. At Tyrone, which was to remain head of the line for fifteen years, large, sturdy corrals were built. Liberal, Kansas, located about five miles northeast of Tyrone and also on the Santa Fe, was started about the same time. When these two places came into existence Kansas had rigid prohibition laws, but law enforcement in the Public Land Strip was almost unknown. Cowboys and cattle dealers wanted their liquor and women after a long drive, or after shipping was over, and enterprising "merchants" did their best to supply the product demanded. As a result, Beer City was established south of Liberal and east of Tyrone in the Panhandle where both seller and buyer would be least disturbed.

At first Beer City was referred to as White City, for it was a tent town. The place never had a post office, church, or school, nor did it have cattle pens or gathering pens for livestock. The townsite was never platted. A part of the main street extended east-west just south of the Kansas border, but there were also north-south extensions, the whole being a "melange of red lights, saloons, and dance halls." The primary business was the selling of whiskey and beer at the numerous dance halls and saloons; thus, the place became known as Beer City.

In addition to liquid refreshments, most places had several games of chance in continuous operation. There were always girls to serve the drinks and provide other entertainment. Much of the liquid refreshment was manufactured locally near a stream named Hog Creek. A large and well-concealed cave, shielded by a leanto and adjacent to an adequate supply of fresh water and plenty of firewood, provided the ideal place for the still. The product was tax free and was said to be bottled dynamite. J. R. Spears, in his

"Story of No Man's Land," stated that Beer City was "composed exclusively of disreputable houses, the only village of the sort ever heard of in America."

The merchants in Beer City advertised in various newspapers, inviting folks to move to "White City the only town of its kind in the civilized world where they is absolutely no law." During the cattle shipping season girls moved from Dodge City, Wichita, and other places to work at Beer City, Tyrone, and, in some numbers, Liberal. Many of the girls lived in Liberal and commuted to Beer City, since a hack made regular runs between the two places.

The leading businessmen did, to some extent, try to provide some law and order. They hired "enforcers" to keep con men, pickpockets, and holdup men away from those who had had too much to drink. Many saloons had drunk pens at the back of the premises where customers would be relatively safe until they could sleep it off. The merchants also provided free wrestling and boxing matches, horse racing, and wild west shows to attract patrons or to celebrate some event. Harry E. Chrisman described some of the action: "At the end of one celebration Pussy Cat Nell, the madam in charge of the house above the Yellow Snake Saloon, put a load of buckshot into the body of the town marshal, who was in turn an active rustler."

With the addition of the Panhandle to Oklahoma Territory in 1890, law and order came to the Public Land Strip. Beer City, which had lived two exciting years, soon disappeared. The entire area is now used for agricultural purposes.

Benton, *ca.* 1887. The first schoolhouse, constructed with blocks of sod plowed from a nearby field, was built by volunteer help. The building was also used for public meetings and as a courtroom. *(Courtesy Beaver County Historical Society)*

Benton

COUNTY: *Beaver*
LOCATION: *(a) Sec. 1, T 3 N, R 26 E, Cimarron Meridian*
             (b) 3 miles south, 18 miles east of Beaver
MAP: *Page 214*
POST OFFICE: *September 13, 1886–October 14, 1899*
NEWSPAPER: *Benton County Banner*

Benton, founded in the early 1880s, had become an important "cultural" center near the eastern edge of the Panhandle by 1886. The town had a large general store, a drugstore, a hotel and livery stable, two saloons, and a blacksmith shop. Although there was no official officer of the law, there was an active vigilante committee. The town therefore had a reputation for sobriety and was not "infected by so-called bad men." A schoolhouse was built of sod, and regular terms of subscription school were held. Church meetings were also held in the schoolhouse. In 1888 the *Benton County Banner*, a weekly paper, started publication.

Many Benton homes were built of sod that had been cut from the adjacent prairie. Most homes had wood floors and window sills. For some years after the town was abandoned, sod walls of buildings remained standing. The town had two hand-dug, rock-walled wells. A ditch was also dug from Mexico Creek so that water flowed by the town.

Before the Panhandle became a part of Oklahoma Territory in 1890, its leaders organized Cimarron Territory, designated Beaver City the capital, and wrote a constitution in which the Public Land Strip was divided into seven counties. The easternmost county was Benton, and the town of Benton was named the county seat.

Benton was a favorite place for gatherings, especially for public dances. Food at the hotel was good, and the saloons kept long hours. Weddings were important events; practically all were invited, and most came. The write-up about the wedding of one popular couple states: "They had a dance every night and a feast every day for three days. The family of the bride kept the tables loaded with food; the men visited the saloons at regular intervals to brighten themselves up. The groom saw that there was plenty of free liquor and beer to drink."

One story is told about a middle-aged cowboy who took time off from work to go to school. In a short while he learned to "read, write, and cipher to the rule of three." Thereafter he was no good as a cowboy, for he had too much education. He quit his job on the ranch and started teaching at a school in the central part of the Panhandle. Another story deals with a man who operated a still near Benton. Most cowboys would not drink moonshine whiskey because of its white appearance. This enterprising operator boiled dried peaches, strained off the juice, and mixed it with the clear liquor to produce an amber-colored, fancy-flavored, sweet taste. The product sold well.

Accessibility to Benton was hindered by the nearness of Beaver and Kiowa creeks, especially during times of flood. Soils in the area were much more suited to grazing than to plowing and planting. Addition of the Panhandle to Oklahoma Territory nullified the town's position as a county seat. Benton was declining rapidly by 1900, and by 1920 everyone had moved from that location. All buildings have now been removed, sod walls knocked down, and caves filled, and the area has been returned to pasture.

Bernice
(NEEDMORE)

COUNTY: *Delaware*
LOCATION: *(a) Sec. 25, T 25 N, R 23 E*
(b) 13½ miles north, 6 miles west of Jay; 1½ miles north, 7 miles west of Grove
MAP: *Page 217*
POST OFFICE: *Needmore: December 14, 1894–February 12, 1913; Bernice: February 12, 1913; transferred to new townsite, then closed on July 31, 1960*
RAILROAD: *Kansas, Oklahoma and Gulf Railroad (K.O. & G.), abandoned 1960*

Bernice came into existence in the late 1880s under the name of Needmore. A small country store was the first business started. Located in the valley of the Grand River, it was surrounded by productive agricultural land. Other businesses moved to the site, churches were established, and a school was built. In 1913 the name was changed from Needmore to Bernice when the Kansas, Oklahoma and Gulf Railroad extended its tracks northeast from Muskogee through the village. By 1940 the population exceeded two hundred.

Bernice was forced out of existence in 1941 by the completion of Pensacola Dam across Grand River, which caused the formation of the

Bernice, 1940. The sign across the front of the store tells the story. *(Courtesy Oklahoma Publishing Company)*

Bernice, 1940. The town area is now covered by the waters of the Lake O' The Cherokees. *(Courtesy Oklahoma Publishing Company)*

Lake O' The Cherokees. Many of the homes and buildings that could be moved were taken from the area. The school building, a large brick and stone structure, burned before it could be torn down. Merchants advertised their goods for sale over a large area. A sign on the largest general store stated: "A Clean Sweep—Must Get Out or Be Drowned Out." The old village is now under twenty feet of water.

A new village still using the name of Bernice overlooks the old site from the lake shore which borders it. Other than the name, there is little similarity between the old and the new.

yon walls are topped by thick layers of gypsum suitable for the making of all kinds of plaster, wallboard, and cement blocks. There the Roman Nose Gypsum Company built a large mill, a commissary, several homes, a hotel for single employees, pipelines for water, and other items needed by the inhabitants. A railroad line was extended to the village.

In the 1920s the mill was closed for economic reasons, and soon thereafter the town was deserted. In 1929 the place was described by Marjorie Everhart: "The mill fell into decay, great powerful engines towering high above man's head rusted and fell into ruin. The bats played about the eaves, the shingles rotted and the rain came through rusting and rotting the great mill wheels, ropes, and leather belts which weighed nearly a ton. All is desolation and ruin where once the busy wheels of industry made a human bee hive. The houses, too, have fallen down or are in a state of dilapidation. The railroad has been torn up and removed and only the ruins of the once thriving industry mark the place where Bickford stood."

Few traces of Bickford remain. All buildings and the mill have been removed. The gypsum hills are again dotted by cedars, and Bitter Creek flows somewhat freely through the canyon. The canyon is now a favorite playground of thousands of Oklahomans each year, and Roman Nose State Park is one of the most popular parks in the state park system.

Bickford, 1918. Mill of the Roman Nose Gypsum Company. *Courtesy John Shriver)*

Bickford

COUNTY: *Blaine*
LOCATION: *(a) Sec. 7, T 17 N, R 11 W*
             (b) 6½ miles north of Watonga
MAP: *Page 215*
POST OFFICE: *November 2, 1904–November 30, 1927*
RAILROAD: *Enid and Anadarko Railway (Rock Island), abandoned 1926*

Bickford was a company-built, company-owned town located in Roman Nose Canyon. The can-

Bickford, 1975. A part of the camping area at Roman Nose State Park near where the mill was located. *(Courtesy Oklahoma Department of Tourism and Recreation)*

Big Cedar
(BIGCEDAR)

COUNTY: *LeFlore*
LOCATION: *(a) Secs. 14/15, T 2 N, R 25 E*
              (b) 27½ miles south of Poteau;
              16½ miles south, 2 miles west of
              Heavener
MAP: *Page 220*
POST OFFICE: *April 3, 1903 – October 15, 1943*

Big Cedar, located in the valley of the Kiamichi River between Kiamichi Mountain to the south and Winding Stair Mountain to the north, occupies one of the truly picturesque sites in Oklahoma. The hamlet is said to have derived its name either from a very large cedar tree that grew nearby or from an enormous grove of large cedars that grew in the vicinity. The settlement may have been located where it was because of the cedars, for most were soon cut and marketed. Records indicate that until the 1940s there was a small sawmill in operation most of the time.

The hamlet probably had its greatest population, about fifty persons, in 1910. One general store in which a post office was located, a blacksmith shop, a gristmill, a sawmill, and a cotton gin formed the commercial activities. Three years later only the store and sawmill remained. Because of the lack of good roads, the area was sparsely populated and isolated.

In the late 1930s activity increased when the white oaks of the area were being cut and made into barrel staves, the stave mill being located in Big Cedar. The staves were dried in the open and sent to a finishing mill in Arkansas. By 1940 the stave mill was closed, and only the small store remained.

Big Cedar, 1936. Barrel staves being dried before shipment to Arkansas. *(Courtesy Oklahoma Publishing Company)*

LEFT: Big Cedar, 1975. Monument erected to the memory of President John F. Kennedy, located at intersection of U.S. Highway 259 and Oklahoma State Highway 63.

BELOW: Big Cedar, 1961. President John F. Kennedy speaking at the opening of U.S. Highway 59 (259). Governor J. Howard Edmondson and Senator Robert S. Kerr are to the President's left; Congressman Carl Albert and Senator Mike Monroney are to his right. *(Courtesy Western History Collections, University of Oklahoma)*

Following World War II, State Highway 63 from Talihina to Mena, Arkansas, through the Kiamichi Valley, was paved. In 1961 U.S. Highway 59 (259), extending from Monterrey, Mexico, to Winnipeg, Canada, was completed through the mountains of eastern Oklahoma. Big Cedar then had its "day in the sun." President John F. Kennedy delivered the address that officially opened the highway on Sunday, October 29, 1961, at Big Cedar. At that time this ghost hamlet had at least twenty thousand visitors. Its natural beauties were shown on television to all parts of the nation. During his talk the President said: "A sympathetic understanding and sound evaluation of present day conditions in Oklahoma necessitates a knowledge of the salient facts of the state's history, for the historical development of any locality determines in large measure the present social conditions of the given region and furnishes a key to an understanding of its peculiar characteristics. The history of Oklahoma has been a unique one, romantic, and in some respects tragic."

Big Cedar today is identified by a roadside monument dedicated to President Kennedy. Two small store–filling station operations compete for business at the intersection. The area is still sparsely populated. Most motorists speed past without realizing the historic importance of the place.

Blackburn

COUNTY:	*Pawnee*
LOCATION:	*(a) Sec. 19, T 22 N, R 7 E*
	(b) 2 miles north, 11½ miles east of Pawnee; 6 miles north, 7 miles west of Cleveland
MAP:	*Page 216*
POST OFFICE:	*December 15, 1893–March 31, 1960*
NEWSPAPERS:	*Blackburn Flash-Light; Blackburn Globe; Blackburn News*

Blackburn was a prosperous agricultural village located on the bank of the Arkansas River in an area of fertile soil. At first a ferry was used to cross the river, but shortly after the opening of the Cherokee Outlet a toll bridge was built by Frank Burdom, an Osage Indian. In 1896 a free bridge connected Blackburn with the Osage Nation, and the village began to grow. The year 1901, however, is remembered as a drought year, for many people moved from the area at that time.

The business people of Blackburn organized a Commercial Club (an early-day Chamber of Commerce) in 1905 and widely advertised their community. As a result the village attained its greatest growth between 1910 and 1915. At its peak Blackburn had two banks, an active newspaper, a telephone exchange, a good hotel, a

Blackburn, *ca.* 1910. Market day sale. *(Courtesy Western History Collections, University of Oklahoma)*

Blackburn, 1974. Two of the buildings shown in the 1910 photograph remain standing; one is still in use.

real estate dealer, and two doctors in addition to the usual stores, livery stable, and blacksmiths. Cotton and corn were the principal crops. A cotton gin was built, and much corn was hauled to nearby markets. Four churches were active, and a high school as well as a grade school held classes. The population was estimated to be between 350 and 400 persons.

Blackburn, however, was destined to become an isolated village. The bridge across the Arkansas River no longer exists, and the former riverbed is now a part of the Keystone Reservoir. A railroad was built to the west of the village, and there are no state or federal highways extending into or by it. Only country roads lead to the community.

Although Blackburn got electricity in the 1940s, natural gas in 1968, and was connected to a rural water system in 1973, the village shows that its days of importance are past. Six old vacant business buildings stand along the main street. Currently, one small grocery store remains. Although there are several families living in the village, 90 percent of the residents are old-timers or retired individuals. The large school structure is falling into ruin, and the churches show the lack of upkeep. The site of Blackburn is an elevated one, and the setting could make a beautiful and picturesque scene if, somehow, the spirit of the early pioneers could be revived.

Boggy Depot

(OLD BOGGY DEPOT)

COUNTY:	*Atoka*
LOCATION:	*(a) Sec. 1, T 3 S, R 9 E*
	(b) 3½ miles south, 10 miles west of Atoka
MAP:	*Page 220*
POST OFFICE:	*November 5, 1849–March 22, 1872*
NEWSPAPER:	*Choctaw and Chickasaw Observer*

Boggy Depot, frequently referred to as Old Boggy Depot, was started in 1837 when a log cabin was built on the divide between the Clear Boggy River and Sandy Creek by some of the early

Boggy Depot, *ca.* 1890. Home of Governor Allen Wright. *(Courtesy Oklahoma Historical Society)*

Boggy Depot, 1922. Remains of the stage line along the former Main Street. *(Courtesy Western History Collections, University of Oklahoma)*

Chickasaw settlers. Since the site was somewhat near the center of the more populated area of the pre–Civil War Choctaw-Chickasaw holdings, the Chickasaws located their annuity grounds in the vicinity. Thus, large numbers of Chickasaws gathered there at the times of payments. Also, as routes of travel from Fort Smith to the west and south joined those from more northern places at this location, the village grew into a place of considerable importance. Streams of migrants followed these roads to California and Texas. Although the place was small, it was thriving, having a hotel, stores, blacksmith shop, and produce markets. In the early 1840s a brick church was built and a school started. Some early travelers referred to the place as "the Depot on the Boggy" and "the Chickasaw Depot" even though large numbers of Choctaws also lived in the village. The post office, when established on November 5, 1849, was officially designated as Boggy Depot, Cherokee Nation, Arkansas. (This designation was in error. It should have read Choctaw Nation. The area had not been a part of Arkansas for twenty-one years.) In 1850 a star route from Fort Smith westward was authorized, thereby assuring mail delivery into and out of Boggy Depot at least once a week. It was one of the two principal stage stations on the Butterfield Mail and Stage Coach Line.

No Civil War battles were fought at Boggy Depot, but it was close enough to actual battle activities to have its people involved. Confederate troops were quartered in the southwestern part of the town, where log cabins were built for their use, the place being the headquarters for Texas and Indian Confederate soldiers. Only once during the war was a raid on Boggy Depot attempted. It failed. After the battle of Honey Springs the Confederates retreated southward. At that time the church was used as a hospital.

Following the Civil War Boggy Depot again became a place of importance. A toll bridge was built across Clear Boggy River about one mile east of town, making the place even more accessible. It served as a meeting point for groups trying to bring order out of the war period. Muriel H. Wright in her article "Old Boggy Depot" (*Chronicles of Oklahoma*, Vol. V, No. 1, pp. 4–17) wrote:

Main Street of Old Boggy Depot bore the appearance of prosperity. Here were to be seen pretentious residences, neat cottages, a hotel, several large two-story buildings, and several smaller buildings, of which one was a bakery and another an apothecary's shop. The north side of the street also boasted a flagstone walk for some distance.

Along this thoroughfare creaked the great tar-pole wagons loaded with provisions and goods for the western military camps. These wagons were drawn by six to eight yoke of huge oxen each of which were branded OT (Overland Transit). In the summer a

Boggy Depot, 1975. Cemetery plot of the Wright family.

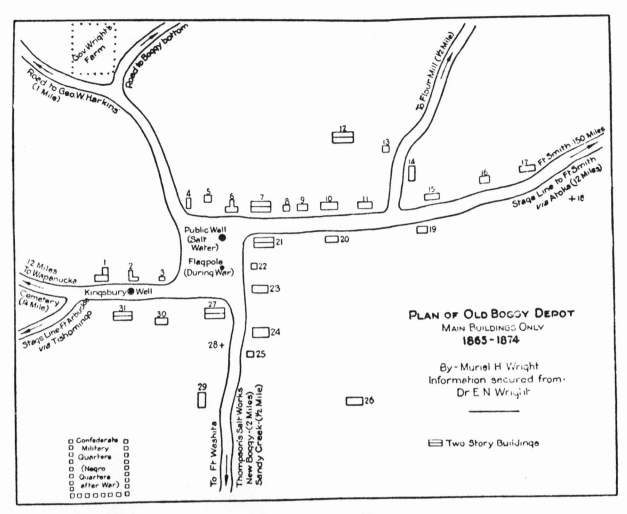

Boggy Depot, 1865–1874

1. Gov. Allen Wright's residence.
2. John Kingsbury residence.
3. House built by Mr. Lowe (cobbler).
4-5. Wood shop and residence of A. J. Martin.
6. Dr. T. J. Bond's residence.
7. Store of Reuben Wright—later store of Edward Dwight.
8. Temporary schoolhouse (hewed logs)—later Aunt Lou's bakery.
9. Apothecary shop.
10. Joseph J. Phillips' store.
11. Mr. Maurer's blacksmith shop.
12. Mr. Maurer's residence.
13. Miss Mary Chiffey's residence.
14. Brick Church-Hospital during the Civil War.
15. Livery barn.
16. J. J. Phillips' residence.

17. James Riley's residence.
18. Old graves.
19. Dr. Moore's residence.
20. Barn for stage coach company.
21. Capt. G. B. Hester & John Kingsbury store.
22. Dr. Bond's office.
23. Store of Mr. Ford.
24. Barn for hotel.
25. Tom Brown's blacksmith shop.
26. Capt. Charles LeFlore's residence.
27. Col. Wm. R. Guy's hotel.
28. Old graves.
29. Capt. G. B. Hester's residence.
30. New schoolhouse.
31. New church—upper floor used by Masonic Lodge.

smell of tar arose from the tar-buckets swinging beneath the wagons, and the oxen, their tongues hanging out, panted with the heat as they slowly but patiently obeyed the crack of the "black-snake" whips and the cries of their drivers.

Boggy Depot was also noted for nearby industries. A cotton gin and flour mill were built adjacent to a creek about one-half mile northeast of town. One man established a bois d'arc (Osage Orange, Horse Apple) seed mill. He crushed the large, green apples, washed out the seeds, and dried them. The seeds were then packaged and sold in the southeastern states, where bois d'arc hedges were used as fences. A salt works was operated about three miles south of Boggy Depot.

When the boundary between the Choctaw and Chickasaw nations was determined, Boggy Depot was found to be in the Choctaw area. Several Chickasaws then moved westward. Also, in the 1870s railroads began to build across the Indian nations. The route of the Missouri, Kansas and Texas Railroad was located about twelve miles northeast of the town. A number of merchants then moved to the rail site at Atoka. About this time the stage road was shifted to a better crossing on Clear Boggy River approximately three miles away. As a result, some businesses moved to that new location. Finally, on December 28, 1883, the post office was moved to what had become known as New Boggy Depot.

Few traces of Old Boggy Depot are now visible. Graves of some of the more notable individuals can be seen in the Boggy Depot cemetery. Bois d'arc still grows in the area, and Clear Boggy River and Sandy Creek show why they presented problems to early travel. The state of Oklahoma has now established the Boggy Depot Recreation Area near the location of the old townsite.

Bridgeport

COUNTY: *Caddo*
LOCATION: *(a) Sec. 4, T 12 N, R 11 W*
(b) 32½ miles north, 8 miles west of Anadarko; 10 miles east of Hydro
MAP: *Page 218*

POST OFFICE: *February 20, 1895–*
NEWSPAPERS: *Bridgeport News; Bridgeport Tribune; Bridgeport News-Tribune; Bridgeport Press; Bridgeport Oklahoman*
RAILROADS: *Choctaw, Oklahoma and Gulf Railroad (Rock Island); Enid and Anadarko Railway (Rock Island)*

Bridgeport had possibilities of becoming an important and progressive town, but two factors (1) physical—the Canadian River—and (2) human—a town feud—caused its downfall. Located on the south bank of the Canadian River in an area of rich farming land, and served by crossing rail lines, the town appeared destined to be the chief shipping point for a large area.

Bridgeport, 1940. Remains of the buildings that once formed the principal part of the business district. *(Courtesy Western History Collections, University of Oklahoma)*

The Canadian River, approximately one mile wide at Bridgeport, was subject to high water and sometimes flood during the rainy season. When water was low it could be forded, but there was always the problem of quicksand. The town received its name in the 1890s as the place where stagecoaches waited to cross the river. During high water they were ferried across; during low water the teams forded the river, following well-chosen paths carefully but never stopping in the channel. In 1893 a toll bridge was built. In 1895 a store with a post office lo-

Bridgeport, 1907. Tremont Hotel on Market Street. *(Courtesy Claren Marie Base Kidd)*

cated at the south end of the bridge, and Bridgeport had its start.

In 1915 a free bridge replaced the toll bridge, but a few years later it was damaged by a flood. The bridge was eventually replaced by the Key Bridge, which charged tolls during the first year. In 1932 the Oklahoma Highway Department constructed a bridge downstream from the Key Bridge and rerouted highways to the south of Bridgeport. In 1948 the Key Bridge was partly burned as a result of a grass fire and had to be removed. In 1958 the bridge for Interstate 40 was completed, resulting in the highway being moved more than one mile south of town. There have been at least five high-water and a dozen low-water bridges across the Canadian near Bridgeport.

In 1898 the Choctaw, Oklahoma and Gulf extended its tracks westward and built its bridge near the toll bridge. The Enid and Anadarko Railway north-south lines, built in 1901, used the same bridge. In 1907 the railroad bridge was demolished when a freight car jumped the track and struck a span of the bridge. This train, carrying cars of livestock and household goods belonging to German emigrants, fell into the sandy river bed. The heavily loaded cars immediately began sinking into the quicksand.

Men trying to save the livestock opened the car doors. Out flew ducks, chickens, and geese to the Bridgeport side of the river. The engine, coal car, and caboose were all that was saved. "To this day the other cars with everything inside as well as the middle section of the bridge lie buried deep somewhere in the shifting sand of the Canadian River bed." The bridge was replaced the next year but in 1914 was washed away during a flood. A new railroad bridge was again built. Later, in 1939, the track south from Bridgeport was abandoned.

In 1901, when the Caddo and Wichita lands were opened for settlement, Bridgeport became a booming new tent town. In a short time frame and brick business buildings and good homes replaced the tents, and a town of over three thousand persons had come into existence. Because of the topography and water a feud developed. Chrystobel Poteet, in the article "Bridgeport by the Canadian" (*Chronicles of Oklahoma,* Vol. XXXIX, No. 2) described it:

People found that water on the west side of Bridgeport was clear and pure while that on the east side, where most of the business buildings had been erected, was filled with gypsum crystals. Instead of trying to find a way to bring good water to the east side a bitter feud developed. The depot was on the west

Bridgeport, 1940. Abandoned church buildings. *(Courtesy Western History Collections, University of Oklahoma)*

Brinkman

COUNTY: *Greer*
LOCATION: *(a) Secs. 9/10, T 6 N, R 22 W*
(b) 8½ miles north, 1 mile west of Mangum
MAP: *Page 218*
POST OFFICE: *June 17, 1910–December 30, 1965*
NEWSPAPER: *Brinkman Courier*
RAILROAD: *Wichita Falls and Northwestern Railroad (Katy), abandoned 1972*

Brinkman was platted in 1910 when the rails of the Wichita Falls and Northwestern Railroad were extended northward from Altus. The site was surrounded by good agricultural lands, and the prospects for the community as an agricultural center were bright. The first settlers sought to attract others by building a good school system as well as needed commercial activities. A twelve-thousand-dollar bond issue was approved for the building of a school. The former Prosperity and Plainview school districts consolidated to form the new Brinkman Consolidated School District, the first in Greer County and one of the first in Oklahoma. A full high school program was developed, and the school became noted for scholastic activities as well as its successful girls' basketball teams. By 1925 the school had 450 students and ten teachers.

Brinkman had its period of greatest importance in the mid-1920s. It was a marketing center for both wheat and cotton, there being two large elevators and two cotton gins. In addition

side near the river but a long hill had to be climbed to reach the post office on the east side. To get mail distributed more conveniently business men on the west side contrived to move the post office one night during dark hours. A two story brick building was erected hurriedly on the west side for a bank. The big three story frame hotel was also moved to a corner location on the west side. Merchants on the east side became so embittered that many of them, in 1902, moved their buildings and stock to Hinton.

In 1904 Bridgeport had seventy-six places of business, including two banks, a flour mill with an output of one hundred barrels per day, and two hotels. A waterworks had been built along with a forty-thousand-gallon elevated tank. By 1909, however, the number of business institutions had decreased to forty-three, and the population was estimated at less than one thousand.

Throughout the years Bridgeport has declined in both population and as a trade center. The changing of the highways resulted in the town being bypassed to the east and south. It is now a somewhat isolated village in which about one hundred people live. The only remaining business is a small grocery store. The depot has been removed, and spurs of the primary track are covered by sand and grass. The place has been described as a rural retirement community.

Brinkman, 1973. Old buildings used for the storing of hay.

to the stores, cafes, and barber shops, the town had a bank, three doctors, a hotel, a telephone system, and a water system. Natural gas for fuel was brought to the community in 1927.

Just when the future looked brightest, disaster struck. In late 1927 the bank consolidated with one in Mangum and moved to that city. In 1929 the Dust Bowl period started, and it lasted for about five years, resulting in the consolidation of farms and the migration of people from the area. During the summer of 1929 fire destroyed the north half of the business district—three grocery stores, two cafes, one barber shop, the Odd Fellows Hall, and the bank building. Since the economic depression of the 1930s was just starting, most businesses were not rebuilt. Later, State Highway 34 bypassed the town one mile east of it.

Since the mid-1930s decline has been continuous. The old water tower, three unused store buildings, wide sidewalks bordering pastures, and an elevator mark where the former agricultural town stood. The school building had been removed and the school district consolidated into a still larger unit. In 1972 the railroad that started Brinkman was abandoned, and in 1974 the tracks were taken up. With the end of this activity Brinkman ceased to exist. As one former resident stated, "Brinkman was born and died with the railroad."

Bromide
(JUANITA, ZENOBIA)

COUNTY: *Johnston and Coal*
LOCATION: *(a) Sec. 32, T 1 S, R 8 E; Secs. 5/6, T 2 S, R 8 E*
8½ miles south, 17 miles west of Coalgate; 10 miles east, 12 miles north of Tishomingo
MAP: *Page 219*
POST OFFICE: *Juanita: October 20, 1905–April 27, 1906; Zenobia: April 27, 1906–June 8, 1907; Bromide: June 8, 1907–*
NEWSPAPER: *Bromide Herald*
RAILROAD: *Kansas, Oklahoma and Gulf Railroad (K.O. & G.), abandoned 1950*

The springs of the Bromide area were important gathering places long before the establishment of the town. There is some evidence that savage warriors fought for possession of the "healing waters" centuries before the coming of the Chickasaws and Choctaws. In the immediate area arrowheads, bones, and stone weapons in a funeral pile bear silent testimony to that fact. The Chickasaws, in whose nation the springs were located, named the springs Oka-Alichi (medicine water) and Popi-Kuli (salt springs). Although the water had a somewhat salty taste, it contained no salt.

Bromide came into existence in the early 1900s as the town of Juanita. In 1906 the name was changed to Zenobia and then in 1907 to Bromide. In 1908 Bromide was incorporated in both Johnston and Coal counties, the county line extending east-west through the northern part of the business district. It was the objective of the town founders to make the place important (1) as a resort area because of the mineral waters; (2) as an industrial center because of the high-grade stone available for crushing, lime kilns, and building purposes; and (3) as an agricultural center because of the fertility of the soil in adjacent areas. For a brief period all three objectives were attained. A booklet, *Bromide and Its Resources*, published by the early businessmen of Bromide states:

Bromide, which takes its name from the medicinal springs that issue from the hills above it, is one of the best finds in the way of possibilities that has been brought to public notice in Oklahoma. Its natural resources are so varied and so great, and its opportunities so vast and apparent, that the investor is amazed. He wonders why all this has not been heralded far and wide, and why development of these stored riches has not taken place long ago. The answer, of course, is a lack of titles to the land until very recently.

Bromide had its greatest development from about 1914 to 1920. The Kansas, Oklahoma and Gulf Railroad laid a spur from its tracks three and one-half miles east of Bromide to the town and the rock crusher. Businesses during the period included three general stores, a bank, two drugstores, two hardware stores, a meat market, two restaurants, a dry-goods store, and a blacksmith shop. Stores were well stocked, fair prices were paid for all produce, and some-

Bromide, *ca.* 1911. Residence of Judge W. H. Jackson, founder of the town. *(Courtesy Mrs. Gladys Channell)*

times free entertainment played to the crowds that flocked to town on market day. Four large hotels, two very modern for the period, were built to serve the regular visitors and those brought in by special excursion trains from Texas and Oklahoma. A large bathhouse and a swimming pool were built by the businessmen of the community to foster the developing tourist industry. One long-time resident of the area commented, "We had everything for the tourist. We were on the Chautauqua circuit, and one time Will Rogers entertained here." Four doctors were located in Bromide to serve those visiting the "best health resort in the southwestern states." Industries included a cotton gin and a cotton yard, a wagon maker, a sawmill, the rock crusher and quarry, a bottler who shipped bromide waters, and a gristmill.

In many respects Bromide declined as rapidly as it was built. In the mid-1920s, with the development of the automobile and better highways, tourists were going to other places more distant from home. By 1930 all excursion trains were canceled, the bank closed, the hotels no longer operated, and the quarry and crusher had stopped their activities.

Bromide today is not at all like the active health spa of yesteryear. No hotels exist; all have burned or have been torn down. The big springs continue to flow but are fenced from public use. Only one grocery store is open. The rock crusher is again in operation, but all material is trucked out, as no train now serves the area. Pasture lands have largely replaced formerly cultivated fields. Shells of a few unused brick buildings remind the visitor of a more successful past.

Bromide, 1912. Hacks meeting excursion trains. *(Courtesy Mrs. Gladys Channell)*

Bromide, 1913. Excursion train arriving from Denison, Texas. *(Courtesy Mrs. Gladys Channell)*

Bromide, 1916. View from the hill north of town. *(Courtesy Western History Collections, University of Oklahoma)*

Burke City

COUNTY: *Okfuskee*
LOCATION: *(a) Sec. 15, T 10 N, R 9 E*
(b) 6 miles south, 1½ miles west of Okemah
MAP: *Page 216*

Burke City came into existence in 1901 when a general store was started on the south bank of the North Canadian River about two miles east of Bearden. The store was successful, and a few other businesses, including a cotton gin, were established. Most of the time there was no problem in fording the North Canadian. The store owners, however, operated a ferry for crossing when the river was swollen.

Although few people other than those having businesses lived in the town, the store did become the meeting place for nearby farmers and ranchers. Outings and parties were held along the river banks. An arbor was built to provide shelter for church services.

Burke City thrived for only a little more than two years. The North Canadian, being an unpredictable river, sometimes flooded wide areas and could cause much destruction. During some floods the river has changed its main channel. Such problems caused abandonment of the site. The North Canadian has now removed all evidence of where Burke City once stood.

Catesby, 1901. Sod building in which the first store and post office were located. *(From* A Pioneer History of Shattuck)

Catesby

COUNTY: *Ellis*
LOCATION: *(a) Sec. 2, T 23 N, R 26 W*
(b) 24 miles north, 10½ miles west of Arnett; 15 miles north, 4½ miles west of Shattuck
MAP: *Page 215*
POST OFFICE: *February 18, 1902–January 31, 1970*

Catesby, located near the western edge of the Cherokee Outlet, developed as a small agricultural hamlet in a sparsely settled area. The place was never incorporated, and its population probably never exceeded one hundred. The period of greatest growth was about the time of statehood, 1907, just before the coming of the automobile and the development of highways. Because of the community's location on the edge of the High Plains and in a region of relatively low rainfall, no large stands of timber were available for lumber. Many families, after staking their claims, lived in covered wagons or tents until a sod shanty or a part sod–part dugout house could be built. Homes of these kinds, used in settlements as well as on farms, were usually one room about ten feet by twelve feet in size. Boards were put across the top of the building and then covered with sod. Such homes were relatively warm in winter and cool in summer. Catesby had both sod and dugout homes until frame ones could be built. In both town and country, getting fuel was a problem. Coal

Burke City, 1902. Ferry on the North Canadian River. A meeting of pioneers of the area. *(Courtesy Western History Collections, University of Oklahoma)*

40
c

was expensive and was used only when necessary. Cedar, locust, cottonwood, and other trees could be cut for fuel, but cow chips were used if available.

In Catesby one of the general stores was built of sod and had chips for sale should a person be unable to gather his own. Much trade in each of the two general stores was by barter. Butter, cream, eggs, and chickens were traded for staple foods, clothing, shoes, and tools. Two livestock dealers, a poultry dealer, two blacksmith shops, a harness shop, and a wagon maker indicated the importance of agriculture. At first the hamlet had a hotel and a meat market, but these soon closed. Since the place never had an elevator, wheat and broomcorn had to be hauled to more distant markets.

Economic conditions, the development of the combine and the electric fence, and the shift from the 160-acre farm to large wheat-cattle ranches brought about the downfall of Catesby. No stores, filling stations, or other businesses now exist. The small homes have been replaced by a few modern farm homes. Only one well-kept and active church remains.

Catesby, 1906. Feed yard and store. (*From* A Pioneer History of Shattuck)

Cayuga

COUNTY: *Delaware*
LOCATION: *(a) Sec. 23, T 25 N, R 24 E*
               (b) 15 miles north, 6 miles east of Jay; 3 miles north, 5 miles east of Grove
MAP: *Page 217*
POST OFFICE: *June 11, 1884–April 30, 1912*

Cayuga, 1910. Wagon factory, in foreground, and store built by Mathias Splitlog. A part of the factory remains standing. (*Courtesy Western History Collections, University of Oklahoma*)

Cayuga, to a great extent, is the story of Mathias Splitlog. He was born in Ohio of French-Canadian–Cayuga Indian ancestry. As a young man he migrated to Kansas City, where he built a flour mill and began dealing in real estate. From these efforts he made a fortune, and, dreaming of building a Splitlog empire, he moved into the Delaware District of the Cherokee Nation.

The site selected by Splitlog lay in the fertile valley of the Cowskin River and had on it a large spring. He named the place Cayuga Springs. Recognizing the need for better and faster means of transportation, Splitlog built a five-story factory for the making of wagons, buggies, and hacks. He also kept a stock of walnut lumber for the making of caskets. In addition to the carriage factory he built a flour mill, a general store, and a blacksmith shop. The factory was operated by steam engines, and the mill was run by water power. Water was piped underground from the spring not only to the mill and factory but also to a few homes. Splitlog operated a ferry across the Cowskin River and built a large barn for his horses and stock.

During the early 1890s Splitlog, who had been adopted by the Senecas, had a church erected as a Catholic shrine. It was of Gothic architecture and built of limestone quarried from the Boone formation. In the belfry he put a large sixteen-hundred-pound bell. It was said that the call to worship could be heard twelve miles

The church stands today as a monument to the pioneer Indian industrialist. A part of the old factory, although dilapidated, still stands. The Cayuga townsite is now bordered by the waters of the Lake O' The Cherokees, and the area is becoming noted as a recreational playground.

Cayuga, 1975. Stone marker at the grave of Mrs. Splitlog.

Cayuga, *ca.* 1955. Church built by Mathias Splitlog in 1896. The building has now been restored. *(Courtesy Oklahoma Historical Society)*

away. For some years the church was not used. The bell was transferred to the Catholic Church in Nowata, but later was returned. Vandals broke into the cornerstone of the old church in search of valuables. Eventually, the church was refinished and refurnished. The Splitlog burial grounds are near it.

Loy Pollan Tullis, in *And Gladly Teach* writes: "The village burned early in 1913. Only the five-story carriage shop, the priest's house, and the Catholic church were left standing. The fire destroyed a hotel, general store, post office, blacksmith shop, and eight or ten dwellings."

Center

COUNTY:	*Pontotoc*
LOCATION:	*(a) Sec. 19, T 4 N, R 5 E*
	(b) 2 miles north, 8 miles west of Ada
MAP:	*Page 219*
POST OFFICE:	*June 9, 1890–February 15, 1928*
NEWSPAPERS:	*Center Expositor; Center News; First Baptist Banner*

Center, established in the mid-1880s, was a white settlement in the Chickasaw Nation before the

Center, 1895. West side of the square. The large building at the left was the courthouse. *(Courtesy Julius Lester Medlock)*

Center, 1975. Area that was formerly the west side of the square.

area was legally open for white ownership. Most of the settlers either leased or rented the land they farmed or on which they built their stores.

By the mid-1890s Center had become the leading town in what is now Pontotoc County. It had a population in excess of five hundred persons, and for a while a courthouse was located in the town. The commercial area was built around a square in which the two principal water wells were located. Most business establishments were on the west and south sides of the square, but there were also some on both the north and east sides. Twenty-five stores of various kinds, as well as two hotels and a "leading" newspaper, the *Center News*, indicate the importance of the place.

Center was described by one of its former residents as a good agricultural trade center and a Saturday town. He stated: "Usually people brought corn to the mill to be ground into meal on Saturday, or they came to buy coffee, sugar, or flour; or if it was the fall of the year they sometimes brought cotton to be ginned; or if they had no other reason they came as they laughingly said because 'their hair got curly' on that afternoon." Saturday afternoon was the community meeting time, and the square was the place where news, gossip, and plans could be discussed.

On March 1, 1900, most of the business buildings on the west side of the square, including the courthouse, were destroyed by fire. No plans had been made to fight such a fire, and no fire-fighting equipment was available. As other towns were beginning to develop in that part of the Chickasaw Nation, some of the merchants moved rather than rebuild. Later, others moved to Ada when it became the recognized city of the area, having been designated the county seat for Pontotoc County by the Oklahoma State Constitution. When the railroad building westward from Ada Junction to Purcell passed to the south of Center, other businesses moved to new places being established by the railroad. As a result, Center rapidly lost importance as a trade center.

The old town square can still be visualized, for the area stands vacant today. A few nearby homes continue to be used. The current village known as Center, one store and a few houses along State Highway 19, is about one-half mile south of the old square. It has little, if any, relationship to the old town. Several persons living there did not know of the older Center when asked about it.

Centralia

COUNTY:	*Craig*
LOCATION:	*(a) Sec. 26, T 27 N, R 18 E*
	(b) 11 miles north, 11 miles west of Vinita; 15½ miles west of Blue Jacket
MAP:	*Page 217*
POST OFFICE:	*April 11, 1899–*
NEWSPAPERS:	*Centralia Standard; Centralia Register*

Centralia, established in the mid-1890s, has always been an isolated community. At the time of its establishment, however, its location was such that it became the trade center for a large area of ranches and farms, the nearest railroad centers being sixteen miles east at Bluejacket and seventeen miles west at Delaware. Most travel was then done by horse and buggy or wagon over usually unmarked and ungraded roads or trails. Thus, when the first store was started and was successful, other commercial activities were soon organized. As most rural citizens of the period preferred not to travel more than ten or twelve miles to a town, a day's journey from home to town and back, Centralia became an active marketing and trading center.

As with most of the towns in the early 1900s, all of the residences and almost all of the business buildings were of frame construction. No water system or fire-fighting system was developed, each home depending upon its own well. There were two public wells in the business area. On January 11, 1907, much of the business district was completely destroyed and a few of the houses were damaged by fire. The bucket brigade, using water from public and private wells, fought a losing battle. Most of the stores, however, were rebuilt.

Centralia had its greatest growth about 1915, when the population was estimated to be between 750 and 800 persons. At that time the town supported three hotels, two banks, an active newspaper, three doctors, and an undertaker in addition to the usual stores, blacksmith shops, livery stables, and feed mills. The town built an electric light plant to serve the local community. Two stage lines helped to meet the transportation needs of the area. Four churches were organized and a school system developed.

The economic depression of the 1930s added to the problems already confronting Centralia. Better roads, the automobile, consolidation of farms and a return to ranching, and the desire for a greater variety of places to buy and sell had caused the town to decline. World War II added to the migration from the general area for work or military duty. Since then the decline has been steady. Today there is a store–post office remaining, but the school has been closed and most of the few standing homes show the lack of care. All roads leading to the town are either gravel or graded dirt roads, the nearest blacktop road being nine miles away. Isolation, which started Centralia, is now slowly strangling it to death.

Centralia, 1899. Interior of Van Ausdal Drug Store. *(Courtesy Western History Collections, University of Oklahoma)*

Centralia, 1899. Grocery store and drugstore. Even at this early date drugstores carried a variety of goods. *(Courtesy Western History Collections, University of Oklahoma)*

Centralia, 1975. Centralia Baptist Church.

Cestos

COUNTY: *Dewey*
LOCATION: *(a) Sec. 11, T 19 N, R 18 W*
               (b) 7 miles north, 7 miles west
               of Taloga
MAP: *Page 215*
POST OFFICE: *November 18, 1898–December*
               15, 1923
NEWSPAPERS: *Cestos Reporter; Cestos News*

Cestos developed as an agricultural service center near the northern boundary of the Cheyenne-Arapaho Reservation when that area was opened for settlement in 1892. The town attained its maximum population, approximately five hundred, between 1905 and 1910. During that period it had fifteen stores of various kinds plus a bank, a hotel, and a newspaper. A local telephone exchange was developed for Cestos

and its immediate rural area. A medical doctor and a veterinarian also served the community.

Cestos became noted for its flour mill, the Cestos Milling Company. The Olympia and Sno Flake Brands, made by the mill, were marketed throughout Oklahoma Territory as it developed and in the Texas Panhandle. The mill advertised: "Our flour and mill products have stood the test above all competitors. Erected June, 1904, and is equipped with Barnard & Lee's latest improved machinery. Bring your wheat and grain where you can get honest weights and best prices." The mill would also exchange best bolted meal with farmers for corn. Since much wheat was grown on farms of the area, and poor roads made the slow transportation to larger markets difficult, the flour mill was a positive factor in the growth of the town.

About 1915 agriculture in the Cestos vicinity began to change from the growing of grains to the grazing of cattle. In the early 1920s, as the automobile developed and highways were improved, the marketing of grain and animals and the buying of supplies for local use shifted to the rail centers to the north and west. Cestos could not compete.

U.S. Highway 60 now follows approximately the old Main Street of Cestos as it passes where the town formerly stood. North of the road no buildings stand, and the entire area is usually planted with wheat. On the south side of the road stands one store building, a building previously used as a church, a home, and a few outbuildings.

Cestos, 1905. Flour mill, the home of Olympia and Swan Lake flour. *(Courtesy Oklahoma Historical Society)*

Cestos, 1906. Kerns & Co., general store. *(Courtesy Oklahoma Historical Society)*

Cestos, *ca.* 1906. Saturdays were always important trade days in early agricultural towns. *(Courtesy Pioneer Museum)*

Cestos, 1906. A street fair was held each fall. Agricultural displays were numerous. *(Courtesy John Windolph)*

Cestos, 1906. Grocery section inside the Kerns & Co. store. *(Courtesy Oklahoma Historical Society)*

Cherokee Town, *ca.* 1890. Dam across Little Sandy Creek (sometimes called Cherokee Creek). Water power was used to run the gin, and the area below the dam was a favorite recreational place. *(Courtesy L. L. Shirley)*

Cherokee Town

COUNTY:	*Garvin*
LOCATION:	*(a) Sec. 25, T 3 N, R 1 E*
	(b) 2 miles south, 4 miles east of Pauls Valley
MAP:	*Page 219*
POST OFFICE:	*August 17, 1874–May 10, 1877*

Prior to the Civil War a small trading post was started near Little Sandy Creek about a mile from where a much-used trail crossed the Washita River. The post remained unnamed until a band of Cherokees who were forced to move from Texas at the time of the Texas Revolution settled in the vicinity. Because the Cherokees built homes and operated farms within the area, the trading post with its blacksmith shop became known to travelers as Cherokee Town, and the Washita River crossing as Cherokee Crossing.

Although the village remained small, it was the best-known place in the vicinity. It was here that General Pike asked the Plains Tribes to join him for a conference shortly before the outbreak of the Civil War. His aim was to enlist sympathy and gain aid for the Confederacy. He did not, however, consider the meeting successful.

Following the Civil War, especially during the 1870s, the trail became one of the most important roads across the Choctaw and Chickasaw nations, as it connected Boggy Depot and Fort Sill. It was, however, sometimes difficult for individuals to secure transportation from place to place. As Joseph F. Murphy writes in his book *Tenacious Monks*: "The two travelers sought some means of conveyance from Tishomingo to Cherokee Town. They finally found a rather extraordinary way to arrange it. A hog merchant offered to take them to their desired destination. He agreed to haul them for the same price that he charged to haul hogs, one cent a pound. When asked what that would come to for both men, he gave a very definite reply as follows: 'Well, I reckon both of you don't weigh more than 150 pounds apiece, so I'll take three dollars for the trip.' They arrived in Cherokee Town two days later."

Cherokee Town gained in importance when a cross-country stage line was started and stage stands were designated at twenty-mile intervals. It was not unusual for freight wagons pulled by twelve to sixteen yoke of oxen to stop or pass through the town. Coaches, pulled by four to eight horses, always stopped to rest or change

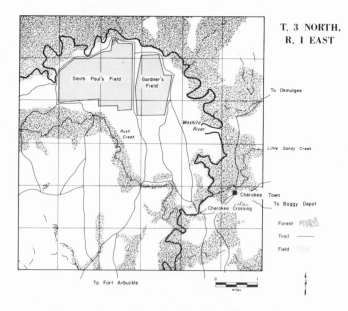

Cherokee Town, 1875. Cherokee Town was located about three-fourths of a mile from the Cherokee Crossing of the Washita River. The area identified as Smith Paul's Field is now the location of Pauls Valley. *(Courtesy L. L. Shirley)*

animals and permit passengers a chance to stretch. Military personnel and wagons hauling military supplies made constant use of the road. As a result of such activity, the town increased in population. Stores were added, and a hotel and campsites were provided. There was also a Masonic Hall, and the town had a doctor. Blacksmithing was a necessary trade and may have been the most important occupation in town. Horses and mules had to be shod and the wagons and stage coaches kept in repair. The smith was an important person in the community. Church services were held, usually by circuit riders, and itinerant teachers sometimes held subscription schools.

As population throughout the Chickasaw Nation increased, new roads were developed and the routes of travel changed. In the mid-1880s the Gulf, Colorado and Santa Fe started building its line north from Gainesville, Texas, to meet with the tracks being extended south to Purcell by the Southern Kansas Railroad (Santa Fe). The tracks, located about three miles west of Cherokee Town, attracted the remaining businesses to a new site on the railroad, where the town of Wynnewood was established.

All signs of old Cherokee Town have been removed, and the land has been returned to agricultural use. Some wagon tracks at old Cherokee Crossing can still be seen.

Cloud Chief
(TACOLA)

COUNTY:	*Washita*
LOCATION:	*(a) Sec. 13, T 9 N, R 16 W*
	(b) 2½ miles south, 8 miles east of Cordell
MAP:	*Page 218*
POST OFFICE:	*March 29, 1892–December 30, 1964*
NEWSPAPERS:	*Cloud Chief Beacon; Cloud Chief Herald; Cloud Chief Witness; Cloud Chief Bulletin; Cloud Chief Herald-Sentinel; Tacola Chief*

Cloud Chief, 1898. Drilling the well at the east end of Main Street, near the courthouse. *(Courtesy Western History Collections, University of Oklahoma)*

Cloud Chief, originally called Tacola, was born with a rush when the Cheyenne-Arapaho Reservation was opened by run in 1892. Because the place had been designated the county seat of H County, it was laid out with streets, blocks, and lots before the opening. For the purpose of establishing claims within the 320-acre townsite, a second race, which had to be made on foot, was started at 1:00 P.M. on the same day the reservation was opened. Within a two-hour period a tent city with saloons, gambling establishments, and grocery stores was started. During the following few weeks the population jumped to over three thousand, and the number of businesses increased to about fifty. All businesses and homes were housed in tents.

Many settlers left almost immediately after their claims were legally staked and recorded, since they had six months from the time they filed to the time they had to settle on the claim. Also, as some merchants sold out their stocks of goods they would strike their tents and leave town. Within a few months the population had decreased to only a few hundred persons. The primary reason for the decline was the lack of transportation facilities. All goods coming to Cloud Chief were dependent on irregular stage or freight lines from El Reno or Minco. One

Cloud Chief, *ca.* 1899. A sketch of the frontier town by an unknown pioneer. The courthouse is the building in the upper left. *(Courtesy Western History Collections, University of Oklahoma)*

year after its founding the town had only four saloons and two stores.

In 1893 a small sawmill was started about two miles south of town to supply cottonwood lumber for the building of a courthouse and a hotel. With these additions the population began to increase. Some of the buildings constructed in the town were unique. The courthouse was a twenty-foot by thirty-foot, one-story structure made of badly warped cottonwood lumber. There were no partitions, but it housed the sheriff, county judge, county clerk, and county superintendent of schools, each being provided with a chair and a desk. There were also two improved jail cells in the building. One hotel, called the Iron Hotel, was made of sheets of galvanized iron on both the sides and the roof. Guests there said it was impossible to sleep when it rained or hailed, and it was noted for its high temperature during the summer. A public watering trough was located at the east end of

Main Street. Nearby was a wagon yard, where, for twenty-five cents, one could rent a stall with a feed trough for his horse and a bunk for himself if he desired to stay overnight. At the west end of Main Street was the town blacksmith shop. The residential sections of town had about fifty small frame houses and some thirty-five dugouts and half-dugouts. By 1898 the population had increased to over seven hundred, and the town had two hardware stores, two restaurants, two general stores, two saloons, a barber shop, a bank, a print shop where the county newspaper was printed, a blacksmith shop, a wagon yard, and a livery stable. Churches had been organized and a school was in operation about six months of each year. It was generally noted that "the two saloons were the best equipped and best kept establishments there."

As H County, now Washita County, became more densely populated and better organized, there was considerable agitation to move the county seat. A petition by those living in the western and central parts of the county was filed with the County Commissioners asking that the county seat be moved to Cordell. After a series of court battles an election to decide the issue was called in spite of the fact that there was an injunction prohibiting it. An appeal to block the election was drawn up by the county attorney. The papers were to be delivered to the federal court in El Reno by a young lawyer who was the son of the county attorney. Instead of delivering them as instructed, the young lawyer mailed the papers. They arrived in El Reno too late, and the injunction died. Upon hearing this, the outraged citizens of Cloud Chief tarred and feathered the young lawyer and rode him out of town on a rail. The County Attorney fled from the county, never to return. After another election, which Cloud Chief claimed was held illegally, the county seat was moved to Cordell. As late as 1904, however, the Supreme Court of the United States held that the county seat could not be moved and ordered county officials to remove their offices to Cloud Chief within thirty days. Two of the County Commissioners then went to Washington and got a bill through Congress legalizing the election that had been

Cloud Chief, ca. 1900. This structure is representative of most frontier hotels. *(Courtesy Oklahoma Historical Society)*

held. This bill, signed by President Theodore Roosevelt, ended the county seat fight.

With the loss of the county seat, Cloud Chief declined rapidly. By 1913 business establishments were reduced to a cotton gin, a wagon yard, a hotel, and two small general stores. Even though a large consolidated school was later located in the town, it continued to lose population.

Cloud Chief today has no stores in operation. Old buildings still standing are used for storage. The remains of the consolidated school building stand unused, with windows broken and some doors swinging in the wind. A church continues in operation, and a few homes, used by farm families or old-timers, remain.

Cloud Chief, 1898. Interior of H County Courthouse. *(Courtesy Western History Collections, University of Oklahoma)*

Cold Springs

COUNTY:	*Kiowa*
LOCATION:	*(a) Sec. 29, T 4 N, R 17 W*
	(b) 15½ miles south, 4½ miles east of Hobart; 9 miles north, 3½ miles west of Snyder
MAP:	*Page 218*
POST OFFICE:	*November 25, 1903–September 15, 1909; January 27, 1913–March 15, 1956*
RAILROAD:	*Blackwell, Enid and Southwestern Railway (Frisco)*

Cold Springs, *ca.* 1902. Types of homes found in newly established frontier towns ranged from small frame structures to tents and dugouts. *(Courtesy Western History Collections, University of Oklahoma)*

Cold Springs was established in the valley of Otter Creek shortly after the opening of the Kiowa-Comanche-Apache Reservation by lottery in 1901. The site selected was in an area of fertile farm and pasture lands, had an adequate supply of water, and was adjacent to the recently constructed Frisco railroad. For a brief period two towns, North Cold Springs and South Cold Springs, existed about a mile apart. North Cold Springs ceased to exist, however, after the citizens of South Cold Springs loaded the depot of the former on a flatcar and moved it to their town.

North Cold Springs was recognized as a recreation and health area. A large hotel was built, and "special" trains from Hobart brought hundreds of visitors to the "living springs, nature's health and pleasure resort." With the advent of the automobile and improved highways the recreation industry soon faded. Near South Cold Springs quarries were developed because of an "unexhaustible supply of blue and black granite." Two polishing plants were opened, and both polished and unpolished granite was shipped to various parts of the nation.

Cold Springs never developed into a large town, although about 1915 it did have a hotel, a lumberyard, a dry-goods store, a meat market,

Cold Springs, 1910. Quarry and plant of the Oklahoma Granite and Monumental Company. *(Courtesy Oklahoma Historical Society)*

Cold Springs, 1973. One of the last buildings to be destroyed. Note the old-style gasoline pump. *(Courtesy Steve Wilson)*

a blacksmith shop and filling station, four general stores, a cotton gin, a granite company, and a telephone exchange. Later a cheese factory existed for a brief period. In the 1930s, as with most small and dominantly agricultural towns, Cold Springs lost population, and the number of businesses decreased. During its last years fewer than fifty people lived in the town.

As early as 1903 the United States Geological Survey sent an engineer into western Oklahoma Territory to survey for dam sites. The Otter Creek area was recommended because of the granite base on which a dam could be built. The dam across the narrows on West Otter Creek, under control of the Bureau of Reclamation, formed Tom Steed Reservoir. Practically all of the good agricultural land is in the reservoir basin. Although the site of Cold Springs will not be under water, it is in the reservoir basin. All buildings of the former town have been cleared away, and no visible signs remain.

Cooperton was platted, and its blocks, lots, and streets were laid out on a half-section of prairie land before the opening of the Comanche, Kiowa, and Apache Reservation in 1901. Lots were drawn in the same drawing that was held for the adjacent farmland. Within the townsite certain blocks were designated for schools, parks, and municipal buildings. Tradesmen, merchants, and others, along with their families, came to Cooperton at the time of settlement. Businesses initially were in makeshift facilities and tents. As soon as possible homes and permanent buildings for stores and offices were built. Clearing the land was a difficult job. In March, 1904, some of the citizens decided to clear the western half of the townsite by burning the grass. The prairie fire that resulted not only cleared the townsite but an additional four and one-half square miles. Some livestock was killed, a few buildings were destroyed, and one person was burned critically.

During the first ten years Cooperton grew rapidly. In addition to general stores and grocery, drug, and hardware stores, the town had a bank, a cigar factory, three cotton gins, a flour mill, livery stables, and blacksmith shops. Two creameries operated for a while, but they closed because of the difficulty of getting butter to market. Although a railroad was promised, and the grade for tracks was partly completed, the project was abandoned and Cooperton remained an inland town. The best years, insofar as number and variety of businesses were concerned,

Cooperton, 1906. Cotton gin. *(Courtesy Mrs. Florence Peterson)*

Cooperton

COUNTY: *Kiowa*
LOCATION: *(a) Sec. 34, T 5 N, R 16 W*
(b) 10 miles south, 12 miles east of Hobart
MAP: *Page 218*
POST OFFICE: *February 1, 1902–*
NEWSPAPER: *Cooperton Banner*

Cooperton, *ca.* 1908. Crowd gathered for a trade day. *(Courtesy Mrs. Florence Peterson)*

were the 1915–1925 period. The peak population, however, was not reached until the late 1930s.

The appearance of Cooperton was somewhat typical of small frontier towns on the Great Plains. Most buildings and houses were unpainted frame structures. Only a few had more than one story, permitting church steeples, cotton gins, and mills to appear with prominence on the skyline. Streets were not paved, and many shown on the original plat were never opened. The only street to completely cross the townsite was Main Street. Blocks set aside for parks were never developed, but where Main Street crossed Rainy Mountain Creek a dam had been built. The reservoir formed a popular playground area for local residents.

In 1925 Cooperton and other school districts consolidated so that a high school could be developed. Later, as population in the school district decreased, Cooperton made a practice of employing chiefly teachers with large families. An effort was made to entice large families to move to the district in order to keep the school operating. The high school closed in 1965, and the grade school in 1971. The school building has now been torn down.

The automobile, the Great Depression of the 1930s, World War II, and the desire of farmers to trade where there is a greater range of services and a greater choice of merchandise have caused a loss of population and business in Cooperton. Today the town has one active church, a community building, a small grocery store, and a garage. A few old buildings, including the bank, still stand. Most people living in Cooperton, probably about thirty-five, are old-timers or retired individuals.

Cooperton, 1974. Remains of the last bank building.

Corbett, *ca.* 1910. Group of young men on their best horses in front of the Corbett store. *(Courtesy Mrs. Franklin Morris)*

Corbett

COUNTY: *Cleveland*
LOCATION: *(a) Secs. 19/20, T 6 N, R 1 E*
             (b) 17 miles south, 12 miles east
             of Norman; 3 miles south, 6 miles
             east of Lexington
MAP: *Page 219*
POST OFFICE: *Higbee: August 23, 1901–February 19, 1902; Corbett: February 19, 1902–January 2, 1907*

Corbett, an agricultural village, had its beginning in 1893 when J. P. Corbett purchased eighty acres of farmland and platted one corner for the village he planned. After deciding upon the exact location for his home and orchard, he designated specific sites for a "store, then for a blacksmith shop, a cotton gin, sawmill, a pond, a gristmill, a rent house for the farmer, a church and the pastor's home." The sites were either leased or given to an individual for the development of what was indicated. They were to revert to Mr. Corbett if used otherwise. Specifically, there was to be no saloon in the village, nor was there to be any liquor sold in the village. A post office, first known as Higbee, was housed in one corner of the store. In 1902 the post office name was changed to Corbett. Children of the community attended a one-room school, known as Valley Grove, one mile east of the village. A few years later two other stores and a sorghum mill were added.

Located just two miles north of the Canadian River, the trade territory of Corbett was confined largely to the area east and west of the village. Corn, cotton, and fruit, especially apples and pears, were the chief farm products. During seasons in which the weather had been favorable, several wagon loads of fruit would be hauled to Purcell, where boxcars filled with various fruits were shipped to market.

Corbett had its greatest growth in the last half of the 1920s, when the population in the immediate vicinity was estimated to be about 125 persons. The village declined rapidly after

Corbett, *ca.* 1910. Baptism service in the Corbett pond. *(Courtesy Mrs. Franklin Morris)*

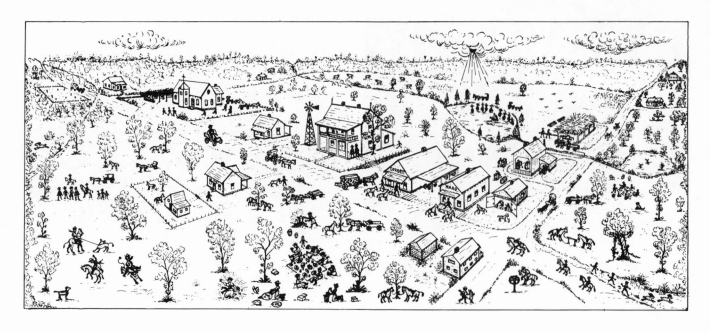

Corbett, *ca.* 1925. This sketch by Robert G. Campbell shows two stores, a blacksmith shop, a cotton gin, and a thatch-covered sorghum mill. The church and the baptism pond are shown. The largest home and the church remain. *(Courtesy Mrs. Franklin Morris)*

1930. The cotton gin burned, the soil "wore out," the dry years killed many of the orchards, and the depression caused financial problems. First the young folks, then the older ones left the community and did not return. The church continues active for those remaining. Stores and mills have been torn down or moved. The first home built still stands, but it is rapidly falling into ruin.

Cornish

COUNTY:	*Jefferson*
LOCATION:	*(a) Sec. 35, T 4 S, R 4 W*
	(b) 22 miles east of Waurika; 1 mile south of Ringling
MAP:	*Page 219*
POST OFFICE:	*July 10, 1891–March 15, 1918*
NEWSPAPERS:	*Cornish Reasoner; Cornish Herald; Orphans' Home Journal*

Cornish, founded in the late 1880s, became an important town in the southwestern part of the Chickasaw Nation. It was the last notable stop between the rail center at Ardmore and Fort Sill. Like most such frontier towns, it had a variety of commercial enterprises, churches, a school, and a well on Main Street which supplied most of the citizens with water.

The principal story of Cornish, however, revolves about the activities of one man, M. E. (Mose) Harris. Mr. Harris was not a minister or social worker, nor was he a man of financial means. He loved children and was touched by their needs in the days when their neglect and suffering was little noticed. With the statement: "I'm going to build a home for orphans and neglected children right here in Cornish," he started. In February, 1907, Harris began construction of the first building of the Cornish Orphans Home. Even before the first building was complete he rented a house, and he and his wife began the care of orphans. He believed in the pay-as-you-go policy for construction work. There was very little lag in his building program, for as his activities became known, contributions came from all parts of Oklahoma and many other states. In 1910 the Oklahoma Legislature recognized the value of his work and appropriated five thousand dollars for the operation of the institution. In 1912, ten thousand dollars was appropriated. The Cornish Orphans Home continued to function for some forty years and helped influence the lives of over fifteen hundred children.

In 1913 the Santa Fe extended its tracks westward from Ardmore to Ringling, a new town about one mile north of Cornish. Soon thereafter the various businesses of Cornish moved to the new rail center, and the importance of the town rapidly declined. A few of the old homes still stand, and most are occupied. No commercial activities remain. The largest building of the orphanage stands unused and neglected.

Crawford, 1910. The large building was a general store; the smaller storelike building was the print shop; the building at the upper left corner was the bank. *(Courtesy Willard Young)*

Cornish, 1975. The largest building of the Cornish Orphans Home stands unused.

Crawford

COUNTY:	*Roger Mills*
LOCATION:	*(a) Sec. 30, T 16 N, R 24 W*
	(b) 15 miles north, 7 miles west
	of Cheyenne
MAP:	*Page 215*
POST OFFICE:	*September 12, 1902–*
NEWSPAPER:	*·Crawford Blade*

Crawford was platted in 1910 in the hope of enticing the Wichita Falls and Northwestern Railway, then extending its tracks northward, into coming through the village. Because the attempt was unsuccessful, Crawford did not incorporate. Before 1910 the village served as the trade center for a large ranch and farm area. Poor roads and horse and buggy or wagon transportation discouraged traveling greater distances than necessary. In 1909 the village had a population of about thirty persons, but the businesses of a general store, bank, weekly newspaper, drugstore, and blacksmith shop as well as the personal services of a doctor, a well driller, and two carpenters indicate the importance of Crawford to the area.

By 1912 Crawford had had substantial growth. A barber shop, hotel, cafe, lumberyard, and produce house had been added to the business community. Another doctor had established his practice in the village, and the population had increased to over 125 persons. A school had been started, and there were three churches. The post office served as the center for rural routes in the area. Most buildings and homes were frame, but a few sod houses remained. The chief problem was the bank. It had been robbed in 1908 and again in 1910. Because it was never a strong bank, it did not recover completely from the second robbery and had to be liquidated in 1912.

Crawford held its own through the World War I years and then gained again during the first half of the 1920s. It became noted as a Saturday town. The merchants staged Saturday drawings, frequently there were horse races, and often dances were held on Saturday nights. Population in the area had increased enough so that by consolidation a high school was established.

The 1930 Dust Bowl years were hard on Crawford, for the village was located near the heart of the Oklahoma Dust Bowl. The lack of rain prevented crops and grass from growing, topsoil blew away, many animals died of thirst, numerous farmers as well as merchants went broke, and people moved away, often abandoning

Crawford, 1925. Gathering for a township fair. *(Courtesy Willard Young)*

dreds of tents, shacks, and temporary houses were hastily built to care for the thousands of workers that came to the new oil field. Restaurants, hotels, mercantile stores, dance halls, and many other businesses developed overnight as merchants of every kind flocked in to get in on the payload. "A Baptist church was organized during the boom, but it was poorly attended since most of the people were too busy to think of religion."

Cromwell soon became noted for the great amount of petroleum produced, and at the same time it became notorious as the "wickedest city in the world." It has been said that there were no places in the United States worse than Cromwell during its boom days. In addition to the

homes and farm implements or small stocks of goods. Those who stayed consolidated farms, began to practice soil and water conservation, and developed large ranches. Thus, with the advent of improved roads and automobiles, Crawford practically disappeared.

The present population of Crawford is less than twenty-five. No business establishments exist, and two of the eight houses are vacant. Some old buildings stand, but are too ramshackle to be used. Two churches, the post office, and an elementary consolidated school remain open.

Cromwell

COUNTY:	*Seminole*
LOCATION:	*(a) Sec. 16, T 10 N, R 8 E*
	(b) 13½ miles north, 2 miles east of Wewoka
MAP:	*Page 219*
POST OFFICE:	*May 17, 1924–*

Cromwell boomed into existence in October, 1923, when oil was discovered in paying quantities on a farm about fifteen miles northeast of Wewoka. "Oil rigs sprung up like sunflowers." Within a few months the rural district became a city of from eight to ten thousand people. Hun-

Cromwell, *ca.* 1918. Bill Tilghman, noted frontier marshal and later chief of police in Oklahoma City, was killed in Cromwell on October 30, 1926. *(Courtesy Oklahoma Historical Society)*

Cromwell, 1924. View of Main Street. *(Courtesy Western Histoy Collections, University of Oklahoma)*

hundreds that came seeking work, there were also large numbers of gamblers, prostitutes, hop peddlers, and swindlers. "On one occasion the sheriff of Seminole County came to Cromwell to rid the wicked little city of all its women of easy virtue. He raided their establishments, seized them, lined them up in the street, handcuffed and chained them together, and marched them to the county jail in Wewoka, fifteen miles away" (Loos, *Oil on Stream* [Baton Rouge, Louisiana State University Press, 1940]).

Numerous liquor joints operated openly even though prohibition was the law. Since there had been no town at all, the only officer that could police the place was the county sheriff. The result was that the town was wide open. Robbery and hijacking were nightly offenses. It was reported: "It was not safe to be out at night without some money. Several times when men were

Cromwell, *ca.* 1925. Intensive drilling was characteristic in the various pools of the Greater Seminole Area as no conservation laws existed.

held up that did not have money on them, they were knocked in the head and told to carry a few dollars next time." One officer stated that there were ten unsolved murders during the first year and that the murderers were free because no bodies were ever found. (Later some bodies were found when the large oil tanks were torn down and moved away.)

Reliable merchants and law-abiding citizens decided law and order must be brought to the town. The sheriff, however, refused to appoint a deputy approved by the citizens. As a result they appealed to the Governor of Oklahoma, Martin E. Trapp, for assistance. At the same time, the citizens wrote former U.S. Marshal Bill Tilghman asking him to become chief of police in the newly organized town. The letter to Tilghman said: "I'm afraid the sheriff and county attorney will not back us up. The gamblers pay $2,500 each; each lodging house that has women, $40 a month—we have 31 of them. We also have a few hijackers here and we want to change their place of residence." A call from Governor Trapp to Tilghman was made shortly after he received the letter. Even though the famous lawman had retired (he was past seventy years of age), he accepted the challenge.

The day after his arrival in Cromwell, Tilghman became acquainted with Wiley Lynn. Lynn was the federal prohibition enforcement officer for the area and had been in Cromwell for some time. Tilghman soon became aware of Lynn's activities and believed he was "on the take." On one occasion the marshal and his assistants thought they had Lynn trapped along with a planeload of dope, but at the last minute the smugglers somehow were given warning. As progress was being made in bringing order to the town, Lynn left no doubt about his hatred for Tilghman. On the night of October 30, 1926, Lynn became drunk and started shooting up the town. Tilghman met Lynn on the street and grabbed and held him until his gun was taken away. Lynn, however, had a second gun. When released by Tilghman, Lynn drew the second gun and shot the marshal three times. Tilghman died within a few minutes. Tilghman's death did much to clean up Cromwell. Lynn fled that night, followed by most of the gamblers and prostitutes out of fear of what might happen as a result of Tilghman's death. (Lynn was soon captured and tried for murder in Wewoka. In spite of the evidence presented, he was acquitted. A few days after the acquittal Lynn was killed during a brawl in southern Oklahoma.)

In the third year of its existence the Cromwell pool began declining in production, and people started moving away. About that time there was also a devastating fire that practically burned out the town. Houses, business buildings, and tents were dry and oil-soaked. After the fire started there was no stopping it until it had burned out. Fire trucks from neighboring large communities came to help, but could do little. Many business establishments, including the bank, did not rebuild. As other oil pools, including the Greater Seminole Area, were being opened, people left Cromwell almost as rapidly as they had come. Population figures for the 1920s show vividly the rise and decline of Cromwell: 1920—0; 1925—8,000 to 10,000; 1930—249.

Refineries and gasoline plants have now been removed from the area. A few wells remain on the pump. Several school districts have consolidated and use the excellent school plant built in Cromwell but known as the Butner School. A few residents live in the old boom town, a few new homes have been built, and there are two stores. The present Cromwell, however, has little relationship to the brawling, booming, lusty town of the 1920s.

Cross

COUNTY: *Kay*
LOCATION: *(a) Sec. 22, T 26 N, R 2 E*
                 (b) 11 miles south, 1½ miles west of Newkirk; within the incorporated limits of Ponca City
MAP: *Page 216*
POST OFFICE: *Dates not definitely known, as records of the office are mixed with those of Ponca City. Opened a few days after the run into Cherokee Outlet.*
NEWSPAPERS: *Cross Resident; Oklahoma State Guide*
RAILROAD: *Southern Kansas Railroad (Santa Fe)*

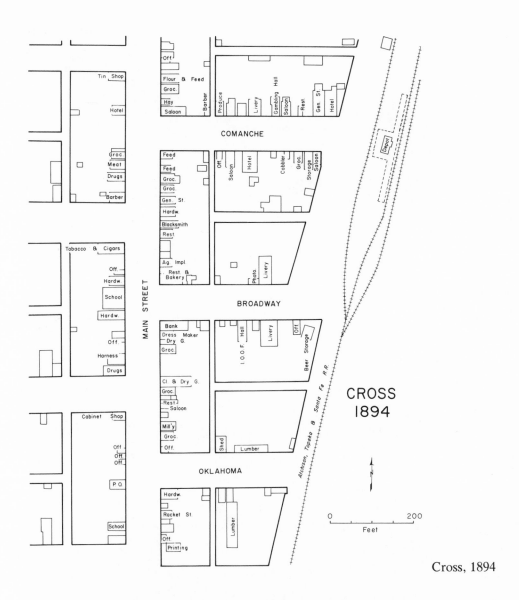

CROSS
1894

Feet
0   200

Cross, 1894

The Santa Fe Railroad planned for Cross to be the dominant city of the Cherokee Outlet. There were also visions of it becoming great as a "midway" city between Kansas City and Galveston as well as the freight terminal between Newton, Kansas, and Purcell. The town was platted before the Outlet was opened for settlement so that claims could be staked without too much confusion. A depot, express office, freight office, and telegraph office were established at the time of settlement, and a post office was approved soon thereafter.

Within a few months Cross had a population of approximately two thousand persons. Retail stores of all kinds supplied a variety of goods. The first factory built in the Outlet was erected in Cross; it manufactured furniture, fixtures,

and sundries. Other factories, including a distillery, were soon started. The town's hotels, one said to be the largest in northern Oklahoma Territory, were noted for their excellence. The bank was rated as sound financially as those in Guthrie or Oklahoma City. There were four organized churches, a good school employing three teachers, and newly constructed homes spread over a large area. The future of the town appeared to be guaranteed.

About a mile south of Cross a group of men secured a tract of land they considered to be the gateway to the Osage and Ponca Indian reservations. There was an adequate water supply, the site was adjacent to the railroad, and the men involved were a "bunch of live wire town builders." Thus, the city of Ponca City was born.

Cross, *ca.* 1895. Post office. *(Courtesy* Ponca City News*)*

Cross, 1898. This distillery began operation soon after the opening of the Cherokee Outlet. *(Courtesy* Ponca City News*)*

Rivalry between the two towns was intense. Outsiders stated that it was like taking his life in his hands for a Cross man to visit Ponca City, and vice versa. There were many fistfights and sometimes free-for-alls when bodies of the citizenry got together. It is recorded that when the Perry baseball team played the Cross team on July 4, 1894, a group went from Ponca City to cheer for the Perry team. A general fight resulted, during which it appeared that those from Ponca City would be annihilated.

At first the Santa Fe refused to stop in Ponca City, but after a year they finally agreed to do so, but did not build a depot. Soon thereafter men from Ponca City started boarding the south bound trains at a station north of Cross. Since such passenger trains carried many prospective settlers, the Ponca City boosters gave cigars to the men and small bouquets to each of the women along with a talk about the advantages of Ponca City over Cross.

The bitter struggle ended somewhat abruptly when an agreement was reached between the railroad station agent in Cross and the mayor of Ponca City. The agent was promised two good lots in Ponca City, plus the free moving of his home to those lots, if he would ask to have the depot and its offices moved to Ponca City. The agent agreed, made the request, and received permission to make the change. The house was moved after dark on a Saturday night and Sunday so the people of Cross could not secure an injunction to prevent the move. Shortly afterward a citizen of Ponca City bought the largest hotel in Cross and moved it to the new town. It was said: "These were the straws that seemed to break the camel's back. Although the people of Cross were angry—in about a week another house was on its way. At the end of the month the prairie was dotted with homes destined for Ponca City, and at the end of six months nearly all of the business buildings and residences had moved to the metropolis on the south."

All of the former city limits of Cross are now within the incorporated limits of Ponca City.

Denoya

(WHIZBANG)

COUNTY: *Osage*
LOCATION: *(a) Sec. 6, T 26 N, R 6 E*
(b) 7 miles north, 20 miles west of Pawhuska; 1½ miles north, 1½ miles west of Shidler
MAP: *Page 216*
POST OFFICE: *December 31, 1921–September 30, 1942*
RAILROAD: *Atchison, Topeka and Santa Fe, abandoned 1939*

Denoya, better known locally as Whizbang, was the "wildest" of the boom towns that developed with the opening of the Burbank Oil Field. The Post Office Department thought the name Whizbang was an undignified identification, so they named the new town Denoya after a prominent Osage Indian family.

Denoya came into existence almost overnight after a six-hundred-barrel well was brought in just north of where the town located. The well was drilled by E. W. Marland, later Governor of Oklahoma and also United States Congressman. The second well was a heavy gas and light oil producer. The oil would burn in an automobile. The third offset well was topped the day before Christmas. On New Year's Day, while the crew was on vacation, the well started flowing one barrel per minute with the tools still in the hole. The only tank available was a thousand-barrel wooden storage tank. A flow line was laid to it, and help was summoned from Tulsa immediately. By dark, trucks had delivered three-inch pipe, and by three o'clock the next morning a pipeline three miles long had been laid to adequate storage facilities. The flow from the well increased to a little over twenty-five hundred barrels per day.

With an oil play of such magnitude, businesses of all kinds, desirable and undesirable, were soon established in the new town. Large oil-field supply houses were started, and a railroad was extended to Denoya. In the early 1920s there were more than three hundred business buildings ranging in size from the very small hamburger shacks to two moderately large hotels. Many people living in Denoya were not connected with oil companies. Shootings were more frequent in Denoya than in other towns in the Burbank area. The bank was robbed twice, and "it wasn't safe for a woman to be on the streets of Whizbang after dark."

José Alvarado, probably the most controversial law officer to serve in an Oklahoma oil field area, was a special officer for oil companies during a part of the boom period. His

Denoya, *ca.* 1924. Long-range view of part of the business district with its frame buildings and traffic problems. (*Courtesy Western History Collections, University of Oklahoma*)

64
D

Denoya, *ca.* 1924. Shotgun houses built for workers by oil companies on leases they owned. *(Courtesy Western History Collections, University of Oklahoma)*

name was actually Bert Bryant, he was a Texan, and he had served in the revolutionary army of Pancho Villa. During World War I he worked with General Alvarado of Mexico, and in the early 1920s he came northward to the Oklahoma oil fields. Stories of his activities describe him as everything from a cold-blooded killer to a Robin Hood. One story says that during a raid on a notorious "boarding house" he seized twenty-five hundred dollars from the woman

manager. Later, although he returned the money to the woman in the presence of two bankers and received a receipt for it, he was arrested for stealing it, but was finally tried and acquitted. On another occasion, when a fire started in the post office of Denoya, Alvarado refused to let the oil companies help extinguish the fire until all postal records were burned. After that the oil companies refused to help, and an entire business block was burned. During the fire Alvarado had a shootout with a lawman from a neighboring town, probably over a married woman. The visiting lawman killed the woman and then shot Alvarado in the chest. Alvarado returned fire and shot the other man four times in the body while he was hunting for cover. Alvarado then took cover behind a merchandise-laden table that had been moved into the street from a burning store, but since his legs were exposed below the tabletop he was shot in the shins, and both his legs were broken. (The two men were taken to the same hospital; they recovered, forgot the woman, and became good friends.) Such was a day in the life of Whizbang.

Denoya died almost as rapidly as it was built. In the late 1920s, as production declined, people started moving away. Good roads to large cities, changes in agriculture and cattle business, the depression of the 1930s, with the loss of property evaluation, and abandonment of the railroad resulted in the death not only of Denoya but also of most Burbank Oil Field towns and camps. All that remains of Denoya today are foundations of some buildings and a few oil rigs.

Denoya, 1927. E. W. Marland was one of the principal developers of the Burbank-Denoya field, founder of the Marland Oil Company (later Conoco), congressman (1932–34), and governor of Oklahoma (1935–39). *(Courtesy Oklahoma Historical Society)*

Denoya, 1975. Location of the town is marked by the remains of a few buildings and crumbling foundations.

Devol, *ca.* 1910. Main Street before Devol became a boom town. A bandstand at the principal business intersection was common in early towns. *(Courtesy Western History Collections, University of Oklahoma)*

Devol

COUNTY:	*Cotton*
LOCATION:	*(a) Sec. 20, T 4 S, R 13 W*
	(b) 10½ miles south, 16 miles west of Walters; 1 mile north, 7½ miles west of Randlett
MAP:	*Page 218*
POST OFFICE:	*November 30, 1907–*
NEWSPAPERS:	*Devol Dispatch; Devol Review; Devol Oil Journal; Cotton County News*
RAILROAD:	*Wichita Falls and Northwestern Railway (Katy)*

Devol came into existence as a rural center, developed as an oil boom town, and nearly ended as a disaster area. The oil boom fizzled about 1922, two banks failed in 1927, and a tornado destroyed several places in 1959. During the boom period the population was estimated at over four thousand; today there are fewer than one hundred persons residing there.

Devol was started by private enterprise when Colonel J. F. Devol divided a part of his farm into town lots and sold them at auction. The site, about midway between the two government towns of Randlett and Eschiti, which were formed when the Big Pasture was opened, was adjacent to the railroad. On the day of the auction more than three thousand persons came to bid for land, and all lots were sold. One block was reserved for a school and another for a park, and each church was given a free lot. A post office had been established before the sale.

By 1916 the town had a waterworks, an electric light plant, and a telephone exchange. In addition to seventeen stores and shops, there was a hotel, a bank, a motion picture show, two cotton gins, two elevators, a flour and feed mill, and a newspaper. Three churches had been established and a consolidated school formed.

In 1918 the Burkburnett Oil Field, just across the Red River from Devol in Texas, boomed in. The people of Devol expected to find oil north of the river within a short time, but even though many wells were sunk no oil was ever found. Devol, however, did become a boom town as a result of the overflow of people and business from Texas. A private toll bridge was built across Red River. People came to the Devol area to find places to live, and companies came to establish offices. Within eighteen months the population jumped from about 425 to 4,500. Tank farms, gasoline plants, and a refinery, with their adjacent camps, added people to the trade territory. In addition to numerous stores and shops, the town was headquarters for several oil well supply firms and oil company

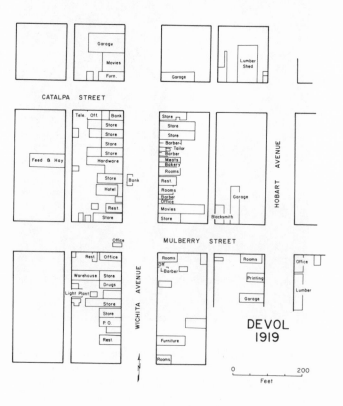

Devol, 1919

offices and was served by a "number of doctors, dentists, and lawyers and a number of illicit operations. Anything that one needed or wanted he could get in Devol." The town, to its credit, made several civic improvements.

By 1923 the boom was over. Before the crash of the stock market in 1929 both papers had folded, and most stores and shops had closed their doors. Two of the banks closed before the crash, and the third went with it. Most people had to move, for there was no work in the area. The depression and the Dust Bowl also took their toll. Devol became a town of empty business buildings and empty houses, and eventually it had no elected officials from 1948 to 1961. The people voted to change from a corporate city to a village.

On August 30, 1959, a tornado struck what was left of Devol. The post office, the Masonic Hall, two homes, a service station, and the depot were destroyed. Numerous houses and other structures, including the Baptist Church, were damaged. The town jail, a very solid structure, served as a shelter for most of the town's people that night.

Devol now has a post office and a small store. The school system has been closed, but the Baptist Church remains active. Many of those living in Devol are retired people or older citizens. Some will argue that it is not a ghost town, but the chief topics of conversation are about the past.

Doaksville

COUNTY: *Choctaw*
LOCATION: *(a) Sec. 13, T 6 S, R 19 E*
(b) 1½ miles north, 13 miles east of Hugo; ½ mile north, ½ mile west of Fort Towson
MAP: *Page 220*
POST OFFICE: *November 11, 1847–June 12, 1903*
NEWSPAPERS: *Choctaw Intelligencer; Choctaw Telegraph*

Shortly after the treaty called Doak's Stand between the Choctaw Indians and the United States was signed in Mississippi in 1820, Josiah S. Doak and his brother moved westward, for they believed the Choctaws would soon migrate. Thus, they loaded their goods on boats and navigated the Mississippi and Red rivers to a point near the mouth of the Kiamichi River. From that point the goods were moved inland to a place near Witches Hole. Dr. W. B. Morrison wrote: "It would appear that these brothers have a right to be classed among the earliest Sooners in Oklahoma history."

Soon after the establishment of the Doak store, other settlers began to move into the area for mutual protection. Raids from Plains Indians, but more especially raids from Indians living in Texas, caused Fort Towson to be established some few miles to the northwest. Shortly

Doaksville, *ca.* 1895. The former capital of the Choctaw Nation was near oblivion when this picture was made. Businesses include a blacksmith shop on the far left, a store, and a barber shop in the tent. *(Courtesy Oklahoma Historical Society)*

Doaksville, *ca.* 1926. Home of Colonel Folsom, built about 1840, continued to be used until the mid-1930s.

after the Fort was garrisoned in 1824, the store and many of those living in the vicinity moved to a location on the bluffs above Gates Creek about one mile west of Fort Towson. After that move, Doaksville began to grow and gave every indication of becoming a permanent town.

Large numbers of Choctaw Indians who did not move to Indian Territory until after 1830 settled in or near Doaksville, making it one of the three important towns of the Choctaw area. By 1840 Doaksville had five large merchandising establishments, two owned by Choctaw Indians and the others by licensed white traders. There was also a harness and saddle shop, wagon yard, blacksmith shop, gristmill, hotel, council house, and church. The *Choctaw Intelligencer*, printed in both English and Choctaw, was available to all—"terms only $2.00 per year, invariably in advance." Trade was brisk. In the 1830s and 1840s Red River boats, coming upstream to the mouth of the Kiamichi River, brought firearms, ammunition, and other necessities and luxuries for the Doaksville merchants and returned with tallow, peltries, bear grease, and cotton grown by the Indian farmers and Indian plantation owners. Traders dealing with the Plains tribes frequently acquired their supplies in Doaksville, and it was not uncommon to see a trader and his train of pack animals following a trail westward to be gone two or three months.

Doaksville was one of the centers where the Indians collected their annuities. Alvin Goode, a missionary, described the scene (Indian Archives, Oklahoma Historical Society):

The trading establishment of Josiah Doak and Vinson Brown Timms, an Irishman, had the contract to supply the Indians their rations, figured at 13¢ a ration. A motley crowd always assembled at Doaksville on annuity days to receive them. Some thousands of Indians were scattered over a tract of nearly a square mile around the pay house. There were cabins, tents, booths, stores, shanties, wagons, carts, campfires; white, red, black, and mixed in every imaginable shade and proportion and dressed in every conceivable variety of style, from tasty American clothes to the wild costumes of the Indians; buying, selling, swapping, betting, shooting, strutting, talking, laughing, fiddling, eating, drinking, smoking, sleeping, seeing and being seen, all huddled together.

Doaksville was also an important political center. In 1837 the Choctaw and Chickasaw leaders met at Doaksville and entered into an agreement with each other and a joint agreement with the United States whereby the Chickasaws acquired land in Choctaw territory. From 1850 to 1863 Doaksville was the capital of the Choctaw Nation. The Choctaw Convention of 1860, meeting in Doaksville, drafted the Doaksville Constitution, under which the nation operated thereafter. And the Civil War in Indian Territory actually ended in Doaksville on June 23, 1865, when Brigadier General Stand Watie

Doaksville, 1975. Former townsite is now overgrown by various types of vegetation. The area is now controlled by the Oklahoma Historical Society.

rode into town and laid down his arms, the last of the Confederate generals to surrender.

The coming of the Civil War was the start of the decline of Doaksville. In 1863 the Choctaw capitol was moved to Chahta Tamaha (Academy). Following the war, plantation and farming operations either ceased or were greatly curtailed by the lack of labor, thereby decreasing the amount of goods to be marketed. (The Choctaws had large numbers of slaves.) More western forts and towns were started in the area of the Plains Tribes; thus, the western trade disappeared. Within a few years most of the important stores either quit business or moved. The town continued to struggle for existence until the early 1900s.

No part of the old town now remains. The area where it stood has been designated a National Historic Site. Many of the important people of the area for that period are buried in the cemetery just west of the townsite. The old townsite and cemetery are both interesting places to visit.

some newly organized, prepared to contest Buffalo.

After its founding in 1907, Doby Springs continued to grow and expand. Plans for future growth were carefully kept before the public throughout the county by columns printed in *The Monitor*, especially since the time was drawing near for the selection of the county seat by popular vote. By 1909 Doby Springs had a population in excess of 250. (Buffalo was not much larger.) In addition to the usual stores and shops the town had a telephone exchange, a foundry, a cotton gin (probably the most northern one ever built in Oklahoma), and a doctor. The Congregational Academy, although it existed for only one term, offered good educational advantages in 1908. Buffalo, however, won the election probably because it was nearer the center of the county. The decline of Doby Springs started shortly thereafter. By 1912 population had decreased to fifty persons and within a few years the town ceased to exist.

The Doby Springs are now owned by the city of Buffalo and furnish water for that community. A well-kept park has been developed around the springs and is well used.

Doby Springs

(BELLAIRE)

COUNTY:	*Harper*
LOCATION:	*(a) Sec. 10, T 27 N, R 24 W*
	(b) 7½ miles west of Buffalo
MAP:	*Page 215*
POST OFFICE:	*January 13, 1908–April 29, 1922*
NEWSPAPER:	*The Monitor*

The Doby Springs area was well known to cattlemen before the opening of the Cherokee Outlet in 1893. Drovers following the Great Western Cattle Trail to northern markets often camped near the springs. The first patent to land around Doby Springs was issued in 1901, but the townsite was not surveyed until 1907. When land in the Cherokee Outlet was organized into counties. all of what is now Harper County was included in Woodward County. The Oklahoma Constitutional Convention, however, outlined the boundaries for Harper County and named Buffalo the county seat. As soon as this fact became known, several towns,

Doby Springs, 1914. Post office. *(Courtesy Harper County Historical Society)*

Doby Springs, 1974. Former townsite is now a park area. The springs furnish water for Buffalo.

The developers believed the town would thrive for two reasons: (1) The townsite was laid out on a survey line of the proposed Midland Railroad, "an important railroad certain to be built within the next eighteen months from Coffeyville, Kan., to the McAlester coal fields and forming a part of the Missouri Pacific System." (2) The townsite developers offered to donate twenty acres to the state for the location of the Territorial Normal School for Negroes. The railroad, however, was never built, and the school was located at Langston.

The Douglas community continues to exist in name. The school remained in operation until it was consolidated with Luther. The church has been moved to a different location. The Turner Turnpike now crosses the former townsite.

Douglas City

COUNTY: *Oklahoma*
LOCATION: *(a) Sec. 1, T 13 N, R 1 W*
               (b) 11 miles north, 15 miles east of Oklahoma City central business district; 1½ miles south, 3 miles west of Luther
MAP: *Page 216*
POST OFFICE: *May 12, 1894–June 15, 1900*

Douglas City, like many other new towns in the Unassigned Lands, exemplified the hopes and dreams of numerous town builders in the early 1890s. Douglas City was to be a black town, developed by black capital and managed by black entrepreneurs. The townsite was to contain 160 acres and have large blocks, wide streets, and lots 25 feet by 140 feet. A tract of ten acres was reserved for a public school. In 1893 the town had a general store, a cotton gin, a gristmill, a number of residences, and a church. Later a school was built. It was reported that more than two hundred lots had been sold to black families.

Downs

COUNTY: *Kingfisher*
LOCATION: *(a) Sec. 1, T 15 N, R 5 W*
               (b) 3½ miles south, 13½ miles east of Kingfisher; ½ mile north of Cashion
MAP: *Page 216*
POST OFFICE: *August 12, 1889–May 14, 1900*
NEWSPAPERS: *Downs Democrat; Oklahoma Congregationalist*

Downs, about midway between the two developing cities of Guthrie and Kingfisher, became an important stage stop shortly after the opening of the Unassigned Lands. The town soon had a population of about 250 to 300. Business establishments included two grocery stores, two blacksmith shops, a drugstore, a hotel, a saloon, a hardware store, and a harness shop. Two churches were established, and a school was started. The town incorporated and had a reputation of being progressive and public-spirited.

Many people in the community were politically oriented. Lee Boecher, in the book *Shortgrass Country*, writes: "A. N. (Artie) Daniels of Frisco was elected to represent Canadian county in the first Territorial legislature. When it convened at Guthrie on August 25, 1890 he was

Downs, 1898. Part of the business district. *(Courtesy* Kingfisher Free Press)

elected speaker of the house. Almost immediately he introduced a bill to make Downs
capital of the Territory. The bill passed both
houses but in a few days was vetoed by Governor
Steele." Once when Governor A. J. Seay was
traveling from Guthrie to his home in Kingfisher
he found it necessary to spend the night in
Downs. Since he had the Great Seal of Oklahoma Territory with him, Downs claimed the
honor of being the capital for one night.

In 1900 the Guthrie and Western Railway
(Santa Fe) started laying track toward Kingfisher. At the same time the Guthrie and Kingfisher Railway (Rock Island) commenced put-
ting down track toward Guthrie. The two lines
agreed to meet about halfway at a point approximately one-half mile south of Downs. When
the line was completed, the town of Cashion
was established. Up to that time all supplies had
been moved to Downs by wagon. Realizing the
advantages of rail delivery, the merchants of
Downs moved to the new town. Many homes
were also moved. Most of the former townsite
of Downs is now used for agricultural purposes.

Eagle

(EAGLE TOWN, EAGLETOWN)

COUNTY:	*McCurtain*
LOCATION:	*(a) Sec. 7, T 6 S, R 26 E*
	(b) 10 miles north, 11½ miles east of Idabel; 1 mile north, 5½ miles east of Broken Bow
MAP:	*Page 220*
POST OFFICE:	*July 1, 1834–; moved to present location in Eagletown in 1920*

Eagle (later known as Eagle Town and then, in
1892, officially as Eagletown) was one of the
earliest Choctaw settlements in the new Indian
Territory. George Shirk, in his book *Oklahoma
Place Names*, attributes the community's name
to the many eagles that nested in the nearby
swamps along Mountain Fork River. However,
some elderly Choctaws stated that the place got
its name from a Choctaw joke. When a Choctaw
needed to consult the U.S. Army or the Indian
Agent, he jokingly said he was "going to the
eagle," referring to the newly adopted U.S. sym-

Eagle, *ca.* 1910. Courthouse for Eagle County, Apukshunnubbee District, Choctaw Nation. Built in 1884, it was used until 1906, when the Choctaw government was abolished. *(Courtesy Lewis Stiles)*

Eagle, 1975. Home of Chief Jefferson Gardner, built in 1884. It remains in use as a home. *(Courtesy Lewis Stiles)*

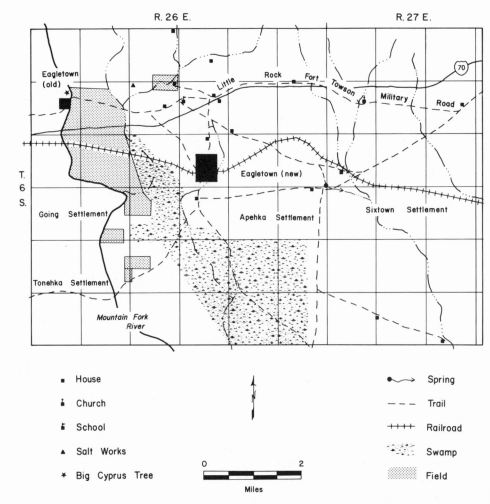

■ House	●—⤳ Spring
⛪ Church	- - - Trail
⚑ School	+++++ Railroad
▲ Salt Works	Swamp
✳ Big Cyprus Tree	Field

0   2
Miles

Eagletown area

bol. The Choctaw name for the place was Osi Tamaha.

In the early 1830s many of the thousands of Choctaws migrating to their new lands entered them by way of the Fort Towson Road. Where the road crossed Mountain Fork River was an enticing area to the worn and weary immigrants after so long and hard a journey. There was much wild game in the country—bear, wild turkey, deer, and a variety of smaller animals. The canebrakes along the banks of Mountain Fork were especially alluring to the hunter, and the river was just as captivating to the fisherman. Finding good camping grounds, hundreds of Choctaws remained in the area, causing it to become one of the first densely settled communities in the new Choctaw Nation.

Eagle was never a town in the sense that it developed a town square or a large commercial district. Neither was it ever platted. But a government ration station located in the vicinity was conducive to permanent settlement. Moreover, the country south of the crossing was an area of fertile land. Soon cotton plantations were established, and cotton gins and gristmills began operation. In 1832 Reverend Loring S. Williams established a mission school, which he called Beth-a-bara (Hebrew for "a crossing"), on the west side of Mountain Fork near a very large cypress tree. In 1834 the first post office and a general store were also located on the west bank of the river. In 1837 Reverend Williams had to leave the area because of ill health, and Beth-a-bara closed. The settlement, however, without waiting for assistance from tribal funds, erected a new schoolhouse and started a term of school the same year. By 1850 Eagle County, Apukshunnubbee District, Choctaw Nation, had been organized, and the first courthouse, built of round pine logs, was erected. A blacksmith shop and a cotton buyer also located there. By the late 1850s a store had located east of the river, and the post office was moved to that store.

Following the Civil War, which had little effect on Eagle Town, as the community was then known, activities rapidly returned to normal. In 1874 Jefferson Gardner, later Principal Chief of the Choctaw Nation, opened a general store about two miles east of the Mountain Fork crossing. He was also a buyer of hides, snakeroot,

Eagle, 1975. The largest tree in Oklahoma, a cypress. The tree is 43 feet around at its base and approximately 150 feet tall, and is said to be about two thousand years old. *(Courtesy Oklahoma Department of Tourism and Recreation)*

and cotton. In 1884 a frame building replaced the log courthouse at the original site. Gardner then moved his store and the post office to the west side of Mountain Fork. He also built a large T-shaped residence. Shortly after his term as Principal Chief, in 1896, Gardner lost his fortune, which included several stores at places other than Eagletown. The post office was then once again moved to a place east of Mountain Fork River.

When the Texas, Oklahoma and Eastern Railroad laid its tracks from Valliant to DeQueen, Arkansas, in 1920, a depot was located about two and one-half miles southeast of the river crossing. The post office and business establishments then moved to the new location. Little reminiscent of the old townsite remains. U.S. Highway 70, which crosses the nation from coast to coast, has a large concrete bridge near the old river crossing. The Jefferson Gardner house is still lived in, a rock at the courthouse site known as "execution rock" can be seen, and the giant cypress, the largest tree in Oklahoma, still stands at the eastern edge of old Eagle.

Eagle City, 1975. Old and unused business buildings on the north side of Broadway.

Eagle City

(DILLON)

COUNTY:	*Blaine*
LOCATION:	*(a) Sec. 20, T 17 N, R 13 E*
	(b) 6½ miles north, 10 miles west
	of Watonga
MAP:	*Page 215*
POST OFFICE:	*Dillon, July 26, 1902–September 4, 1909; Eagle City, September 4, 1909–*
NEWSPAPERS:	*Eagle City News; Eagle City Record; Eagle City Star*
RAILROAD:	*Blackwell, Enid and Southern Railroad (Frisco)*

Eagle City was established in 1902 by a syndicate from Kansas City that knew the route to be followed by the Frisco railroad as it built through western Oklahoma. When the tracks crossed the North Canadian River the syndicate purchased three farms, surveyed the land, and platted the streets and lots. There were visions of

greatness. Main Street, as shown on early maps, was to extend one mile north-south, Broadway one mile east-west. The site selected was a good one, for there were no towns north, west, or south for distances of fifteen to twenty-five miles and no rail competition for even greater distances. After the survey a large office building was constructed, and lots were offered for sale.

Stores of various kinds were soon established. Lumberyards did a big business as many sod and dugout farm homes, which had been built earlier, were replaced by frame ones. Business buildings, barns, and new homes were also built. A livery stable that rented horses and buggies to traveling salesmen and others was profitable. (An early day Hertz or Avis concern.) Doctors settled in the community, drugstores were started, and a telephone system with several rural lines was developed. A bank added to the importance of the town as a trade center. A school system and churches were organized. Dancing was the important form of recreation. At first the Townsite Building was used for dances, but later a granary was made into a dance hall, where dances were held every Saturday night. During the Christmas season masquerade dances were popular.

There was trouble with the post office. The first one was named Dillon. Eagle City was not acceptable as a name because of its similarity to Eagletown. Eventually, however, the name of the post office was changed.

About the time of statehood the Kansas City,

Mexico and Orient Railroad built a line across western Oklahoma paralleling the Frisco about eight to ten miles west of Eagle City. As new towns developed along the Orient, the trade territory of Eagle City decreased and some stores moved away. From 1915 to 1928 the population remained at about three hundred. At the start of the depression the bank consolidated with one in Custer City. As a result of better roads, faster transportation, the lack of utilities, and the consolidation of farms, all businesses except one, a feed and fertilizer plant, have closed. Old store buildings, some with their high boardwalks, line the north side of one block of Broadway. Across the dirt street stand the remains of a lumberyard and other business buildings. The remaining part of the school plant is used as a community building. A few homes are occupied, and a church is still organized. Even though remaining residents are few and the last store closed in 1971, the post office continues to operate—for about a dozen boxes. A large arrow, with Eagle City dimly painted thereon, points toward Broadway from State Highway 58.

Eagle City, 1975. A few large homes, all dilapidated, indicate the former prosperity of the town.

Earlsboro

COUNTY:	*Pottawatomie*
LOCATION:	*(a) Sec. 8, T 9 N, R 5 E*
	(b) 4½ miles south, 7 miles east of Shawnee; 7 miles east of Tecumseh
MAP:	*Page 219*
POST OFFICE:	*June 12, 1895–*
NEWSPAPERS:	*Earlsboro Border Journal; Earlsboro Echo; Earlsboro Plain People; Earlsboro Times; Earlsboro Journal; Earlsboro Messenger*
RAILROAD:	*Choctaw Coal and Railroad Company (Rock Island)*

Earlsboro has twice been a boom town of considerable importance and twice a decaying, disintegrating, and dilapidated village. It was formed in 1891 a few days after the Choctaw Coal and Railroad Company extended its tracks westward from the Seminole Nation. The town was platted under the name of Boom-De-Ay. A post office by the name of Tum was moved to the new site, and the name was changed to Earlsboro.

The fact that Earlsboro was situated near the Indian Territory boundary aided its early growth. Liquor was prohibited in Indian Territory, but saloons in Oklahoma Territory were legal. Because of the demand of the people living in Indian Territory for liquor, Earlsboro became known as a "whiskey town." Three of the first four businesses established were saloons; the other was a grocery store. The number of saloons and stores handling liquor continued to increase and to dominate the business activities of the village until 1905. During that year it was estimated that 90 percent of the merchants were dealing profitably in liquor. With approaching statehood, however, many liquor dealers started moving their activities to other states, and the first boom period ended.

Along with the whiskey trade, Earlsboro developed as a small commercial center serving nearby farmers. A blacksmith shop, gristmill, and cotton gin were built. Churches were started and a school district organized. Some streets were graded, and homes were constructed. The railroad located a boxcar next to the track to

Earlsboro, *ca.* 1926. Five miles of traffic in the nearby oil fields slowed or stopped as a result of heavy rainfall and flooding.

Earlsboro, 1927. Fire at Twin States No. 2 Hearn well. One person was killed, several injured.

serve as a depot, and the village became a regular stop for passenger service.

During its first year of existence Earlsboro had a population of about 100 persons. By 1900 the population had increased to 400, and it continued to increase until 1905, when it reached an estimated 500 persons. The special census of 1907 recorded only 387 persons, the decrease being accounted for by the moving of liquor dealers. Population continued to decrease gradually, the 1920 census showing a total of 317 persons.

During the early 1920s the commercial activities of Earlsboro were like those of many other small, farm-centered communities. Poor roads and slow transportation caused farmers in the vicinity to trade in Earlsboro. Subsistence stores supplying the most essential needs dominated the business area. A bank and a newspaper also aided in making it an active rural center.

The situation was completely and abruptly changed on March 1, 1926. On that day the first oil well to be a commercial producer in the Earlsboro Sand, the well that caused the active development of the Earlsboro Field, "blew in." The Earlsboro Sand was penetrated at a depth of 3,557 feet, and oil started flowing at a rate of two hundred barrels per day. Although this well was minor compared to some drilled shortly thereafter, the discovery started a violent oil boom; speculation in royalty rights and leases mounted rapidly, and drilling became frenzied.

Once begun, Earlsboro grew rapidly, so rapidly that in two or three months the town had a population variously estimated at from five thousand to ten thousand people. Main Street was lengthened from one to five blocks, with numerous side and parallel streets added to the business section. The streets were lined with stores of all types in addition to pool halls, picture shows, beauty shops, lumberyards, and cafes. A large four-story brick hotel was soon under construction. Doctors, lawyers, engineers, and geologists sought office space in any type of building. The residential area expanded as rapidly as the business section. Shotgun houses of all varieties were built on land once used for gardens or lawns. Tents frequently occupied unused spaces, and often tent space in a back yard rented for as much as twenty-five dollars per month. No streets in the residential area were paved or graveled. Public utilities were almost unknown to Earlsboro when the boom started. There was no sewage disposal, the water supply was furnished by individual wells, and most of the homes used kerosene lamps for light. The post office was entirely inadequate to handle the increase in mail. Earlsboro was too small to have delivery service, so everybody received his mail at the general delivery window or from a box in the post office. Two general delivery windows were soon opened, but this procedure only slightly relieved the situation. The people waiting to receive their mail often formed lines over a block in length.

One of the biggest problems that faced Earlsboro during the boom period was transportation. There were no paved roads in the community or town. Because of the heavy traffic, every road leading to Earlsboro was either a cloud of

Earlsboro, 1928. Traffic at the west end of the principal business street. Usually it took about thirty minutes to drive the two to three blocks. *(Courtesy E. D. Keys)*

Earlsboro, 1975. Same street as shown in the 1928 photograph.

dust or a sea of mud. Automobiles, teamsters, and trucks all moved at a snail's pace. Rainfall was exceptionally heavy during the fall of 1926, greatly exceeding the normal. Roads and fields were so boggy that it seemed drilling would have to be temporarily discontinued. Trucks were practically abandoned in favor of horses. Rail transportation was even more inadequate than the roads. Trackage and storage space were missing.

By 1928 the boom was beginning to settle as the limits of the producing fields were determined. New oil developments in nearby fields resulted in many of the single workers seeking steadier employment elsewhere. New city leaders, working with the older ones, began to bring order out of chaos and to improve the facilities of the community. Main Street was paved, a city water system was developed, and electricity was brought to the town.

In 1928 the population within the incorporated limits of the community was estimated at 4,000, but by 1930 it had decreased to 1,950. Also in 1928 the number of business establishments, as listed in the *Earlsboro Journal*, totaled 286. The 1940 population census (486) and a count of business establishments in the same year (19) showed that the second boom period had definitely ended and that the second stage of decay was well advanced.

Present-day Earlsboro is but a broken hull of the twice-booming community. About forty homes, many unpainted since the 1930s, remain scattered about the incorporated limits. Several residential streets have been closed and a few plowed and planted. Only uncared-for trees and broken foundations occupy previously densely populated blocks. The business area definitely shows that the boom is over and that the town is dying. Once busy streets are now almost unused. One block of brick buildings remains, and only three of them are in use. Grass and weeds grow in cracks along the sidewalks and in places once occupied by buildings. The depot built to replace the first boxcar has long since been removed, and trains no longer stop.

The 1970 census recorded only 248 persons. The population continues to decrease. How long will Earlsboro continue? As one of the oldest residents stated recently, "We can always hope for another boom."

Eschiti
(ESCHITE)

COUNTY: *Tillman*
LOCATION: *(a) Sec. 3, T 4 S, R 14 W*
(b) 10 miles south, 20½ miles east of Frederick; 1 mile north, 1½ miles east of Grandfield
MAP: *Page 218*
POST OFFICE: *October 31, 1907–January 21, 1909*
NEWSPAPERS: *Eschiti Banner*

Eschiti, advertised as the Princess of the Pasture, was one of five chartered townsites planned, platted, and sold by the Department of the Interior in 1907 after the opening of the Big Pasture. (Apheatone, Isadore, Quannah, and Randlett were the other four, and of these only Randlett is now in existence.) Eschiti was so named to honor the second chief of the Comanches.

The life of Eschiti was brief but hectic. Shortly after the bidding for town lots closed, the population was estimated to be in excess of twelve hundred. Soon after the founding of Exchiti the Wichita Falls and Northwestern Railroad extended its tracks across the Red River into Oklahoma. Expectations were that since the town was a government-approved site, the railroad would build through that site to its destination. Frank Kell and others had secured the right-of-way across the Big Pasture from the U.S. Government. Since Kell was also a townsite promoter, he refused to route the railroad through Eschiti, but did establish a place called Kell City about two miles southwest of Eschiti. A switchyard and sidings served as an inducement in securing settlers for Kell City. The U.S. Government, however, established a post office in Eschiti but refused to locate one in Kell City. Thus, a rivalry, sometimes bitter, developed.

The *Kell City Enterprise*, in an editorial on October 17, 1907, proclaimed: "Kell City is only a small town, yet we jar the earth and strike fire from the cobblestones as we walk. . . . Eschiti essays to be the business rival of Kell City, but she is not making any more noise than the passing of a regiment of pussy-footed caterpillars." The *Eschiti Banner*, of course, replied with a full-page editorial. More sarcastic exchanges followed. On one occasion individuals from Kell

OFFICIAL MAP OF ESCHITE, OKLAHOMA.

Compliments of M. A. WERT,
Real Estate, Loans and Insurance.

If you have a lot in this city and desire to sell it, place it on my list and I will sell it, or buy if price is right. Should you want to buy a lot, write me or see me, as I have the name and address of every one who purchased a lot in this townsite.

I expect to open an office at this townsite about July 1st, and be identified with the upbuilding of this city as I have lots there and a farm close by. With my main office at LAWTON, the county seat of COMANCHE County, I shall be in a position to do you good and look after your interests. There will be nothing in my line of business in the way of loans and insurance but what I will be in a position to accommodate you if the security will justify it.

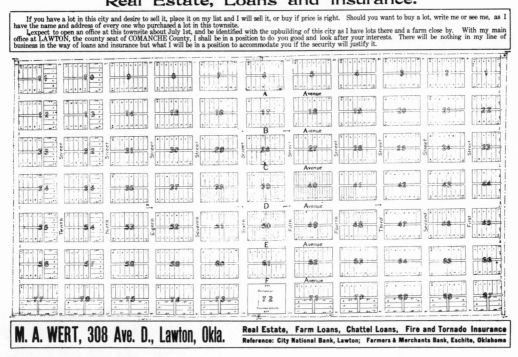

M. A. WERT, 308 Ave. D., Lawton, Okla. | **Real Estate, Farm Loans, Chattel Loans, Fire and Tornado Insurance**
Reference: City National Bank, Lawton; Farmers & Merchants Bank, Eschite, Oklahoma

Eschiti

City loaded the frame post office building on a wagon and moved it to that city during the night. A clerk sleeping in the post office said that when he awoke he was surprised to find the building had been moved. U.S. marshals came to Kell City during the day following the move and asked a few questions. During the night the post office was again moved, this time back to its original location. The people living in Kell City refused to go to Eschiti for their mail. Instead, some citizen of Kell City served as a carrier each day, taking outgoing mail to Wichita Falls and picking up incoming mail.

In 1908 Eschiti had an estimated population of three hundred. Twenty businesses of various kinds, plus a bank, two doctors, an undertaker, and two cotton gins, served the community. Cotton was the prime agricultural product. One gin in the last three months of 1907 bought and shipped over twenty-five hundred bales of cotton. Two churches were active, and a school was started. In spite of the positive factors,

Eschiti was having problems. The water supply was largely "gyp" (gypsum water), transportation facilities were very poor, and a fire had burned out a part of the business area.

The feud between Eschiti and Kell City continued, to the detriment of both. Reverend A. J. Tant, who owned a quarter-section of land between the two towns, platted a part of his land and offered free lots to those from either place who would move their buildings to the new site or would build on the site. Since the new site had advantages greater than those in either Kell City or Eschiti, the citizens of both soon moved, and the new town of Grandfield was formed. Both Eschiti and Kell City had disappeared by 1909.

The last official act of Eschiti was to establish a cemetery. Today it still marks the memory of what was once a promising town. A part of the former townsite of Eschiti is now occupied by the Grandfield Cemetery; the remainder of the townsite is used for agricultural purposes.

Fallis
(MISSION)

COUNTY: *Lincoln*

LOCATION: *(a) Sec. 29, T 15 N, R 2 E*
(b) 13 miles west, 2½ miles north of Chandler; 3½ miles north, 3 miles west of Wellston

MAP: *Page 216*

POST OFFICE: *Mission, December 28, 1892–January 13, 1894; Fallis, January 13, 1894–April 30, 1970*

NEWSPAPERS: *Fallis Blade; Fallis Gazette; Fallis Star*

RAILROADS: *Missouri, Kansas and Oklahoma Railway of 1901 (Katy) abandoned 1976; Missouri, Kansas and Oklahoma Railway of 1903 (Katy), abandoned 1916; Fort Smith and Western of Oklahoma, abandoned 1939*

Fallis was an unusual little town. Located in a wooded area and "on a long red hill," it became an agricultural center, a railroad town, and an oil community. More importantly, however, it was the home of five nationally recognized authors plus two well-known state poets. The original natural setting was beautiful, and, as one author noted, it was a source of inspiration.

Founded in 1892 at the western edge of the Iowa Reservation, Fallis developed as an agricultural trade center. Cotton was the principal crop, and two cotton gins were in operation. In 1902 the Katy railroad built through Fallis when completing its line from Bartlesville to Oklahoma City. In 1903 the Katy built a line from Fallis to Guthrie. Also in 1903, the tracks of the Fort Smith and Western Railroad from Fort Smith to Guthrie crossed the Katy line at Fallis, making the community a trans-shipment center. For a while it was believed a roundhouse and repair shops would be located in the town. The first oil well drilled in Lincoln County, in 1904, was near Fallis. Although it was of little importance, it did add income to the community. At the time of statehood Fallis had a population of about 350. Four general stores, a bakery, two lumberyards, two blacksmith shops, three hotels, a bank, two doctors, and four saloons, as well as other businesses, attested to the importance of Fallis as a trade center.

For so small a town to produce, or help to produce, so many well-known authors is remarkable. Blanche Seal Hunt wrote children's stories, notably the "Little Brown Koko" series which appeared in *Household Magazine* for more than twenty years. She was a good friend of Beulah Rhodes Overman, a writer of popular and detective short stories. Jenny Harris Oliver was Poet Laureate of Oklahoma in 1940. Her works include several books of poems as well as such short stories as "It Is Morning" and "The Singing Hand of Joe Fitzpatrick." Vingie E. Roe, a close friend of Mrs. Oliver's, was a writer of western novels, including such books as *West of Abilene, Guns of Round Stone Valley,* and *Dust above the Sage.* Her novel *Divine Egotist* used Fallis for its setting. Aletha Caldwell Connor

Fallis, *ca.* 1940. Jennie Harris Oliver, Poet Laureate of Oklahoma. *(Courtesy Oklahoma Historical Society)*

Fallis, 1939. Home of Jennie Harris Oliver. *(Courtesy Western History Collections, University of Oklahoma)*

The Fort Smith and Western and a part of the Katy railroads have long been abandoned, and the remainder of the Katy tracks are unused. Two remaining brick buildings, which are falling apart, and the old bank vault still stand in the former business district along with the closed post office. The dozen homes remaining give evidence of the town's demise. Streets are almost impassable, and yards are uncared for and full of weeds. The "wishing well" at the Oliver homestead remains. Koko Knoll, the Hunt homestead, occupies an excellent site, and the view to the east and south could be beautiful. It is the one remaining indicator of the former "golden period" of Fallis.

edited the yearly *Anthology of Poetry*, written by various Oklahoma authors, during the 1930s. Her most noted novel was *Pisces's Child*. Cecil Brown's most important book of poems, *Journey's End*, was published in 1948. Delbert Davis, Poet Laureate of Oklahoma in 1963, has written such poems as "Pipe Dreams," "The Wild Cat," and "Evening in the Hills." Most of these authors knew each other and at times served as critics for one another.

Fallis today is, for the most part, in shambles.

Fleetwood

COUNTY:	*Jefferson*
LOCATION:	*(a) Sec. 32, T 7 S, R 6 W*
	(b) 18 miles south, 7 miles east
	of Waurika; 5 miles east of Terral
MAP:	*Page 219*
POST OFFICE:	*December 2, 1885–July 21, 1961*

Emily Fleetwood, an Indian who was a large landholder, established the Fleetwood post office and gave her name to it. The village was located three miles west of the Chisholm Trail on the north side of Red River. It was the first trading post in the Chickasaw Nation where drovers and trail bosses could buy supplies. The trading post was indeed a general store, for it carried not only such staples as flour, coffee, potatoes, and beans, but also tobacco, saddles, blankets, hats, and anything else the cowboy might need. There was also a blacksmith shop where horses could be shod or wagons repaired. The last herd of longhorns went up the trail in 1885.

Following the cattle drives, rural population in the area increased and farming largely replaced ranching. Cotton became the chief money crop, so a cotton gin was built in Fleetwood. At the time of greatest growth the village had two general stores, two cotton gins, a blacksmith shop, and a telephone exchange. About sixty people lived in Fleetwood. There was a

Fallis, 1975. Entrance to Koko Knoll, home of Blanche Seal Hunt.

Fleetwood, 1974. Remains of store and cotton gin. The Chisholm Trail was about two miles to the east (right) of the gin.

good rural school. The school building also served as a community building for preaching, pie suppers, political meetings, and school programs. A doctor served the countryside either by horseback or by horse and buggy.

Most roads are now all-weather roads. Farms have enlarged, and people have moved from the area. The schoolhouse has been torn down, and homes have been moved to other locations. One dilapidated store building and a part of a cotton gin still stand, both separated from the road by a barbed wire fence, as the land is now used for grazing. In some places east of Fleetwood parts of the old Chisholm Trail can still be followed.

Department of the Interior. Located in the northwestern part of the Osage Nation (now Osage County) in an area of rolling plains, the town in 1908 advertised itself: "In the heart of this farmer's and stockman's paradise flourishes Foraker—one of the best 'Little Towns' in the state."

Shortly after its settlement, Foraker became an agricultural boom town. In 1909 the population living within the incorporated city limits was estimated at five hundred, and the trade territory had a radius of approximately twenty-five miles. The town was served by the Midland Valley Railroad, and a second line had been surveyed through the area, crossing at Foraker. (The second rail line was never built.) Corn and alfalfa were the principal crops in an area rich in natural pasture; thus, "it was bound to become one of the best hog and cattle producing sections in Oklahoma." Although it was only four years old, Foraker resembled a much older place. Concrete sidewalks had been put down throughout the business district, and much building was in evidence. Already in operation were two banks, two drugstores, three hardware stores, six mercantile stores, two grocery stores, two lumberyards, two livery stables, two grain elevators, and other necessary retail establishments. There were also two "live" newspapers, two churches, and active fraternal organizations. Two blocks had been designated for a

Foraker

COUNTY:	*Osage*
LOCATION:	*(a) Secs. 28/29, T 28 N, R 7 E*
	(b) 13 miles north, 12 miles west of Pawhuska; 6 miles north, 5 miles east of Shidler
MAP:	*Page 216*
POST OFFICE:	*February 13, 1903–*
NEWSPAPERS:	*Foraker Tribune; Foraker Free Press; Foraker Sun*
RAILROADS:	*Midland Valley Railroad, abandoned 1968; Osage Railway, abandoned 1953*

Foraker, settled in 1905, was a government townsite platted under the supervision of the

Foraker, 1965. Large school building in the foreground has now been torn down. The business district was to the right. During the 1920s each block had at least four houses. *(Courtesy Robert H. Burrill)*

Foraker, 1975. All that remains of the once large business district.

businesses now operate, and only a few people live in the once thriving community. As one long-time resident still living in what remains of the town stated: "Stores gone, post office gone, train gone, school gone, oil gone, boys and girls gone—only thing not gone is graveyard and it git bigger."

public park, thirty thousand dollars in bonds had been voted for a light and water system, and a new twenty-thousand-dollar school building had been completed. Freight and passenger service into and out of Foraker had tripled within the year.

After its rapid beginning Foraker stagnated until about 1920, when oil was discovered in the Burbank area some fifteen miles to the south. Foraker was the shipping point nearest the new oil field; thus, the town had another boom period, when it became the center for the distribution of oil-field equipment and supplies. A branch rail line, the Osage Railway, was extended from Foraker into the oil-producing area for the shipment of tank cars of petroleum products. Population of the town jumped to over two thousand, and several new business buildings and homes were constructed. Since oil was not found in the area immediately adjacent to Foraker, the town did not suffer the rough and lawless times of a true oil-field community.

With the decrease in oil production during the 1930s, Foraker declined rapidly. The development of large ranches, the abandonment of the railroads, the building of highways, and the use of large trucks to move livestock to market have resulted in the demise of the town. No

Foss

COUNTY:	*Washita*
LOCATION:	*(a) Secs. 1/2, T 11 N, R 19 W*
	(b) 11 miles north, 10½ miles west of Cordell; 4½ miles south, 11½ miles west of Clinton
MAP:	*Page 218*
POST OFFICE:	*September 15, 1900–*
NEWSPAPERS:	*Foss Enterprise; Foss Banner*
RAILROAD:	*Choctaw, Oklahoma and Gulf Railroad (Rock Island)*

Foss had its beginning in the late 1890s when settlers living near a post office called Wilson moved four miles northward to the valley of Turkey Creek. They tried to name their new post office Graham, but there was already an office by that name. The Post Office Department named the new place Maharg, an anagram for Graham. The town was making some progress as the population was slowly increasing, and a new store or two had been added, when on May 2, 1902, a sudden flash flood, caused by unusually heavy rainfall on the upper watershed of Turkey Creek, practically wiped out the village. Several persons were drowned, buildings were wrecked or washed away, and goods and animals were destroyed. Immediately thereafter residents moved out of the creek bottoms to higher land adjacent to the railroad already built through the area. A post office named Foss had been established at the rail stop. Foss became the name of the town that developed.

Foss grew rapidly, and by 1905 the population

Foss, 1959. Business district. The bank is located on the first floor of the two-story building. *(Courtesy Oklahoma Publishing Company)*

Foss, 1975. Same business areas as shown in 1959 photograph. Grass and weeds now fill the street. The bank is still in operation.

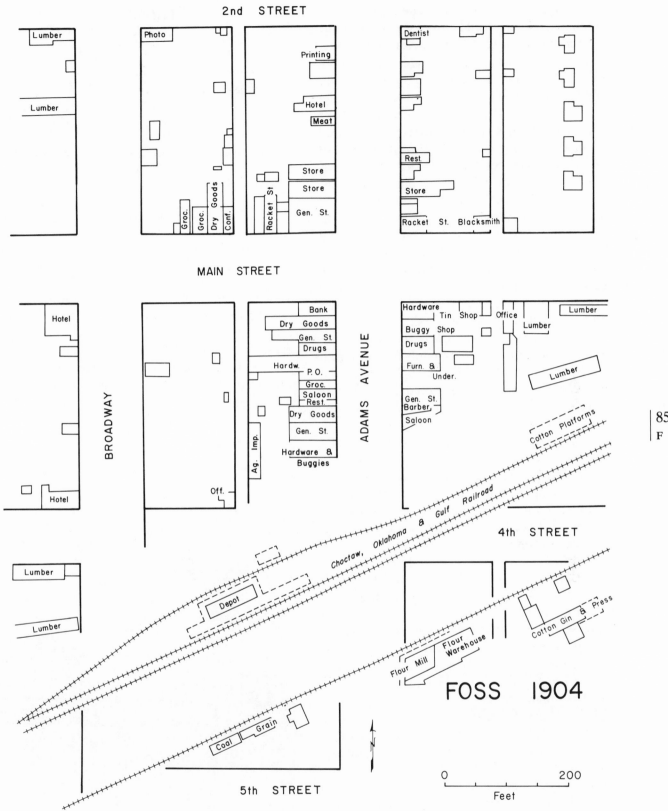

2nd STREET

MAIN STREET

BROADWAY

ADAMS AVENUE

Choctaw, Oklahoma & Gulf Railroad

Cotton Platforms

4th STREET

5th STREET

FOSS 1904

0   200
Feet

85
F

Foss, 1904

was estimated to be between nine hundred and one thousand persons. The town was surrounded by productive farmlands; as a result, a variety of stores and shops carrying large and selected stocks of all kinds developed. Top prices were paid for farm products. The two banks had deposits of over $120,000, much more than those in most rural areas. Three cotton gins operated during the ginning season. In 1908 shipments of cotton approximated ten thousand bales, about seven thousand of which were ginned in Foss. The Foss Mill and Elevator Company could produce two hundred barrels of flour daily, and the elevator had a capacity for seventy thousand bushels of wheat. Rock and brick business buildings replaced frame structures, large up-to-date homes replaced smaller ones, a school system was organized, and several churches built substantial houses of worship.

After the initial rapid growth, the town population leveled off at approximately five hundred. By 1912 Foss had an electric light plant. An opera house had been constructed, and a second hotel had been added. About 1920, however, the town began to have problems. Located almost midway between the larger and rapidly developing rail centers of Clinton and Elk City (about fifteen miles from each), and with the faster transportation of the automobile becoming common, the trade territory of Foss was largely absorbed by those two places, and the town began to decline.

The financial problems of the late 1920s, the depression and the Dust Bowl of the 1930s, and World War II of the 1940s all caused migration from the area and the closing of stores. For a while in the 1950s and 1960s there was some revival caused by the increased use of the large air force installation at Burns Flat, when excess population lived in Foss. With the closing of that base many people moved.

Foss today is but a reminder of the past. The streets are still marked, and some old business buildings remain, but only one is in use. Queerly enough, it is one of the banks which continues to open. One filling station and one grocery are located on State Highway 44, which is west (along Broadway) of the former business district. Several homes, many in poor condition, are occupied, most by retired individuals or transients. (Bank closed September, 1977)

Francis
(NEWTON)

COUNTY:	*Pontotoc*
LOCATION:	*(a) Sec. 29, T 5 N, R 7 E*
	(b) 6½ miles north, 4½ miles east of Ada
MAP:	*Page 219*
POST OFFICE:	*Newton, April 17, 1894–June 5, 1902; Francis, June 5, 1902–*
NEWSPAPERS:	*Francis Wigwam; Franciscan; Francis Banner; Francis Bulletin; Frisco Meteor; Frances Herald*
RAILROAD:	*St. Louis, Oklahoma and Southern Railway (Frisco)*

Francis, located about two miles south of the Canadian River in a hilly area, was first named Newton. Both the eastern and the western sides of the incorporated limits of the village have hills 100 to 150 feet in height, but an area of comparatively level land extends through the central part. In 1902, when the Frisco tracks

Francis, *ca.* 1915. Coal-burning passenger engine and the depot. *(Courtesy George P. Dale)*

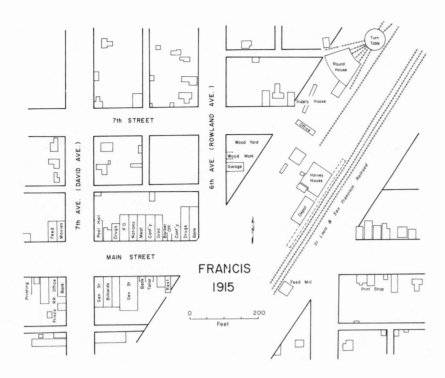

Francis, 1915

were being extended southward from Tulsa to Sherman, Texas, many rail sidings were laid across this level area. Francis then became a place for the collection and holding of box, cattle, flat, and coal cars until they were needed.

In 1904 the Frisco began establishing regional offices in Francis. In 1906 some division offices were moved to the town, and Francis became the chief freight division point on the line. A large roundhouse and car repair shops were built. Because Francis was the place where trains changed crews and where coal and water were taken on, passenger trains were scheduled to arrive in Francis about mealtime; thus, a Harvey House was also established so that those not carrying lunches could buy their meals.

Francis from 1906 to 1916 was definitely a railroad town. A majority of the workers living there were employed by the railroad. Some fifteen stores of various kinds, in addition to two hotels, two banks, and two restaurants, served the people of the area as well as the traveling public. There was a tailor who specialized in the making of trainmen's uniforms and a jeweler who advertised that he kept watches repaired and "railroad accurate." Two doctors and a lawyer maintained offices. Several large homes

were built in the hilly areas. It was estimated that the population of Francis in 1915 was between eighteen hundred and two thousand.

In 1916 the Frisco began to move its offices and shops. Soon thereafter store buildings stood vacant and homes empty. By 1920 population had decreased to less than one thousand. During the 1920s Francis continued to lose population, even though it was surrounded on all sides by the booming oil fields of the Greater Seminole Area. By 1940 population had decreased to fewer than four hundred persons, seven of the remaining business buildings were vacant, and numerous homes were falling into decay.

Currently the population is about two hundred. One store, a cafe, a filling station, and a drugstore in which the post office is located serve what is left of the village. The high school has been closed, and the school district is consolidated with Byng. Most houses near the edge of the incorporated area have been removed, streets have been closed, and the land has been returned to pasture. Many rail sidings continue to occupy the level area and are still used for car storage. The younger people living in Francis work in Ada or Byng, both only a few miles away.

Francis, *ca.* 1915. Roundhouse, turntable, and depot. The Harvey House was located in the end of the depot where the passengers are standing. The two-story frame house behind the depot was "home" for the Harvey Girls. *(Courtesy George P. Dale)*

Francis, 1974. Tracks are now used when needed as sidings for extra cars.

Francis, *ca.* 1925. Station telegrapher with his receiver and sender. *(Courtesy George P. Dale)*

Frazer

COUNTY: *Jackson*
LOCATION: *(a) Sec. 14, T 2 N, R 21 W*
　　　　　　(b) 2½ miles west of Altus
MAP: *Page 218*
POST OFFICE: *February 18, 1886–December 31,*
　　　　　　1895
NEWSPAPER: *Greer County News*

Frazer, the forerunner of Altus, was located in the valley of Bitter Creek. Founded in the spring of 1885, the community consisted of a log cabin, two tents, and a dugout in which three families lived. Being about midway between Doan's Crossing and Mangum, Frazer became a popular stopping place for those traveling in or through Old Greer County. The cowboys referred to the stop as "Butter Milk Station" since that was the principal beverage to be had there. The post office located in the settlement in 1886 was named Frazer because a nearby stream was called the Waters of the Frazer. (That stream is now known as Salt Fork of Red River.)

In 1886 Frazer battled for its life. Rainfall was below average, and the fields were dry. Someone living near the mountains east of the settlement set the grass on fire to clear a field. The fire could not be controlled, and it roared across the prairies, driving cattle and wildlife before it and burning rapidly toward the town. Cowboys, in order to stop the advance of the fire, shot cattle, skinned them, and dragged the fresh sides of beef across the grass in an effort to halt the blaze. Furrows were plowed around the settlement, and wet sacks were used to beat out the flames to save the place from destruction.

Frazer became a trading post for Plains Indians and was patronized by trail drivers, ranchers, and travelers in general. For approximately six years the town prospered. Some three hundred people lived in Frazer, and about twenty stores and shops plus two hotels and a wagon yard were in operation. A gristmill was built on Bitter Creek about three hundred yards west of the town square.

In 1891 torrential spring rains fell. Bitter Creek went on a rampage and overflowed its banks. At the same time, Salt Fork of Red River also overflowed and poured additional water into Bitter Creek. The waters of the two streams completely flooded Frazer. All citizens were forced to flee hurriedly to higher ground, moving everything they could, "lock, stock, and barrel." When the flood subsided it was found that the town was demolished. Buildings had either been wrecked or swept away. The people never returned, but moved to a new and higher location and renamed their town Altus. The area formerly occupied by Frazer is now used for agriculture.

Frazer, 1975. Old cemetery is a short distance from where the town was located.

Frisco
(VETERAN CITY)

COUNTY: *Canadian*
LOCATION: *(a) Sec. 6, T 12 N, R 5 W*
　　　　　　(b) 10 miles east of El Reno; 2
　　　　　　miles north, 1 mile west of Yukon
MAP: *Page 216*
POST OFFICE: *May 18, 1889–March 30, 1904*
NEWSPAPERS: *Frisco News; Frisco Herald;*
　　　　　　Frisco Times

Frisco was one of the two towns in Canadian County platted before the opening of the Unassigned Lands in 1889. The town, settled largely by a colony of Civil War veterans, was for a time known as Veteran City. The group assembled in Kansas, where the members exercised their veteran preference rights, filed upon the lots in advance of the opening, and then moved to the new townsite in May, 1889. Shortly after its founding, the population of the town was estimated to be over one thousand persons.

Frisco, *ca.* 1895. The Occidental Hotel was noted for its excellent food. *(Courtesy Canadian County Historical Society)*

Frisco started with a boom. Although the town was located on the north side of the North Canadian River, its citizens believed that the Choctaw, Gulf and Oklahoma Railroad (Rock Island), building westward from Oklahoma City, would come through. Soon after its founding, in addition to numerous stores, the town had a bank, a cotton gin, a sawmill, and two active print shops. Substantial buildings, considerably better than those in most frontier towns, were erected. One large stone building housed a general merchandise store and another a drugstore. A large building that had been erected for use as a hotel in another town was moved to the north edge of Frisco and used as one of two buildings for a private school campus. In addition to elementary and secondary studies, courses for college credit in commercial, normal, and pharmaceutical studies were offered. The school was known as Oklahoma Frisco College and was reported to have had an enrollment of 150 students.

Frisco was an active political center. The town had the first Grand Army of the Republic (GAR) post in Oklahoma Territory. Frisco contested El Reno for the location of the county seat and won by a small margin of the popular vote. El Reno, however, took the matter into court and through political action, with the aid of the railroad, won the contest. The representatives to the territorial legislature from the Frisco area campaigned vigorously for the town to be designated as the territorial capital. This campaign resulted in the first political convention in Oklahoma Territory being held in Frisco.

One of the most frequently recalled happenings in the new town was the "Indian uprising." While a revival meeting was in progress, and with a large number of people in attendance, a blacksmith rushed in while the minister was praying and shouted that "the Indians had broken out." Women and children were immediately taken to the large stone store buildings, and breastworks of baled cotton were put up around the outside. The GAR immediately organized and patrolled the streets. The "uprising," of course, was entirely a false alarm. It had been started by a drunk railroad worker from Fort Reno.

The railroad built its tracks south of the North Canadian River, resulting in the establishment of Yukon about five miles south of Frisco. Within a short time many stores and homes were moved to the new town, and most of the remaining residents moved to areas opened after the town of Frisco was started. As late as 1968, however, the ghost of Frisco asserted itself when a court action was filed seeking a decree

Frisco, 1897. Meat market located in one part of a grocery store. *(Courtesy Charles E. Webb)*

Frisco, 1975. This large stone in the Frisco Cemetery shows the movement of the Warner family to the Unassigned Lands.

Gene Autry is an old village with a relatively new name. The first store, started in the 1870s, was located on the banks of the Washita River about one mile east of what now remains of the village. In July, 1883, a post office named Lou was opened in the store. In November of that year the post office was moved, and the name was changed to Dresden. In 1887, when the Gulf, Colorado and Santa Fe extended its tracks through the area about one mile from Dresden, the post office and stores moved to the railroad, and the name was changed to Berwyn. The name of the Berwyn post office was officially changed to Gene Autry on January 1, 1942. The name of the town had been changed previously on November 4, 1941.

vacating a portion of "the plat of the town of Frisco." The property was within the city limits of Yukon but had not been accepted by the government of Yukon for town or city purposes, streets and alleys not being used. The owner wanted to plow and plant the area.

A cemetery, located nearby, is all that remains to show where an important frontier town was once located. Frisco, with all its possibilities, existed for only about fifteen years.

Gene Autry
(LOU, DRESDEN, BERWYN)

COUNTY:	*Carter*
LOCATION:	*(a) Sec. 24, T 3 S, R 2 E; Sec. 19, T 3 S, R 3 E*
	(b) 7 miles north, 5 miles east of Ardmore
MAP:	*Page 219*
POST OFFICE:	*Lou, July 11, 1883–November 22, 1883; Dresden, November 22, 1883–September 1, 1887; Berwyn, September 1, 1887–January 1, 1942; Gene Autry, January 1, 1942–*
NEWSPAPERS:	*Berwyn Light; The Guide*
RAILROAD:	*Gulf, Colorado and Santa Fe Railway (Santa Fe)*

Gene Autry, 1941. Gene Autry riding his horse Champion at the Flying A Ranch. *(Courtesy Western History Collections, University of Oklahoma)*

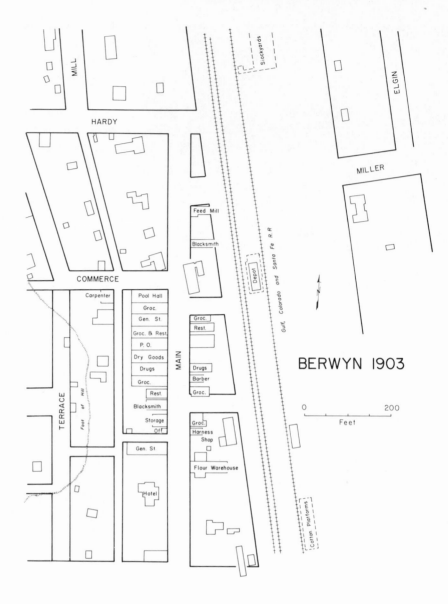

Berwyn, 1903

The site of the village is a picturesque one. The southern flank of the Arbuckle Mountains is to the north and west, with rolling hills to the south and the Washita River and its fertile valley to the east. Just west of the principal north-south street is a steep hill that somewhat limited expansion in that direction, although a few early-day homes were built near the summit and stores fronting on the street backed into it. Berwyn, with its various stores and shops, was a good agricultural Saturday town.

The biggest day in the life of the village was November 16, 1941. Gene Autry, the famous cowboy movie star, had purchased a twelve-hundred-acre ranch about two miles west of Berwyn. With approval of the Santa Fe and the U.S. Post Office Department it was decided to change the name from Berwyn to Gene Autry. Plans for a gigantic celebration were developed. November 16 was selected as the date because it was a Sunday and also statehood day, being the thirty-fourth anniversary of Oklahoma. A special train of twenty-one cars and many buses was chartered. It was estimated that a crowd of thirty-five thousand attended the ceremonies. As early as Friday before the program Main Street was teeming with traffic. One visiting newsman reported that "you couldn't see the

Gene Autry, 1941. Some of the thirty-five thousand persons who jammed the streets on the day the name was changed from Berwyn to Gene Autry. *(Courtesy Oklahoma Publishing Company)*

town for the people." Another stated that "you couldn't see the people for the dust fogged by countless cars." Food and drink stands were set up and operated by church groups. Some had the featured delicacy of buffalo meat. Indians were brought from western Oklahoma to set up tepees to add to the color.

The four-hour program on Sunday included a parade and stage show. Four roundup clubs and a dozen bands participated. A network of Oklahoma radio stations aired one hour of the program before a thirty-minute national broadcast. Movie companies sent newsreel cameramen, and metropolitan papers had reporters present. Governor Leon Phillips and Autry both made talks. Autry stated that he would spend $250,000 on improvements at his ranch, including a headquarters building for his traveling rodeo.

Three weeks later, on December 7, 1941, the

Gene Autry, 1959. Deserted Main Street after the inactivation of the Ardmore air base. *(Courtesy Oklahoma Publishing Company)*

United States became involved in World War II. Autry went into the armed services and did not follow through with his plans for the ranch. Later he sold the property and moved his headquarters.

During World War II Gene Autry was given a brief period of growth. Large aviation facilities were located just north of the village, and many people working there lived in the community. One rock building, completed in 1904, still stands; it houses a small grocery store. The store, a church, and the post office, plus a few homes, are all that remain of the place that in 1915 had ten stores, a newspaper, two lumberyards, a hotel, an oil mill, two cotton gins, an elevator, and its own electric light plant. There were also two lawyers, two doctors, and an undertaker. The population has dropped from over 600 to 120 in 1970 and an estimated 90 in 1975. The consolidated grade school which continues to function is known as the Berwyn School.

Grand, *ca.* 1905. Temple Houston, son of Governor Sam Houston of Texas, was one of the prominent lawyers frequently appearing in court in Grand. *(Courtesy Western History Collections, University of Oklahoma)*

Grand

COUNTY:	*Ellis*
LOCATION:	*(a) Sec. 31, T 18 N, R 24 W (b) 9 miles south, 2½ miles west of Arnett*
MAP:	*Page 215*
POST OFFICE:	*November 4, 1892–September 30, 1943*
NEWSPAPERS:	*Canadian Valley Echo; Day County Progress; Day County Tribune; Day County Progress and Grand Republican*

Grand, because of the amount of material that has been written about it, is probably the best-known ghost town in western Oklahoma. It was established in 1892 when the Cheyenne and Arapaho Reservation was opened for settlement. The site was almost adjacent to the north bank of the Canadian River and east of the Antelope Hills south of the river.

E County was organized in the northwest corner of the Cheyenne-Arapaho lands. Ioland, some sixteen miles east of Grand, was designated the county seat. The courthouse in Ioland, a frame structure, burned on November 18, 1893. Because of the exceedingly bad quality of the water at Ioland, plus the loss of the courthouse, the County Commissioners moved the county seat to Grand. (Later the Territorial Legislature approved the move.) Grand was located in a grove of trees, and on a nearby low hill was a spring, known as Robinson Springs, of good-quality water. Leslie A. McRill has said: "Grand is the only place I have ever seen where you climb for water and dig for wood. The roots of the shin oaks were large and furnished good firewood."

Grand prospered as most small county-seat towns did in territorial days. The town had about one hundred inhabitants, "most of whom were county officials and lawyers." There were four law officers and six resident lawyers. The legal business was good, as there was a lot of "proving up" on the claims and "contests" against settlers who had not stayed on their claims and im-

Grand, 1905. Business district of the county seat. The *Echo*, leading newspaper in the area, was printed in the building at the right. *(Courtesy Oklahoma Historical Society)*

Grand, *ca.* 1905. Store and post office. *(Courtesy Ellis County Historical Society)*

proved enough. Both territorial and federal courts were held in Grand. The town was about three blocks long and had the usual hotel, saloons, general stores, blacksmith shop, and livery stable. A three-room courthouse was built. There were at least two newspapers much of the time, and always their political views differed.

Grand should be remembered for both its prominent people and its activities. Dr. O. C. Newman, who later established the widely known Shattuck Hospital, practiced medicine in Grand from 1900 until statehood. Temple Houston, son of Sam Houston and noted frontier attorney, often had cases before the courts. The Fourth of July was always a special day, for loyalty on the frontier was strong. This special day was a meeting time for people from all parts of the county to enjoy games, visiting, listening to patriotic speeches, and being "brought up on the gossip." The county normal school, conducted each summer, brought to town several young women teachers, which usually resulted in a romance or two.

The Territorial Legislature changed the county name from E to Day. During the writing of the state constitution by the Constitutional Convention meeting in Guthrie, it was decided to abolish Day County. The Canadian River would sometimes go on a rampage, with walls of water two and three feet high sweeping down it, and at such times people south of the river could not get to the county seat. Crossing the river even during periods of low water was always a problem because of possible areas of quicksand. Therefore, two new counties, Roger Mills south of the Canadian and Ellis north of

the river, were formed. Grand was designated as county seat of Ellis County. However, since Grand was at the southern boundary of the new county, the people soon voted to change the county seat from Grand to Arnett; thus, on August 26, 1908, the records of old Day County were moved to Arnett.

Soon thereafter Grand was almost a deserted town. Some buildings, including the large two-story lodge hall, were moved to Arnett. A store and post office continued to operate for a few years. Currently a dirt road leads to the site of old Grand. A small grove of trees and a part of an old bank vault are all that remain.

Grand, *ca.* 1905. The Grand Hotel was the popular meeting place for farmers, ranchers, and politicians. *(Courtesy Ellis County Historical Society)*

Gray Horse

COUNTY: *Osage*
LOCATION: *(a) Sec. 22, T 24 N, R 6 E*
             (b) 8 miles south, 14 miles west
             of Pawhuska; 1 mile south, 3
             miles east of Fairfax
MAP: *Page 216*
POST OFFICE: *May 5, 1890–December 31, 1931*

Gray Horse, *ca.* 1930. Native American Church. *(Courtesy Osage Museum)*

Gray Horse, located in the southwestern part of the Osage Reservation, served as a subagency center for the Osage people. The area surrounding the village is hilly, and as such it serves as the home of the "Big Hills People," one of the five physical divisions of the Osage Indian Tribe. Legend has it that a great flood spread over the land in which the Osage lived, forcing them to move for safety. The results of the flood are told by John Joseph Mathews in his book *The Osages* (p. 147):

> *Wah'Kon-Tah* had desired that the Little Ones break up into five villages, so that one village would not grow to be too large, and if the enemy struck one village suddenly, the other would be free to come to their aid, and also each village would be a scout or guard for all.
>
> Obedient to *Wah'Kon-Tah*'s wishes, the five groups ever after lived on the type of topography to which they fled that day long ago. They settled in the places where they had camped with their drying fires, and when they migrated, each group chose a spot most closely resembling the topographical features where they had taken refuge—the hill people on the hills, the plateau people on the plateau. . . .

The first store at Gray Horse was started in 1884. After the village was made a subagency it became an important place not only for trade and government business, but also for general meetings of the Big Hills People. The large, round dance house was built about 1908. Later the Native American church was constructed. Population in 1905 was estimated to be about 150 persons.

Gray Horse, 1910. Osage Dance or Round House. *(Courtesy Osage Museum)*

Gray Horse, 1975. Remains of U.S. Indian Trading Store.

Gray Horse, 1975. Gray Horse Cemetery, in which many noted Osage leaders are buried.

Hanson

COUNTY: *Sequoyah*
LOCATION: *(a) Sec. 7, T 11 N, R 25 E*
(b) 1½ miles south, 5½ miles east of Sallisaw
MAP: *Page 217*
POST OFFICE: *July 13, 1888–November 30, 1954*
RAILROAD: *Saint Louis, Iron Mountain and Southern Railway (Missouri Pacific)*

Hanson started in 1888 in a store-post office combination. Two years later the store was moved about one mile west to be near the Iron Mountain Railroad, which was then laying tracks through the area. Soon thereafter the village began to grow. Hanson was headquarters for the railroad crew, and many people came there to work. A depot, a bunkhouse, a section house, a cotton loading platform, and cattle pens were built. A big public well was dug to supply water. A large pumphouse and water tank were constructed so that the steam engines could get necessary water.

The decade of the 1890s saw Hanson develop to its greatest extent. A hotel, several general stores, and two cotton gins, besides a clothing store and drugstore, located in new buildings south of the tracks. One of the buildings was a large two-story frame structure. The village also had three churches and a school. Several of the Cherokee families built new homes in Hanson after receiving the "Strip Payment" in 1894. There were no telephones at first, but when they came into existence they were called the "whoop and holler" system. They had hand cranks. The party called was determined by the number and combination of long and short rings, and they were real party lines. At this time Hanson exceeded Sallisaw in importance and population.

Hanson became noted for the amount of cotton grown in the area and the number of cattle shipped to Kansas City. During the cotton picking season people came into the region to work, and the gins ran twenty-four hours a day. Trains loaded with bales of cotton left every few days. Cattle roundups were of extreme importance. It was said: "The townspeople didn't get much

Currently, one dilapidated store building remains standing. The original dance house no longer exists, but an old store building and a few homes remain. Although the village is no longer the site of a subagency, meetings are still held in the once important center.

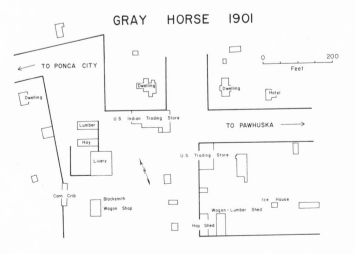

Gray Horse, 1901

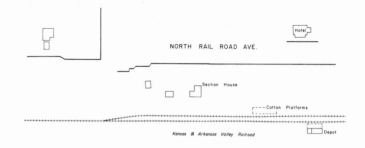

NORTH RAIL ROAD AVE.

Section House

Cotton Platforms

Kansas & Arkansas Valley Railroad   Depot

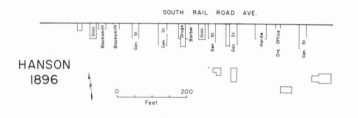

SOUTH RAIL ROAD AVE.

HANSON
1896

0   200
Feet

Hanson, 1896

Hochatown

McCurtain
LOCATION: *(a) Sec. 22, T 4 S, R 25 E*
(b) 14 miles north, 8 miles east
of Idabel; 5 miles north, 3 miles
east of Broken Bow
MAP: *Page 220*
POST OFFICE: *September 5, 1894–December*
28, 1963

Hochatown history is summarized by Len Green in his article "Rise and Fall of Hochatown: Interesting Community Saga" (*Idabel Gazette*, June 19, 1972): "Over a span of more than 60 years, Hochatown grew from a brawling lumber camp to become the 'Moonshine Capital of Oklahoma' and later a quiet farming and ranching community before disappearing forever beneath the waters of Broken Bow Lake."

When the Choctaw Indians first came to Oklahoma, about twelve families followed the trail northward from old Eagle to the valley in which Hochatown was later located. These early inhabitants planted a few crops and spent a great deal of time hunting and trapping. About 1900 the Choctaw Lumber and Coal Company (later Dierks) established a lumber camp where the village developed. To get the logs out they built a spur railroad into the area from Eagletown. The lumber camp had a commissary that sold largely personal items plus whiskey on Saturdays only, a cook shack, and a bunkhouse. After the prime timber had been cut, the tracks were removed and the lumberjacks shifted to new camps, but the old buildings remained standing.

Toward the end of the operation by the Choctaw Lumber and Coal Company a small private sawmill and a stave mill were started. Farmers moved into the area, making use of the partly cleared land by planting cotton, corn, sorghums, hay, and truck crops. As a result of the population increase, a general store and a school were started, and a post office was established. No state highways were ever extended through the area, and no bus line ever served the village.

During the 1920s and 1930s the area became noted for its moonshine whiskey. Green writes: "Since the clear waters of Mountain Fork River were ideal for distilling mountain dew, and because the creek canyons furnished concealment

H

sleep the night before the cattle were to be shipped. The cattle train would arrive about 3 A.M. Sunday morning, arriving in Kansas City for Monday morning market. The cowboys would be on hand to load them up, which would arouse the town. Many came to watch them load."

Disaster struck in 1899 when all the business houses except one burned. The fire was such a blow to the town that it was never overcome. A few of the merchants rebuilt, but most moved away. Just before the fire the Kansas City Southern Railroad selected Sallisaw instead of Hanson as the site of its rail junction with the other lines. Hanson residents then began moving to Sallisaw. About 1910 another fire, the death blow to the town, burned most of the business district that had been rebuilt.

Hanson now is an isolated community of a few homes. There are no stores, and all of the evidence of the former business district has been erased. The depot, along with the cotton platform and the cattle pens, has been removed. As a large number of people have moved from the area, the school has been consolidated with other districts. Both U.S. Highway 64 and Interstate 40 bypass the village to the south.

from federal revenuers, Hochatown became the center for a thriving illegal whiskey operation." During a trial in federal court in Muskogee, one federal agent referred to the village as the "moonshine capital of Oklahoma."

Before the Broken Bow Dam was ever considered, people were leaving the Hochatown community. Because of the lack of economic and social opportunities, very few of the younger people remained, and many of the older people moved to nearby towns where medical and transportation facilities were available. With the building of the dam, the cemetery and church were moved and most other structures were either moved or destroyed. The last family left the village in 1966. Hochatown is now covered by forty feet of water.

Independence, *ca.* 1897. A parade along the main street to celebrate the Fourth of July. *(Courtesy Clinton Daily News)*

Hochatown, 1963. The post office and last store in town. *(Courtesy Eugene Burke)*

Independence

COUNTY: *Custer*
LOCATION: *(a) Sec. 32, T 15 N, R 16 W*
               (b) 10 miles north, 1½ miles east of Arapaho; 4 miles north, 3 miles west of Custer City
MAP: *Page 215*
POST OFFICE: *October 5, 1892–July 15, 1922*
NEWSPAPERS: *Independence Courier; Independence Herald*

Independence was one of two government townsites established before the opening of the Cheyenne-Arapaho Reservation in 1892 in what has become Custer County. At the time of the run a general store and a blacksmith shop were started. In due time each moved from its tent home into frame buildings. Farmers claiming land adjacent to the village built homes either in it or nearby. Within a week or so there was a population of about forty persons.

The first robbery occurred soon after the founding. All of the men of the community, except the blacksmith, had gone to Kingfisher after lumber for the construction of homes. During the morning three strange men rode into Independence. The men staked their horses in an adjacent pasture and loafed about. The women suspected that the men planned to rob the store. During the day the women carefully hid all items of value and then gathered in the one house to wait. In the evening the strangers rode in, broke open the door of the store, and rushed to the cash box to find it contained only one nickel. They then went to the blacksmith and asked where the women were. When told they were all in one place and had shotguns, the men rode back to the store, put on new clothes, discarded their old clothes, and vanished.

By 1900 Independence had a population of about three hundred. The place reached its peak in 1902, when it had four general stores, a lumberyard, two blacksmith shops, two churches, a newspaper, two barbers, two doctors, a bank, and a livery stable. There were two schools, white and colored, and three active organizations—the Odd Fellows (IOOF), the Modern Woodmen, and the GAR.

The editor of the *Independence Courier* wrote, "Independence, with the railroad facilities she is sure to get, is destined to become the metropolis of western Oklahoma." The people of Independence, however, made the fatal mistake of thinking that the railroad could not afford to miss the town. The Kansas City, Mexico and Orient Railroad, making its survey in the area, stated that the town must secure a right-of-way for them and advance eighteen hundred dollars in cash. The right-of-way was secured, but not the cash. The Orient continued to build on a straight-line course northeastward, Custer City was founded, and in less than two years Independence was a ghost town. The first store started in Independence was also the last to leave it.

The old townsite is now used completely for agriculture. No traces of the place remain.

Ingalls, 1938. Monument erected by the citizens of Ingalls. The inscription reads: In Memory of U.S. Marshals *Dick Speed—Tom Huston—Lafe Shadley* who fell in the Line of Duty September 1, 1893 By Dalton and Doolin Gang.

Ingalls

COUNTY:	*Payne*
LOCATION:	*(a) Sec. 28, T 19 N, R 4 E*
	(b) 1 mile south, 9½ miles east of Stillwater
MAP:	*Page 216*
POST OFFICE:	*January 22, 1890–October 31, 1907*

Ingalls was founded in 1889 a few weeks after the opening of the Unassigned Lands. A year later it was reported to be "a thriving town with a post office and several stores." The land in the area was good for the growing of cotton and grain crops, and the settlers had hopes that a proposed railroad through the area would make the town an agricultural trading and shipping center.

Ingalls, however, is remembered primarily as the headquarters of the Doolin outlaw gang. The town, located only about fifteen miles from the Creek Nation, in which the gang had its hideout cave, was the general meeting place for Doolin and his associates after a bank or train robbery. The OK Hotel served as headquarters. Mary Pierce, the wife of the owner, planned entertainment for the men when they gathered for relaxation. The people living in Ingalls were divided into three groups as far as the outlaws were concerned: (1) those friendly to the outlaws, (2) those who were afraid of the outlaws, and (3) those who found it best not to know anything about their activities or whereabouts.

During the last of August, 1893, Bill Doolin, Arkansas Tom Jones, Bob Yocum (Bitter Creek),

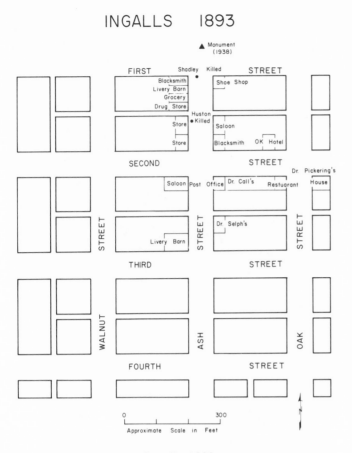

INGALLS 1893

▲ Monument (1938)

FIRST   Shadley Killed   STREET
Blacksmith   Shoe Shop
Livery Barn
Grocery
Drug Store
                Huston
            Killed
Store   Saloon
Store   Blacksmith   OK Hotel

SECOND   STREET

                            Dr. Pickering's
                                House
Saloon Post Office Dr. Call's   Restuarant

STREET   Dr. Selph's

Livery Barn

THIRD   STREET

WALNUT   ASH   OAK

FOURTH   STREET

0   300
Approximate Scale in Feet

N

Ingalls, 1893

Bill Dalton, Dan Clifton (Dynamite Dick), George Newcomb, Tulsa Jack, Red Buck, and a few lesser outlaws gathered in Ingalls at the hotel. Red Lucas, a marshal unknown to the group, drifted into town and played poker with the outlaws. After studying the situation, he returned to Guthrie and helped make plans to capture the gang. On the night of August 31, three covered wagons carrying U.S. Marshals E. D. (Ed) Nix, A. H. Houston, Lafe Shadley, Red Lucas, James Masterson, Dick Speed, and others, with their supplies, camped near the town. As they made final plans they noticed a small boy listening. The marshals decided to hold him all night, but they unwisely let him go the next morning. He immediately ran to town with the news that "the law" was coming.

The "Battle of Ingalls" started shortly before eleven o'clock on the morning of September 1, 1893, when the three wagons drove into town. The outlaws had saddled their horses but had not left town. Bitter Creek was riding northward toward the town pump when Speed opened fire, and the battle was on. Bitter Creek was wounded. Arkansas Tom, who was in the hotel, opened fire on Speed, wounding him. The other officers were by this time out of their wagons, and the rest of the outlaw gang also took up the fight. The battle was furious but short. A fourteen-year-old boy was killed accidentally by either Doolin or Dalton. Two saloon keepers were wounded, and a neutral citizen was killed. In the end three marshals—Speed, Houston, and Shadley—were killed. Two of the outlaws were wounded but were taken away by other gang members. Arkansas Tom could not get out of the hotel. A Reverend Mason talked him into surrendering. He was later sentenced to fifty years in prison but was pardoned after serving seventeen years. The other outlaws were eventually caught or killed. The Battle of Ingalls marked the effective end of the Doolin gang. During the battle the doctors and ministers living in Ingalls administered to officers and outlaws alike. (Some stories have identified Rose of the Cimarron, sweetheart of Bitter Creek, as being the heroine. There is no evidence, however, that she was in Ingalls at the time.)

After the "battle" Ingalls declined. As late as 1938, however, it was believed that a new community spirit had developed. At that time the town had two stores, a garage, a church, and a few homes. A monument to the slain officers

Ingalls, 1974. First Sunday School in Payne County was held in this log cabin. It was moved to Ingalls from site northwest of the town.

was erected, and the people living in Ingalls made some attempt to attract tourists. However, when State Highways 51 and 108 were completed they were one mile north and one and one-half miles west of town, respectively.

Today many people drive near the historic site, but few visit. No businesses are now in operation. The monument stands at what was the intersection of First and Ash streets. Nearby is a large map that shows where the shootout took place and where the officers were killed. A small school building, the oldest in Payne County, has been moved to the old townsite, but it has no relationship to the town.

Ingersoll, 1975. This elevator, though in fairly good repair, is no longer used.

Ingersoll

COUNTY: *Alfalfa*
LOCATION: *(a) Secs. 21/28, T 27 N, R 11 W*
                 (b) 2 miles north, 2 miles west of Cherokee
MAP: *Page 215*
POST OFFICE: *September 13, 1901–December 31, 1942*
NEWSPAPERS: *Ingersoll Review; Ingersoll Times; Ingersoll News; Ingersoll Midget*
RAILROADS: *Choctaw Northern Railroad (Rock Island); Denver, Enid and Gulf Railroad (Santa Fe)*

When the Cherokee Outlet was opened for settlement in 1893, many persons of German ancestry migrated to the Ingersoll area. No town was formed until the Choctaw Railroad (Rock Island) reached the site of Ingersoll in the summer of 1901. A townsite was platted and opened for settlement in September of that year. The town was named Ingersoll after the president of the railroad.

It is said that Ingersoll was born full-grown. Within a month it had an estimated one thousand inhabitants, stores of all kinds were either in operation or being built, and temporary homes were being replaced by permanent ones. Soon after the town started, three churches, one the German church, were organized, and a two-story brick school building was under construc-

tion. Because of its rapid growth the County Commissioners declared the town incorporated in January, 1902. At that time Ingersoll rivaled Cherokee in business activities and may have forged ahead for a while in population.

During its development Ingersoll became noted as a "sinful" town, not only because it had seven saloons and two pool halls, but also because many individuals believed the town was

Ingersoll, 1975. A wide sidewalk is all that remains along the west side of the former business street.

Ingersoll, 1974. Even though the sign says it is open, the restaurant has been closed for some time. *(Courtesy Enid Morning News)*

named for the famous agnostic Robert Ingersoll. With the coming of statehood all saloons were closed. At various times four newspapers were printed in the town, the *Ingersoll Times* being the most important and having the longest life. The *Ingersoll News* printed only one issue, then combined with another paper. Many businesses reflected the importance of agriculture in the area, especially wheat growing.

After statehood Ingersoll contested Cherokee for the location of the county seat. Four towns were voted on in the January, 1909, election, with Ingersoll running third behind Cherokee and Carmen but ahead of Jet. At that time the town had four elevators, four general stores, two barber shops, two livery stables, two restaurants, and two banks in addition to a hardware store, a lumberyard, a drugstore, a blacksmith shop, a hotel, a telephone exchange, a billiard hall, a meat market, a coal dealer, a shoemaker, an agricultural implement dealer, a weekly newspaper, and a corncob pipe manufacturing company. Population was estimated at about 375. Shortly after losing its bid for the county seat, Ingersoll started to decline and has continued to do so.

Most of the business buildings have been torn down or have burned down. Wide sidewalks of yesteryear are buckled by tree growth, in part covered by dirt, and encircled by weeds. One former business block is fenced and used as a pen for sheep or cattle. The elevators are out of business, and the schools are closed. There remain, however, a few large, well-kept homes. The only business in full-time operation is a very small grocery store–filling station combination. Since the store is on U.S. Highway 64, it also serves as a bus stop.

Jefferson, 1974. All store buildings in the former business district now stand unused.

Jefferson

COUNTY:	*Grant*
LOCATION:	*(a) Sec. 24, T 26 N, R 6 W*
	(b) 6 miles south, 3 miles west of Medford
MAP:	*Page 216*
POST OFFICE:	*Pond, November 13, 1879–April 14, 1887; Jefferson, July 12, 1894–*
NEWSPAPERS:	*Jefferson Hustler; Old Pond Creek Hustler; Jefferson Review*
RAILROAD:	*Chicago, Kansas and Nebraska Railway (Rock Island)*

Jefferson, located on the low divide between Osage and Pond creeks, is about a mile from the confluence of the two streams. Therein lies one of the principal causes of the demise of Jefferson; the area is subject to heavy flooding.

In 1866 James R. Mead established a trading station at what then was called Round Pond Creek, later the site of Jefferson, on the Chisholm Trail in the Cherokee Outlet. Mead recalled, "Mr. Chisholm's teams and my own were the first which ever passed over the route and marked out what afterward became known as the Chisholm Trail." There, at Round Pond, the cattle route crossed an old Indian warpath, Black Dog Trail, named for an Osage chief. In November, 1879, a post office named Pond was located at this place. The station and post office were closed in 1887. The Cherokee Outlet was opened for settlement in 1893. In 1894 the town of Jefferson came into existence.

Jefferson, surrounded by some of the best agricultural land in Oklahoma, soon became a growing farm center. Within ten years some twenty stores and shops plus two banks and two hotels had located in the town. In addition, there were two produce houses, an agricultural implement dealer, a wheelwright, three blacksmith shops, three elevators, and a feed mill. Better-than-average medical care was available, for three medical doctors and three osteopaths had established offices. A weekly newspaper advertised the virtues of Jefferson throughout the area. The town also had its saloon keepers and liquor dealers who had moved in fast "to quench the thirst of the newly located settlers, townsmen, and others."

Two churches were soon started. The First Methodist Church, which still stands, was built in 1895 of rock quarried along the Oklahoma-Kansas border and brought to Jefferson in wagons pulled by teams. A school system was also organized. In the early 1900s a two-story frame opera house was constructed. Performances by touring theatrical companies and musical organizations were given on the first floor, and dances were held in the upper story. The building also served as town hall for local meetings.

Jefferson reached its peak about 1915, when it

Jefferson, 1975. First Methodist Church, built in 1895, is still in use.

had an estimated population of about six hundred persons. After that there was a gradual decline until 1944. At that time the first big flood in fifty years hit the town. Most homes and businesses were inundated. On October 10–11, 1973, Jefferson had its biggest flood. It was reported that fifteen inches of rain fell in five hours. "After that mess several families moved out." Again, in 1974 there was another great flood and more families moved. During these last two floods water covered the lower floors of homes, store buildings, and churches.

Currently about eighteen families live in Jefferson. Two churches remain open, but all stores and the school are closed. An elevator continues to serve the farmers of the area. There is evidence of repair to homes in some places, but more evidence of flood damage and decay. Boggy places in and about the town can be seen, and in many places driftwood left by the receding waters remains.

Jumbo, 1974. Monuments erected by the Woodmen of the World in memory of those killed in the mine explosion of 1910.

Jumbo

COUNTY: *Pushmataha*
LOCATION: *(a) Sec. 28, T 1 S, R 15 E*
             (b) 15 miles north, 7 miles west
             of Antlers
MAP: *Page 220*
POST OFFICE: *November 11, 1906–*

Jumbo, an isolated community near the western edge of the Ouachita Mountains, became important in the late 1880s when asphalt was discovered in the area. The first big vein of asphalt was somewhat in the shape of an elephant, hence the name.

Four shaft mines and three strip mines were opened between 1890 and 1900. The shaft in the principal mine was about thirty feet deep and then extended eastward at an angle of sixty degrees. The underground mines were interlocked. About forty men worked on each of the two shifts, one during the day and the other at night. In 1905 the mines caught fire, and the men escaped one by one by climbing a ladder through the air vent. In 1910 a mine explosion took the lives of fourteen men. The mines were reopened after the explosion but were largely worked out by 1914. Later, another shaft was put down, but it was closed permanently in 1916. The mined asphalt was moved by wagon or tram to Moyers, a railroad station, for shipment.

At the time of its greatest growth, Jumbo had a hotel, a barber shop, a blacksmith, a pool hall, and three general stores. Its maximum population was about two hundred persons. The Woodmen of the World had a lodge hall and were very active in community affairs. Several of the miners killed in the explosion were members. The lodge erected one of their distinctive monuments at the grave of each. There was an unveiling of the monuments in 1911.

The only commercial activity remaining in Jumbo is one small store–post office–filling station combination. The school was closed in the 1950s, but the church continues to serve a large mountain area. The old cemetery is well cared for. Every year on the Saturday before the first Sunday in June the old-timers and the younger group meet at the cemetery for Decoration Day. On Sunday they have an all-day meeting and a big dinner at the church.

Kaw City, *ca.* 1918. Probably this group gathered to look at and talk about the eighty-pound catfish caught a short time before in the Arkansas River. *(Courtesy Western History Collections, University of Oklahoma)*

Kaw City

COUNTY: *Kay*
LOCATION: *(a) Secs. 1/2, T 26 N, R 4 E*
                   (b) 9 miles south, 12 miles east
                   of Newkirk; 3½ miles north, 13
                   miles east of Ponca City
MAP: *Page 216*
POST OFFICE: *September 12, 1902; moved to*
                   new Kaw City townsite in 1970
NEWSPAPERS: *Kaw City Star; Kaw City Tribune*
RAILROAD: *Eastern Oklahoma Railway (Santa Fe), abandoned 1971*

Kaw City was established in 1902 by William M. Jenkins, a former governor of Oklahoma Territory. Located near the Arkansas River and adjacent to the Santa Fe tracks being laid from Newkirk to Pauls Valley via Cushing and Shawnee, the townsite was platted soon after the railroad bridge across the Arkansas was completed. The first two buildings erected in the new town were north of the railroad tracks because the owners believed the business section would develop in that area. Jenkins, however, erected his office at the corner of Main Street and Fifth Avenue. New arrivals also started building along Main Street. Soon thereafter the two original buildings, which housed a harness shop and a peanut stand, were moved. A dance was held to celebrate the completion of the first store building on Main Street. It was attended by fifty men and six women. A fiddle and mouth organ supplied the music.

The town grew rapidly. Soon after its founding a post office was approved and a newspaper started. In addition to stores and restaurants there were a livery stable, a blacksmith shop, and barber shops. From 1902 until statehood Kaw City was a wide-open town, having five saloons. The three merchants in the nearby village of Longwood moved their stores to Kaw City, and the doctor who had his practice in Longwood also moved. Kaw City became an important trading center for the Kaw Indians, whose reservation was to the north, and the Osage Indians living to the south and east. By 1919 Kaw City was recognized as a prosperous city because of its business with the Indians, farmers, and cattlemen of the area. New business activities had developed as needed, and several professional people had settled in the community. A good school system was in operation, and churches had been organized. The streets, however, had not been paved, nor had a water and sanitation system been developed.

In 1919 oil was discovered in the Kaw City area. As in all oil boom towns, strangers walked

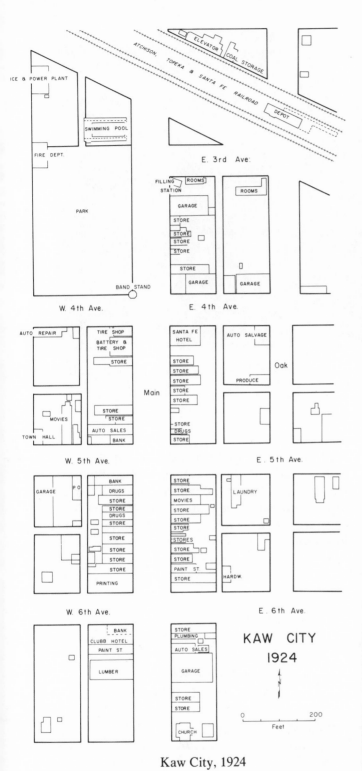

buildings were soon going up in all parts of the town, old buildings were torn down and replaced, streets were widened and graded, Main Street was paved, bonds were voted for a sewer and water system, and gas was piped into the town. Probably the most important building constructed, however, was a modern, four-story hotel built by I. M. (Ike) Clubb. Kaw City in a very short time had become a city of the first class.

The best-remembered citizens of Kaw City are Ike and Laura Clubb. Before their marriage Mrs. Clubb had been a teacher. She attended the first normal school held in what is now Oklahoma, studying public speaking and oratory. After marriage she continued to teach, but she also boarded four cattlemen and raised calves to help pay for additional education. Mr. Clubb continued to develop the ranch and livestock that they owned. When oil was discovered the Clubb lands proved to be near the center of a producing area. With this new wealth the Clubbs built the famous Clubb Hotel in Kaw City. Mrs. Clubb, desiring to add to her education, spent a

Kaw City, 1924

Kaw City, *ca.* 1940. Mrs. Laura A. Clubb, teacher and art collector. *(Courtesy Oklahoma Historical Society)*

the streets—oil company officials and trucking contractors, millionaires and bums. Unheard-of rentals were offered for any and all kinds of places where one could sleep and eat. "Millionaires occupied shabby little rooms at the two-story brick hotel, with outside sanitation." New

Kaw City, *ca.* 1969. Looking east across the town toward the Arkansas River. The entire area was flooded upon completion of the dam. *(Courtesy U.S. Army, Corps of Engineers)*

year at Northwestern University studying oratory and traveling in Europe. While in Europe she visited many of the great art galleries and invested in a few art treasures for her home. What began as purchases for the home so interested her that she created an art gallery of masterpieces. The collection, displayed in the lobby and halls of the hotel, included works by Gainsborough, Kirchbach, Thomas Moran, Corot, Schiavoni, William Chase, Bonheur, and other world-famous artists. Such a collection, located in a small-town hotel, was explained by Mrs. Clubb with: "I made my money here and I give it to the people here." (In March, 1947, Mrs. Clubb gave the choice of her collection to the Philbrook Art Center in Tulsa.)

When the oil boom was over, Kaw City began to decline. As people moved away, businesses closed. With the passing of time, ranches in the area became larger, and farms consolidated. Machinery replaced man in these activities. Many of the Indians, having gained wealth as a result of the oil discoveries, moved to larger cities. As the program for flood control and the development of the Arkansas River Inland Waterway progressed, it was decided that a large dam needed to be built in the Kaw City area. Thus it became necessary for the town to either move or be drowned. Some buildings were moved to new locations, but most were torn down. All of the platted area that was Kaw City is now covered by the waters of Kaw Reservoir.

Kenton
(CARRIZO, FLORENCE)

COUNTY: *Cimarron*
LOCATION: *(a) Sec. 16, T 5 N, R 1 E, Cimarron Meridian*
(b) 11½ miles north, 25 miles west of Boise City
MAP: *Page 214*
POST OFFICE: *Carrizo, September 8, 1886–April 19, 1890; Florence, April 19, 1890–May 12, 1891; Kenton, May 12, 1891–*

NEWSPAPERS: *Cimarron Valley News; Cimarron News*

Kenton, 1916. North side of Main Street. About half the buildings were made from stone quarried nearby. *(Courtesy Western History Collections, University of Oklahoma)*

Kenton is situated in the valley of the Cimarron River, which ranges from one to five miles in width. Lava-capped Black Mesa, located to the north of the town, reaches some five hundred feet above the valley and has a maximum elevation of 4,973 feet, making it the highest point in Oklahoma. Kenton is approximately two miles east of New Mexico and six miles south of Colorado.

The first village, called Carrizo, consisted of a general store and three saloons. It was a roistering place and became known as the Cowboy Capital. After the Panhandle was surveyed and somewhat organized, the store owner moved his store about one mile eastward and platted and laid out forty acres for the townsite of Kenton. The saloons also moved, and the original site was abandoned. Kenton, being the most accessible place within a forty-mile radius, grew into a town with a population of approximately 350 persons.

In 1905 a story about the town in the *Cimarron Valley News*, published in Kenton, stated: "We have three large stores carrying general merchandise; one drug store; one hardware store; one notions store; one furniture store and repair shop, also undertaking goods; one shoe shop; one barber shop; one blacksmith shop; one feed yard and livery; one grain dealer; one tin shop and pipefitter; one alfalfa seed cleaning mill; one laundry; one $2,000 church; two good teachers; many residences of brick, stone, frame, and adobe; twelve wells of fine soft water; and four windmills on the townsite. Come and cast your lot with us and you will do good." The story failed to mention that two saloons continued to operate. Apparently, however, the

Kenton, 1957. Looking east along Main Street. All the buildings shown are either rock or concrete.

Kenton, 1975. Monument on top of Black Mesa marks the highest elevation in Oklahoma. *(Courtesy Oklahoma Department of Tourism and Recreation)*

business structures as well as the sod houses have been destroyed. A few homes, occupied mostly by older persons, and two churches remain. The total population is now less than twenty-five.

Keokuk Falls

COUNTY: *Pottawatomie*
LOCATION: *(a) Sec. 26, T 11 N, R 6 E*
(b) 4½ miles north, 15 miles east of Shawnee
MAP: *Page 219*
POST OFFICE: *January 13, 1892–February 15, 1918*
NEWSPAPER: *Keokuk Kall*

Keokuk Falls, named for Chief Moses Keokuk, was platted at the time of the opening of the Sac and Fox Reservation on September 22, 1891. The location was ideal for supplying goods and services to the Creek Nation, whose western boundary was about one mile east of the town, and the Seminole Nation, about a mile to the south just across the North Canadian River. For several years a ferryboat operated at the river crossing. Later, a floating bridge capable of supporting heavy loads was extended across the river and anchored at both ends. A fee of two cents was charged for the use of the bridge, but there was a fine of two dollars for crossing animals faster than at a walk.

The location and accessibility, however, resulted in Keokuk Falls becoming the most famous of the "liquor towns" that developed near the boundary of Oklahoma Territory and the Indian nations. The Indian nations were "dry" areas, for it was illegal to buy or sell liquor or even have it in one's possession there. Oklahoma Territory was legally "wet" and "wide open." Primarily on the basis of this liquor trade, Keokuk Falls developed into one of the toughest of frontier towns. From 1895 to 1905, in addition to various kinds of stores, cotton gins, and sawmills, the town had three hotels, two distilleries, ten doctors, seven saloons, and one coffin factory. There was one justice of the peace, but

write-up attracted others, for before statehood a bank was started, a hotel was opened, and a doctor and a lawyer moved to the community.

At the time of the writing of the constitution for the state of Oklahoma, Kenton was the only town in the area designated as Cimarron County. It was therefore named the county seat. Immiately after statehood other towns were formed, each wanting to become the county seat. By popular vote the seat of government was moved to Boise City, a new town near the center of the county. Soon after the removal of the courthouse, Kenton began to decline. The bank closed in 1913. The *Cimarron News* moved to Boise City, and the number of business establishments declined to fewer than ten.

Kenton is now an isolated village having one grocery store–gasoline pump business. For a while a grade school and high school with five teachers served the village and a large ranching area. All pupils are now transported to Boise City, thirty-five miles away. Most of the old

Keokuk Falls, *ca.* 1900. Chief Moses Keokuk, Sac and Fox, for whom the town was named. *(Courtesy Oklahoma Historical Society)*

Keokuk Falls, *ca.* 1907. At the time of statehood the saloons closed, and the town became "much quieter and more civilized." *(Courtesy Oklahoma Historical Society)*

eating the mash, caused much amusement as they squealed, staggered, and became affectionate while parading along the main street. An auctioneer who sometimes visited the town rode a saddled ostrich. It is said that "He would race against any horse and rider for a hundred yards. He never lost a race." The biggest party of all, however, was held on the night of November 15, 1907, when most male and many female citizens joined in consuming as much liquid re-

never a marshal or lawman; four to six preachers, but never a church. The first saloon built was named the Black Dog, and the second the Red Front, and it was between these two that most trouble developed over control of the liquor trade in the Indian nations. In 1904 the bitter rivalry between the saloon keepers resulted in several killings and the closing of four of the saloons. In 1907, at the time of statehood, the remaining saloons and distilleries were closed.

Stories about the shootings and killings in Keokuk Falls are numerous. The town became known as the home of the "seven deadly saloons." It is reported that one stagecoach driver, who made a daily run through Keokuk Falls, told his passengers, "Stop twenty minutes and see a man killed." One distillery located at the south edge of town dumped its waste mash in a gully at the back of the building. Hogs, after

Keokuk Falls, *ca.* 1900. Keokuk Falls in the North Canadian River. The falls were about three feet high. *(Courtesy Western History Collections, University of Oklahoma)*

freshment as possible before dry statehood at noon on the next day.

Soon after statehood most merchants moved to other towns where transportation facilities were better. A few businesses continued to operate until the early 1920s. South of the old town the North Canadian River has shifted its bed, and the former two- to three-foot waterfalls are no longer visible. Currently, only a dilapidated and unused building is standing. No good roads lead to what remains of Keokuk Falls.

Keokuk Falls, 1972. The last structure remaining on the old townsite.

Keystone-Appalachia

COUNTY: *Pawnee*
LOCATION: *(a) Sec. 31, T 20 N, R 10 E*
               (b) 11 miles south, 29 miles east
               of Pawnee; 9½ miles south, 10
               miles east of Cleveland
MAP: *Page 216*
POST OFFICE: *Appalachia, January 18, 1905–*
               January 1, 1906; Keystone, May
               6, 1900–November 12, 1962
NEWSPAPERS: *Appalachia Outlook; Keystone*
               Outlook; Keystone News
RAILROAD: *Arkansas Valley and Western*
               Railway (Frisco)

Keystone and Appalachia began as two different towns separated by the Cimarron River. Appalachia started first, but Keystone existed

longer. Both ceased to exist upon completion of the Keystone Dam, for the site of each is now covered by the waters of Keystone Lake.

Appalachia, located near the mouth of the Cimarron River where it flows into the Arkansas, was platted as a scheme for selling town lots in 1903. As Charles N. Gould, in his book *Oklahoma Place Names*, states, the plan was ". . . designed to appeal to the credulity of the gullible. Flamboyant, a birds-eye-view, three color maps were printed. Regardless of the fact that both rivers are sand beds for great periods of the year and can scarcely float a canoe, these maps show steamboats on both the Arkansas and Cimarron. An alluring red-line prospectus sets forth the advantages of owning lots in the new Oklahoma town." A few lots were sold, and some homes were built. Some of the early settlers suggested that the nearby hills reminded them of the Appalachian Mountains, so the town was named Appalachia.

One of the first settlers was a former sheriff from Texas. After "sizing up the situation" and recognizing the fact that Appalachia was in "wet" Oklahoma Territory, while within fewer than five miles was "dry" Indian Territory, he opened a saloon. Word soon spread through the Indian lands, and business boomed. The chief problem for the patrons was crossing the Cimarron River, for many of those who visited Appalachia came from Sapulpa and Red Fork to the south. Appalachia's civic spirit manifested itself in the construction of a narrow, swinging footbridge across the river. Horses with wagons, buckboards, and buggies were hitched near the south bank while their owners crossed the some-

Keystone, 1941. Frisco passenger depot. *(Courtesy Western History Collections, University of Oklahoma)*

Keystone-Appalachia

Cimarron River

Arkansas River

Keystone Dam

State Highway 51

Keystone-Appalachia, 1975. The former townsite is covered by sixty feet of water in Keystone Reservoir. *(Courtesy U.S. Army, Corps of Engineers)*

what shaky bridge. The bridge was soon dubbed the "Carrie Nation Bridge." Sober persons could negotiate it successfully, but those returning with a full load of liquor under their belt were usually ducked in the shallow waters below.

A deputy marshal, who was sent to Appalachia to keep order, after looking the situation over also decided to open a saloon, but on the south side of the river, thereby eliminating the trip across the shaky bridge; thus, Keystone was born. Soon other businesses as well as other saloons were built in Keystone, and a trade center began to develop. Appalachia offered competition for only a brief period.

The first business buildings in Keystone were largely frame structures with high false fronts. Board sidewalks were common, kerosene lamps were the chief sources of nighttime light, and all sanitation facilities were outside. The crowds in Keystone were said to have been "exceptionally well behaved." Those who became intoxicated and decided to right their wrongs or shoot

up the town had their guns taken away or were jailed. One cowboy who decided to burn down the jail, a frame structure, while locked therein received a "thorough scorching which cooked all the desire for blood out of him" before the marshal could get the door open.

Following statehood, Keystone became a fairly progressive small town. Brick and stone buildings largely replaced the frame ones in the commercial area, and several good homes were built. Activities gradually shifted with changes in technology. Blacksmith shops and livery stables closed as garages and filling stations opened, general stores were replaced by grocery and dry-goods stores, and hotels closed as transportation became faster and roads better. Population increased until the early 1930s, when the people began to move to expanding Tulsa, Sand Springs, and Sapulpa. Finally the town ceased to exist shortly after the U.S. Army Corps of Engineers started construction of the Keystone Dam.

Knowles, 1912. A growing agricultural town with several small stores and shops. *(Courtesy Beaver County Historical Society)*

Knowles

(SANDS CITY)

COUNTY: *Beaver*
LOCATION: *(a) Sec. 25, T 5 N, R 26 E, Cimarron Meridian*
                 (b) 4 miles north, 17½ miles east of Beaver
MAP: *Page 214*
POST OFFICE: *March 16, 1907–*
NEWSPAPER: *Farmers News*
RAILROAD: *Wichita Falls and Northwestern Railway (Katy), abandoned 1972*

Knowles, like many other towns in Oklahoma, has moved its location and changed its name. Incorporated as Sands City in 1906, it moved about a half mile eastward in 1912 at the time the Wichita Falls and Northwestern Railroad laid its tracks through eastern Beaver County. The post office, with the name of Knowles, was established in Sands City before the founding of Knowles.

The new city of Knowles soon became a trading, marketing, and shipping center for eastern Beaver and western Harper counties. In 1909 Sands City had nine business establishments; in 1913 Knowles had thirty. In that four-year period the population increased from 25 to 254 persons. In addition to the various stores, the town had a good bank, an excellent grade school and high school system, active churches, and the widely read *Farmers News*. Around the town was some of the best farming land in the state. Between September 1, 1928, and September 1, 1929, some 273 train cars of

wheat, 43 cars of kafir corn and milo, 18 cars of broomcorn, 49 cars of cattle, 5 cars of hogs, and 14,480 gallons of milk were shipped. Turkeys, chickens, and eggs were sent to market by trucks. Most farms had small orchards, and all had gardens. Knowles was a growing agricultural center.

The 1930s, however, changed all that. The depression ruined many farmers economically, and during the Dust Bowl period many saw their farms blown away. A long period of below-average rainfall, dry topsoil, and strong winds dominated the weather of the mid-1930s. Probably the most severe dust storm in the area started on Sunday, April 14, 1935. On that date a reddish brown cloud moved over Knowles from the northwest. It was a large dust cloud carried eastward by a slowly advancing cold front. Light from the sun was blotted out, and visibility was reduced to a few feet. Even though houses were shut as tight as possible, and wet cloths were wedged around windows and doors, the fine silt covered furniture and floors. The storm continued the following day. Stores were closed, school was canceled, driving ceased, and meetings were postponed. Those who had to go outside wore masks to protect their mouth and nose and goggles to protect their eyes.

Knowles, 1919. The most widely known hotel in the eastern end of the Panhandle, the meeting place for farmers and ranchers and a favorite of drummers. *(Courtesy Beaver County Historical Society)*

Knowles, 1927. The most important trade center in the eastern end of the Panhandle. The number of cars indicate the prosperity of the town and area.

Knowles, 1935. An approaching dust storm.

When the wind was not strong, such a storm could last two or three days. If the wind was strong the storm would move on quickly but often would have the effect of a sand blaster on a painted building or car. In the mid-1950s such dust storms again developed.

The town of Knowles now struggles for existence, but that struggle appears to be a losing cause. So many people have moved from the community that the schools are closed, the railroad has been abandoned and the tracks removed, and only one grocery store and the post office continue to operate. U.S. Highway 64 borders the eastern edge of the town, and cars speed by to larger towns and cities. Knowles is a victim of farm consolidation and the return to ranching, advancing agricultural technology, improved highway transportation, and the weather. The town is almost surrounded by a single ranch.

Knowles, 1975. Only remaining business buildings. The building only partly shown at the right has the only store in town.

Kosoma

COUNTY:	*Pushmataha*
LOCATION:	*(a) Sec. 27, T 2 S, R 16 E*
	(b) 8 miles north of Antlers
MAP:	*Page 220*
POST OFFICE:	*November 28, 1888–October 31, 1954*
RAILROAD:	*Fort Smith and Southern Railway (Frisco)*

Kosoma, north of the Kiamichi River and in the rugged Kiamichi Mountains, was an isolated community until the Frisco Railroad laid its tracks through the area in the late 1880s. The town has served as a Choctaw Indian camp and court site, as a place for the logging and lumber industry, and for a period of time as a rural trading center.

Sulphur water was found nearby, and its smell was generally unknown to the Choctaw Indians when they moved into the area, so they named the place Kosoma—"stink water." Deciding that

Kosoma, 1916. Log train unloading at a mill pond in the area. *(Courtesy Claude W. Curran)*

Kosoma, 1966. Remains of an abandoned home and a store.

the water had medicinal value, they would travel as much as fifty miles for their *kosoma*. The site was in Jack's Fork County, Pushmataha District, of the Choctaw Nation, and on a few occasions court was held there. Records indicate that when an individual was sentenced to death he was set free for a period of time to provide for his family and make his peace with this world and the next. On the day he was scheduled to die he would report for execution. (This was true of Indian justice in all of the Five Civilized Tribes.)

After the railroad came through, lumbermen stripped the large pine trees from the mountain slopes. Kosoma became a logging and sawmill center. When lumber production was greatest, Kosoma was reported as having a population in excess of seven hundred people. The town had three general stores, two blacksmith shops, two hotels, a drug store, a restaurant, and a billiard hall. There was also a large sawmill. One and sometimes two doctors served the community.

Two interesting stories are told about law enforcement in Kosoma shortly after statehood. A justice of the peace and a constable were duly elected. The first case before the court dealt with a lumberjack who had drunk too much Peruna, a product with a large alcoholic content. No law books were available, and there was no precedent to follow. The justice therefore opened his Bible for guidance. The book fell open to the first chapter of Acts, and the first line read was in verse five: "but ye shall be baptized. . . ." Accordingly, the prisoner was taken to a nearby lake, and after the light covering of December ice was broken he was thrown in. It is claimed that he was sober when he climbed ashore. Another case, but under a different justice and constable, also involved a Peruna-drinking lumberjack. Since there was no jail, the prisoner was locked in a boxcar to "sleep it off." When it was time to release the prisoner the next morning, the constable found the boxcar had been hooked onto a freight during the night and moved out. The car was finally located in Wister. The prisoner, when released, was reported to be very sober. The lumberjack returned to his wife and family in Kosoma by

Kosoma, 1974. First floor formerly served as a general store, the second floor as a lodge hall and a place for town meetings, dances, and parties.

riding in a passenger car on fare paid by officers of the law.

Not much remains in Kosoma. Logging has ceased, and the sawmill has long since been removed. An old two-story building that once had a store on the first floor and a few other unused and somewhat dilapidated business buildings still stand. No businesses are now in operation, but a few homes continue to be used. A drive through the Kosoma area, although on a gravel road, will be a beautiful and interesting one.

Lawrie

COUNTY: *Logan*
LOCATION: *(a) Sec. 16, T 17 N, R 2 W*
             (b) 5 miles north of Guthrie
MAP: *Page 216*
POST OFFICE: *August 22, 1890–October 15, 1900*
RAILROAD: *Southern Kansas Railway (Santa Fe)*

Lawrie was never much of a village. A general store in which the post office was located, a blacksmith shop, and a family or two kept it alive for a brief period of time. One event entitles it to a place in ghost town history. The following story appeared in the *Choctaw News* on August 7, 1894:

William Cardwell, a Cherokee Strip boomer, who had become hard up, some days ago, announced that he was going to sell his wife to the highest bidder. The sale was held in Lawrie last Friday. There were half a dozen bidders present, and as the woman was buxom and good looking, bidding was spirited.

John Insley, a grass widower of Guthrie secured the prize, for $100 in cash, a cow, a horse, and a lot of furniture. The woman seemed to be wholly unconcerned and departed with Insley, after he had turned over the things in his bid. The strangely mated pair have left for Texas in a covered wagon.

Lehigh

COUNTY: *Coal*
LOCATION: *(a) Secs. 13/14, T 1 S, R 10 E*
              (b) 5 miles south of Coalgate
MAP: *Page 220*
POST OFFICE: *April 4, 1882–*
NEWSPAPERS: *Lehigh Leader; Lehigh News*
RAILROADS: *Oklahoma City–Ada–Atoka Railway, abandoned 1956; Oklahoma Central Railway (Santa Fe), abandoned 1934; Denison and Washita Valley Railway (Katy), leased to O.C.A.&A., abandoned 1956*

Lehigh, named for the noted coal mining center in Pennsylvania, was established in 1880 as a coal camp. The tents, huddle of company-owned shacks, and commissary making up the camp were moved twice before being located in 1884 where the town developed. This final movement was to the vicinity of a shaft known as "Old No. 4." Development in the area continued as shaft No. 5 was excavated. Lehigh, however, became an active town in 1887 following a mine disaster at Savanna. The company closed that mine and moved its equipment and 135 houses to Lehigh.

From 1890 to 1910 the population of Lehigh increased to approximately two thousand. Coal mines, both shaft and strip, were in full operation. The town became known for the quantity and quality of coal mined, about twelve hundred tons per day. Agricultural lands in the vicinity were also productive. In 1900 some five thousand bales of cotton and over fifty thousand bushels of wheat were marketed in Lehigh. Three railroads extended their tracks to the town, making it an important shipping point. During these two decades the town incorporated, developed police and fire departments, started a water system, and organized an active commercial club. The Constitutional Convention in 1907 designated Lehigh as county seat of Coal County. (The county seat was later moved to Coalgate by popular vote.)

The mine payroll, which exceeded $100,000 per month, plus income from other activities caused the development of all types of commercial institutions. In addition to the numerous stores, restaurants, barber shops, and pool halls or billiard parlors, the town had two banks,

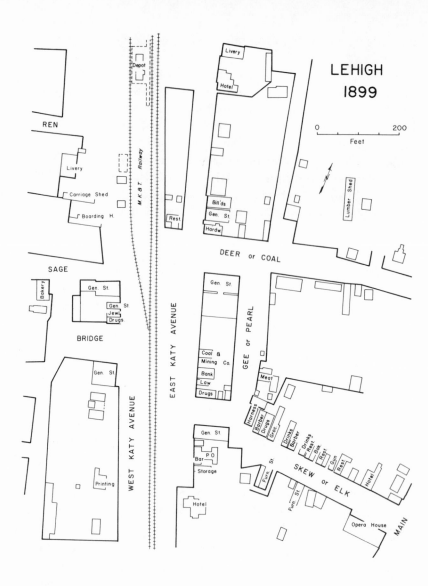

Lehigh, 1899

three large hotels, an ice plant, an elevator and a fifty-barrel flour mill, two cotton gins, a bottling works, and the famous Bijou Opera House. Four or five lawyers, one or two dentists, and five or six doctors resided in Lehigh. Five schools and four churches served the community.

Lehigh had a polyglot population. Many of the miners were Italian, but there were also miners from France, Germany, Belgium, and several east European areas. Mixed with the English-speaking Americans, plus the Chickasaw and Choctaw Indians and a few Chinese who had drifted into the town, all these nationalities must have created a somewhat cosmopolitan atmosphere. The cultural contrast was great. West Lehigh, where many with the larger incomes lived, was known as Quality Hill. The area along the Katy tracks, especially on the two

days each month when the miners were paid, was called Wildcat Row. In 1896 the Masonic groups built the Bijou Opera House, reserving the third and top floor for their hall. Because of the quality of most programs given in the Bijou, many coming from New York, Chicago, and other eastern centers, it became known as the "cultural center of Indian Territory." Numerous programs and dances were formal. Several programs, however, were not booked for the people of Quality Hill, and there were times when those from all parts of Lehigh joined together for special purposes.

One of Oklahoma's most distinguished citizens, Patrick J. Hurley, was born in Lehigh in 1883. At the age of eleven he began working nine and one-half hours each day as a trapper in Mine No. 6 at a daily wage of seventy-five

Lehigh, *ca.* 1905. No. 8 Mine, one of the most productive shaft mines in the area. *(Courtesy Western History Collections, University of Oklahoma)*

Lehigh, *ca.* 1910. In its day Lehigh exported both coal and agricultural products. A trail load of coal is ready to move out, and soon thereafter several cars of baled cotton will be on the way. *(Courtesy Western History Collections, University of Oklahoma)*

cents. After two years he was promoted to mule skinner, a job in which he drove the mules hauling coal from the mine. At the age of fifteen he left the mines to get an education, finally completing a degree in law from National University of Law, Washington, D.C. He served in both World Wars I and II, retiring with the rank of general. During the Hoover administration he was Secretary of War, and during the F. D. Roosevelt administration he served as ambassador to China.

From 1915 to 1930 there was little change in the total population of Lehigh, but there was considerable movement into and out of the town. The importance of coal as a fuel decreased, and mines were shut down as oil production increased. Stores closed, offices moved to other cities, and buildings stood vacant. Fire destroyed some buildings, including the Bijou. During and since the 1930s hundreds of people have moved from Lehigh. Some homes were moved to other communities, but many simply rotted and fell down. Schools were closed, and the few remaining students transferred to either Coalgate or Atoka. All railroad lines were abandoned by 1956, and the tracks have since been removed.

Today, no stores operate in the old business district of Lehigh. A few brick buildings still stand. No houses remain on Quality Hill, but some east of the Katy right-of-way are occupied.

Old city streets can be followed in part. Strip pits, now filled with water and junk, are adjacent to the north part of Lehigh. The water tower still stands on a hill east of U.S. Highway 75, and a business or two faces the highway.

As said one resident who is well along in age: "Wildcat Row and the Bijou will live only in memory—but what a memory."

Lehigh, 1957. Looking east from Quality Hill along Skew or Elk Street. *(Courtesy Oklahoma Publishing Company)*

Lenora, ca. 1906. The crowd is gathered for events, possibly drawings, taking place on a trade day. *(Courtesy Western Trails Museum)*

Lenora, 1975. Remains of the last store building.

Lenora

COUNTY:	*Dewey*
LOCATION:	*(a) Sec. 13, T 18 N, R 18 W*
	(b) 5½ miles west of Taloga
MAP:	*Page 215*
POST OFFICE:	*March 24, 1896–June 30, 1955*
NEWSPAPERS:	*Lenora Leader; Lenora News;*
	Lenora LaPearl

Lenora, entitled by its citizens the "Pearl of the Prairies," was started shortly after the opening of the Cheyenne-Arapaho lands in 1892. By 1896, when the post office was established, it had become a full-fledged and very active frontier town. By 1900 Lenora had a population of approximately four hundred persons, probably the largest town in D County. It was certainly one of the most prosperous and progressive.

Located in a relatively sparsely settled area within the great bend of the Canadian River as it crossed D (present-day Dewey) County, Lenora became a trade and cultural center. The businessmen published the *Lenora Business Directory*, which was widely distributed. Three general stores, a meat market, a confectionery, a drugstore, a hardware store, a harness shop, and a lumberyard were the chief retail establishments. Before statehood two saloons were operated. The town was noted for its hotel and restaurant. The bank was considered "solid," and two doctors served the area by making house calls day or night. Churches and a school system were developed. Several fraternal orders—Woodmen of the World, Masons, Odd Fellows, Eastern Star, and Royal Neighbors—thrived. Industries included a well driller, a cotton gin, and a gristmill. The weekly paper was a dedicated booster of the town and area. At one time there was talk about moving the county seat from Taloga to Lenora.

Lenora became noted as a place where "men were men," but it was also always noted that a woman was cashier of the bank. Stories are still told about one old-time lawman who threatened to throw all his guns away because he failed to hit a dime pitched into the air on his eighty-sixth birthday. Another old-timer, said to be a very hard worker, was noted for the amount of food he could eat during one meal—at one time an entire big roast goose, and another time a huge ham. Two brothers who had a store are remembered for the candy they gave all the children at Christmas.

Lenora, like so many other places, became a victim of technological progress. The one large remaining store building is now used for the storage of hay and farm equipment. A small garage–filling station remains open. The school is closed, but the church is still used regularly. Only a few people now live in what was once the "Pearl of the Prairies," a good town.

A. S. WORWICK, M. D.

Lenora, Oklahoma

Special attention given to
Diseases of the

EYE, EAR,
NOSE
AND THROAT

Complete Stock of Drugs and Sundries.

North Star Saloon

Fine Wines, Brandies and Liquors
a specialty. Plenty of Budweiser and
Pabst always on tap. Complete line
of cigars can always be found here.

Patterson & Purcell, Props.

Lanora, Oklahoma.

HOTEL DAISY

J. H. PILE, Proprietor

Mr. Pile, the genial proprietor, has been a resident
of Dewey county for the past seven years and his
hotel is headquarters for those seeking a good,
clean, quiet stopping place. His tables are
filled with well cooked wholesome food three
times a day. When in Lenora stop at the Daisy.

Best $1.00 a Day House in Dewey County.

LENORA, OKLA.

Richart Brothers

Harness and Saddlery,

Lanora, Oklahoma.

A Complete Line of Farm and Driving Harness, Robes, Whips, etc. Also Fine Line of
Saddles. Repair Work Neatly and Promptly done. Come in and examine our goods.

LANORA BUSINESS DIRECTORY.

J. F. Nickel

Retail Lumber, Lath, Shingles,
Sash, Doors, Glass, Putty, Lime
and Cement ∴ ∴ ∴ ∴ ∴

Lenora, - - - Oklahoma

When in Lenora Remember the Big Store of

General
Merchandise
and Implements

Kingman, Moore & Company's Plows and Listers;
Bain and Everett Wagons. Our past eight successful
years in business tells the merits of our goods.

Ventioner & Company

WM. BADER, Pres.   E. S. DIXSON, Vice-Pres.   ROSS J. BADER, Cashier.
HATTIE A. SNODE, Assistant Cashier.

THE LENORA STATE BANK

OF LENORA, OKLAHOMA

(Established 1902)

We loan money on real estate; we loan money on chattles;
we pay interest on time deposits; we are a depository for Dewey
county. We solicit your banking business and are ready to extend accommodations when consistent with careful banking
methods.

GO TO

E. F. SMITH'S SHORT ORDER

For a Good, Quick, Wholesome Meal.

I Also Conduct a

BILLARD PARLOR and ART GALLERY

PHOTO ENLARGING A SPECIALTY

E. F. SMITH

LENORA - - - OKLAHOMA

Lenora, *ca.* 1907. A section of advertisements in a business directory. Notice the misspelling of the town
name. *(Courtesy Western Trails Museum)*

Lodi

COUNTY: *Latimer*
LOCATION: *(a) Sec. 12, T 6 N, R 21 E*
(b) 6 miles north, 15½ miles east of Wilburton; 5 miles north, 2 miles east of Red Oak
MAP: *Page 220*
POST OFFICE: *March 23, 1894–March 15, 1955*

Lodi (pronounced "low-dye") was a mountain hamlet on the southern slope of the Sans Bois Mountains. No stage lines, post routes, or trails ever passed through the community, but a small service center developed there to supply the needs of the farmers and lumbermen who lived in the isolated area. Lodi was founded in the early 1880s when a general store, commonly referred to as the commissary, was started. Soon thereafter a blacksmith opened a shop in the community, and a cotton gin–gristmill–sawmill combination was also developed. A post office was eventually located in one corner of the store. The store, the blacksmith shop, and the mills, largely developed by and under the supervision of one family, were located at the base of the hill where the valley farmers and loggers could have the easiest access. Later, a second general store was opened near the top of the hill. (Although Lodi was the name of the entire community, the store near the ridge crest was sometimes referred to as Hidi.) A one-room school, Big Sandy, was located about one mile southeast of the community.

The mountain slopes were covered with tall, straight, virgin pine, and the valley soils were fertile. Cotton became the chief cash crop of the valley farmers, and the lumbermen cut the pine. The cotton was ginned and baled in Lodi, and the pine was rough sawed at the mill. Oxen, three yoke in the mountainous areas, two yoke in the valleys and on the more level lands, pulled the loaded carts and wagons to Red Oak for shipment. It was an all-day trip, a difficult and slow seven miles getting the community products to market.

The first homes in Lodi were built of logs chinked with rock and mud. Rooms were added as needed. Later, frame homes replaced some of the log cabins. Although the total population of Lodi never exceeded eighty or ninety people, there were not more than ten families. One home had seventeen children; two others had ten each. One person who was born in Lodi and moved from the area only a few years ago stated that the "mountain community adequately supported the country doctor who lived there."

Lodi as a hamlet is now history. Roads to the area have been graded and graveled. The stores and the mills are gone. Trees are again covering the mountainsides, and cattle graze on the formerly plowed fields.

Logan, 1962. Small middle building was the post office. It, along with the stores, is now closed.

Logan

COUNTY: *Beaver*
LOCATION: *(a) Sec. 2, T 1 N, R 26 E, Cimarron Meridian*
(b) 16 miles south, 17 miles east of Beaver
MAP: *Page 214*
POST OFFICE: *December 10, 1888–; moved to new site in 1973.*

Logan was typical of numerous small communities that developed in agricultural areas in the Panhandle. Established in a somewhat isolated area, the village reached its greatest growth about 1910, when it had a general store, hardware store, blacksmith shop, small hotel, and livery stable. A local telephone exchange also served the village and surrounding community. The post office was the starting place for two rural routes. A one-room school and a church were located about one mile from the settlement.

In the days when the horse and wagon or buggy were the chief means of transportation, Logan served the people living within a radius of about fifteen miles. Necessary food supplies were purchased at the local general store, since trips to the larger places required two or three days to go and return home.

The post office has been moved to a new location five miles northwest, and the general store, the last business to close, stands mute against the almost unceasing winds. Faster transportation, better roads, and consolidation of farms caused the death of Logan. Even the nearby cemetery stands neglected.

Loveland, 1974. The postmark attracts valentine mailers.

Loveland
(HARRISTON)

COUNTY:	*Tillman*
LOCATION:	*(a) Secs. 9/16, T 3 S, R 15 W*
	(b) 6 miles south, 14 miles east
	of Frederick; 5 miles north, 5
	miles west of Grandfield
MAP:	*Page 218*
POST OFFICE:	*October 23, 1908–*
NEWSPAPERS:	*Harriston Herald; Loveland Herald*
RAILROAD:	*Wichita Falls and Northwestern Railway (Katy)*

Loveland came into existence in 1908, reached its peak about 1918, and began to die during the 1920s. The town was carved out of parts of two cotton farms when the railroad extended its tracks from Wichita Falls to Frederick through the area. The land was platted, and lots were sold at auction. As the first sale was far from successful, a second auction was held. Between auctions, however, promoters built houses on some of the lots. Those bidding on lots during the second auction did so without knowing which lot they were to get. After the bidding ended, a drawing was held to see who got the prize lots with houses. The second sale was very successful.

During the town's best years the streets were crowded with farm wagons, especially on Satur-

Loveland, 1975. Remains of the water tower at the west end of Main Street.

Loveland, 1914. Main Street. The photographer added lightning to his picture for dramatic effect. *(Courtesy Mrs. Mable Kinder)*

Lovell
(PERTH)

COUNTY: *Logan*
LOCATION: *(a) Sec. 9, T 18 N, 4 W*
(b) 12 miles north, 12 miles west of Guthrie; 7 miles north, 2 miles west of Crescent
MAP: *Page 216*
POST OFFICE: *Perth, May 22, 1889–February 12, 1906; Lovell, February 12, 1906–March 8, 1957*
RAILROAD: *Denver, Enid and Gulf Railway (Santa Fe)*

days. Loveland had six stores, a blacksmith shop, a livery stable, two hotels, a bank, and two cotton gins. It was also a railroad center; four passenger trains made daily stops. A high school was started in 1918 and continued until 1957. The first school building was destroyed by a tornado, and twice school buildings were burned. During the 1920s fires destroyed several business buildings, usually one at a time. Most were not rebuilt. A water system was developed, but no fire department was ever formed. The last store closed in 1968.

The post office remains in operation largely because of its name. When the town was first organized it asked to be named Harriston. The request was denied because of the similarity of other town names in Oklahoma, and the name of Loveland was chosen. The postmaster states that quite a few valentines and letters are sent to that office to be canceled with the Loveland postmark and then mailed. The office also receives requests from collectors of postmarks.

Several reminders of more prosperous days are evident. The old water tower stands at the west end of Main Street, although bricks are falling from it. Some business buildings stand vacant, and the remains of the bank vault are surrounded by tall weeds. An elevator continues to operate, a church is still active, and a few homes are occupied. Roads leading to Loveland are rough and dusty. Few strangers now drive through the town.

Lovell, first known as Perth, developed as an inland town when the Unassigned Lands were opened for settlement. Located in an area of fertile soil, the village became a rural agricultural trade center after the railroad route from Enid to Guthrie was established in 1902. In 1906 the name was changed to Lovell in honor of the man who developed the townsite.

In 1907, at the time of statehood, Lovell had a population of approximately two hundred persons. The commercial area had nine stores fronting on the principal street. There were also a bank and a hotel. The importance of agriculture was shown by the town's two elevators, two cotton gins, feed store, and large blacksmith shop. The total population remained fairly constant until 1926, when oil was discovered in the Roxana area about three miles to the northwest. During the years of this short-lived boom, many persons moved to Lovell, all houses were occupied and some new ones built, freight service was increased, and a few stores were added.

On January 3, 1928, a fire that started in a

Lovell, *ca.* 1927. Lovell oil field. Storage tanks for McCully No. 1 well are in the foreground.

Lovell, 1975. Looking west toward the windmill in the middle of street which was an important source of water for the town. The principal business area extended north (right) from the corner along the concrete sidewalk.

barber shop wiped out the east side of the main business block in one and one-half hours. The town had no fire fighting equipment or water supply other than the town pump and a few private wells. The heat was so intense that it broke windows across the street. Places destroyed included two barber shops, two cafes, a grocery store, a drugstore, a furniture store, a storage building, and the IOOF Hall. In all, eleven buildings were burned. Because the loss was not covered by insurance, very little rebuilding was done.

Except for a feed mill, Lovell now has no stores or shops. The old windmill that was the source of much of the town's water supply still stands. Concrete foundations and some sidewalks on both sides of the former main street show where business buildings once stood. The area is overgrown with trees and weeds. One brick wall remains standing on the east side; the west side has been fenced and is used as a pasture. Most of the fifteen houses are lived in. The church and school are no longer used.

Lugert

COUNTY:	*Kiowa*
LOCATION:	*(a) Sec. 26, T 5 N, R 20 W*
	(b) 8½ miles south, 10 miles west of Hobart; 6 miles south, 1 mile west of Lone Wolf
MAP:	*Page 218*
POST OFFICE:	*April 18, 1902–September 30, 1950*
RAILROAD:	*Kansas City, Mexico and Orient Railway (Santa Fe)*

Lugert, 1909. Main Street. *(Courtesy Western History Collections, University of Oklahoma)*

Lugert, 1916. Store established by town founder. Brick buildings replaced many frame buildings after the 1912 tornado. *(Courtesy Mrs. Florence Peterson)*

Lugert, 1912. Damage caused by tornado on April 27. *(Courtesy Western History Collections, University of Oklahoma)*

Lugert, 1941. Abandoned townsite. *(Courtesy Western History Collections, University of Oklahoma)*

Lugert was started in 1901 when a family by that name opened a store at the edge of the Quartz Mountains. Shortly thereafter a blacksmith shop and a cotton gin were built nearby. In 1908 the Orient Railroad, extending its line from Clinton to Altus, built through Lugert. A bank, an elevator, and a few other stores were soon added, making the town an important local trade center. At its peak in 1911 it had a population of approximately one hundred. In April, 1912, a tornado destroyed a part of the town, and some stores were not rebuilt.

In 1940 the United States Government condemned the town and land for use as a storage area for Altus-Lugert Lake. By 1942 the dike that protects adjacent land had been built, and the lake started to form. When the lake is low, ruins of the inundated town—water wells, building foundations, cellars, and highway bridges—can be seen along the southeast shore of the lake.

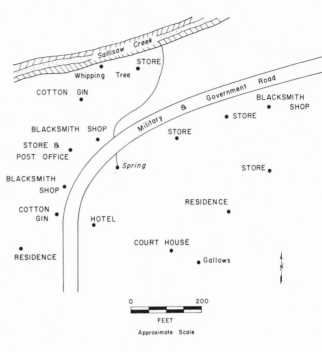

Mayes, 1894

Mayes

COUNTY: *Adair*
LOCATION: *(a) Sec. 20, T 15 N, R 25 E*
(b) 4 miles south, 2½ miles west of Stilwell
MAP: *Page 217*
POST OFFICE: *June 7, 1888–September 19, 1896 (located in Stilwell last two years)*

Mayes was a settlement which developed about the Flint Courthouse of the Flint District, Cherokee Nation. Court was held at this site from 1883 to 1902. During that time five small stores, two blacksmith shops, two cotton gins, and a hotel located in Mayes because of the importance of government activities, the productive agricultural land in the area, and the road which furnished transportation to Fort Smith, Fort Gibson, Fayetteville, and other points. The spring also furnished a good supply of fresh water for both men and animals. The Flint Courthouse was designated one of the centers where each Cherokee could collect his or her payment from the federal government after the sale of the Cherokee Outlet. The town ceased to exist after Stilwell was developed.

The Flint District had two courthouses. A replica of the second has been built on the site where it stood. No other buildings now stand. The spring still flows good water, and the stream from the spring follows the same path to Sallisaw Creek. The area adjacent to the creek has many trees, so one may decide for oneself which was the whipping tree. Gravel and dirt roads lead to the historic place.

Mayes, 1975. Replica of Flint Courthouse built on the site where the original stood.

Mayes, 1975. Trail follows, in part, the old Government and Military Road through the townsite.

Meers

COUNTY: *Comanche*
LOCATION: *(a) Sec. 33, T 4 N, R 13 W*
(b) 12 miles north, 10½ miles west of Lawton
MAP: *Page 218*
POST OFFICE: *March 12, 1902–*
NEWSPAPERS: *Mount Sheridan Miner*

Prior to the opening of the Comanche-Kiowa-Apache lands for settlement in 1901 there was much speculation about the mineral wealth in the Wichita Mountains. Stories were frequently told about old Spanish mines in the area, and numerous Indian legends had Spanish and Mexican miners digging for gold and silver. Miners from various parts of the nation had worked briefly in the Wichitas. During the 1890s a few small strikes were reported, and in late 1896 the mining fever boomed. Persons living in nearby towns organized stock companies. Newspapers reported startling stories. The December 24, 1896, issue of the *Marlow Review* carried the headline, "New Mines Are Opened." The story stated that Colorado miners

Meers, 1957. Old arrastre (ore grinder) near the Meers gate of the Wichita Mountain Wildlife Refuge. It was probably used by miners in the late 1890s. *(Courtesy Oklahoma Publishing Company)*

working in the area believed the ores were as good as those at Cripple Creek. The article also reported that thirty-eight pounds of ore were sent to an assayer and netted the owner $17.80. As a result, people flocked to the mining camps.

Because the Wichita Mountain area had not been opened to settlement, it was illegal for non-Indians to enter it. Early in 1902, after the opening of the Comanche-Kiowa-Apache lands, the federal government ordered all persons not actually engaged in mining to move from the Wichita Forest Reserve. Many moved northward across Medicine Creek, forming the town of Meers. Soon after the movement began, a grocery store opened and a post office was established. A smelter was built, five additional stores were started, three doctors moved to the town, and the *Mount Sheridan Miner* began publication later in the year. Most people lived in tents, but there were also numerous small frame houses. Church services were conducted in a home, and a school was built near the town. The peak population has been estimated at five hundred persons. The town flourished until 1905, when the mining fever died.

A few mine shafts, none very deep, were sunk in the Meers vicinity. Traces of gold, silver, copper, and zinc were found. Some ore was shipped from the area, but paying quantities were never found. An arrastre located near the Meers entrance to the Wichita Mountains Wildlife Refuge, perhaps used by the miners in the 1890s, shows how the ore was crushed. The store that makes up present-day Meers is one-half mile north of the original location.

Meers, 1974. All that remains of the once active mining town.

Milton

COUNTY: *LeFlore*
LOCATION: *(a) Sec. 15, T 8 N, R 23 E*
(b) 8 miles north, 12½ miles west of Poteau; 11 miles west of Panama
MAP: *Page 220*
POST OFFICE: *June 20, 1890–November 10, 1942*
RAILROAD: *Fort Smith and Western Railway, abandoned 1959; tracks from McCurtain via Milton taken over by Kansas City Southern Railway*

Milton was established about 1870 when a single store was opened at that site. At first the place was known locally as Needmore, since the store

JOIN THE PIONEERS
AT
MILTON, OKLAHOMA
✦ ✦
Settling the Choctaw Country
✦ ✦
TREASURES OF INDIAN EMPIRE WITHIN REACH OF THE WHITE MAN
✦ ✦
GET A HOME FOR YOUR FAMILY
✦ ✦
CHANCE TO INVEST IN TOWN PROPERTY, A FARM, A COAL MINE, A SAW MILL AND DRILL FOR OIL IN A VIRGIN FIELD
✦ ✦
NOT MUCH MONEY NEEDED

Milton, 1912. Front cover of a pamphlet describing the Milton Colony. *(Courtesy Mary Langthrop)*

was so often out of needed items. About 1885 a second store located nearby, and soon other services were added. In 1901 the Fort Smith and Western extended its tracks westward through the Milton community. As coal mines were being opened and some logging was being done in the area, Milton became a small shipping center. By 1910, in addition to a few regular commercial outlets, there were a cotton gin, a gristmill, and two hotels in the village. Schools and churches had been organized and Milton was recognized as a "nice little town."

In 1912, Dr. S. T. Peet, a Muskogee philanthropist interested in the social and industrial welfare of the working classes, organized the Milton Colony. The stated purpose was to establish a "co-operative industrial colony of actual workers, where each worker could own his own job and participate in the various earnings of the colony." Peet acquired 168 acres embracing the Milton townsite plus another 80 acres for farming purposes. He also secured a twenty-five-year mineral lease on 20 acres of allotted land containing a sawmill and a coal mine.

People from various parts of the United States bought into the project and moved their families to Milton. It was an extremely diverse group. Some were "sophisticated New Yorkers," while one family "came from Arkansas in a covered wagon drawn by oxen." Religious beliefs ranged from fundamentalism to agnosticism and atheism. Many had experienced hard work; a few had no work experience at all. "The only bond the people had was their belief in socialism." The financial success of the group was linked to the sawmill and the coal mine.

The colonists addressed each other as "comrade." It was to be a classless society, but the manager lived in luxury compared to the remainder of the group. A few built frame houses, but most lived in tents. The sawmill operated only part of the time, largely because of the untrained work force and poor management. The largest working group labored in the coal mine, and, because of the thickness of the coal seam, mining was somewhat profitable. The mine, however, was often closed because of poor working conditions. A few worked on the farm. The colonists were paid in scrip which was good only at the colony commissary. Dr.

Milton, 1919. Buildings from the left are the general store, the doctor's office, the coal mine office, the post office, and the general store. *(Courtesy Ben Sharp)*

Peet died soon after the founding of the Milton Colony. His successor and a group of Guthrie businessmen who took over the project either did not know how to direct such a colony or diverted most of the income to their own use. Advertisements of the colony led people to believe they would find almost instant wealth. After their arrival they were soon disillusioned and disappointed.

When World War I started, many jobs became available elsewhere. Colonists soon left for these better paying jobs; thus, the attempt at socialism in Oklahoma failed. By 1916 the Milton Colony had ceased to exist. The town of Milton continued into the early 1950s, but currently little remains to mark its location.

Mineral, located in the far western part of Cimarron County, was laid out as Mineral City in 1886 when two coal mines were opened. The beds of lignite were found in the top of the Purgatoire formation. Coal men from other areas advertised the quality of the coal as equal to that of eastern bituminous. Because the extent and general character of the coal beds could not be determined, it was impossible to trace them for any considerable distance, and the two mines failed. The mines were never worked commercially, and very little of their coal was used for local consumption.

Mineral City was a boom town for only a short period. With the opening of the mines there was talk of extending a railroad into the area. There were two or three general stores, a saloon, and a blacksmith shop. The largest population attained was about seventy-five. With the closing of the mines, most of the people moved.

One of the stores moved a short distance southward to a more accessible location and continued to operate. The name was shortened from Mineral City to Mineral. A post office was located at the store, a rock school building was constructed, and for a brief period a U.S. land office was located in the town. Church activities, held in the schoolhouse, and community socials drew crowds from homes and ranches fifty miles away. By 1910 the population of Mineral had decreased to ten, and soon thereafter the store and post office closed.

The old store building and schoolhouse continue to stand. They now form a part of the buildings making up a ranch headquarters.

Mineral

(MINERAL CITY)

COUNTY: *Cimarron*
LOCATION: *(a) Sec. 13, T 4 N, R 1 E, Cimarron Meridian*
(b) 5½ miles north, 21 miles west of Boise City
MAP: *Page 214*
POST OFFICE: *Mineral City, February 6, 1888–March 29, 1895; Mineral, March 29, 1895–February 11, 1911*

Mineral, 1974. Old store building now used for the storage of hay and feed at the ranch headquarters.

Mouser

COUNTY: *Texas*
LOCATION: *(a) Sec. 26, T 5 N, R 15 E, Cimarron Meridian*
(b) 12½ miles north, 2 miles east of Guymon; 12 miles west of Hooker
MAP: *Page 214*
RAILROAD: *Beaver, Meade and Englewood Railroad (Katy), abandoned 1972*

Mouser was platted in 1928 when the Beaver, Meade and Englewood Railway extended its line through Texas County. The land on which the tracks were laid was given to the railroad by the owners. The streets extending east and west were identified as First, Second, and Third, but those running north and south were more appropriately named: Angora, Persian, and Maltese.

The primary function of the village was to serve as a shipping point for wheat and livestock. One large and two small elevators were built, and many thousands of bushels of wheat were shipped each year. Although some cattle and sheep were unloaded for grazing in the area, none were ever shipped out.

The population of Mouser never exceeded one hundred. Two stores and two filling stations made up the retail establishments. The village never had a post office, school, or church. The railway has now been abandoned and the tracks removed. Most of the platted area has been plowed and planted to wheat. The smaller elevators are no longer used, and the stores and filling stations are closed. The land that was given to the railroad was sold back to the original owners.

Mouser, 1975. Abandoned elevator adjacent to the abandoned rail line. The stacked ties were later picked up and sold.

Navajoe

COUNTY: *Jackson*
LOCATION: *(a) Sec. 35, T 3 N, R 19 W*
(b) 3 miles north, 9 miles east of Altus
MAP: *Page 218*
POST OFFICE: *September 1, 1887–November 15, 1905*
NEWSPAPER: *Buckskin Joe's Emigrants Guide*

Navajoe, located in the eastern part of Old Greer County, was started in 1887 when Joseph S. Works, a land promoter usually known as Buckskin Joe, settled at the site and built a two-story frame hotel. It was there that he published a small paper called *Buckskin Joe's Emigrants Guide,* which was widely circulated in Texas and brought many people to the area.

Navajoe soon became a center of commerce and activity. The first store built had one corner partitioned off for the post office. This store faced the east, causing the Main Street to extend north-south. North of the first store was a "long red building housing a stock of general merchandise." Beyond the second store was a saloon, a drugstore which "compounded prescriptions and sold a considerable amount of high alcoholic-content patent medicine to Indians since under federal law they could not buy liquor," and at the north end on the west side of the street another grocery store. On the east side of the street, across from the drugstore, was the home and office of a doctor. The church, a small unpainted building, was directly across from the saloon. The church had originally been a dance hall and later a skating rink. Also on the east side of the street was a barber shop. The hotel was southeast of the business district. It had a tall post topped by a large bell which was rung at noon and 6:00 P.M. each day to call the hungry boarders from town.

After the first year, additional businesses included a meat market, a pool hall, a blacksmith shop, and another barber shop. A school and several new homes were also built. Nearby ranchers and farmers traded in the town, since the nearest railroad point, Vernon, Texas, was fifty miles away. Settlers bartered butter and eggs for sugar and coffee or used hard-earned cash to buy shoes, dry goods, or clothing. Frequently a trail boss would bring in a chuck

THE EMIGRANT GUIDE

VOL. 1   AUGUST, 1888.   No.

J. S. WORKS, Prop'r.   OFFICE AT NAVAJOE, GREER COUNTY, I. T.

Navajoe

Is situated one and one-half miles south of North Fork of Red river, and twenty-five miles north of South Fork, and is situated at the foot of the Navajoe mountains (a spur of the Wichita range of mountains;) and we can say, without fear of successful contradiction, that from the summit of the Navajoe mountains, for twenty miles around the base, lies as grand and magnificent a country, take it as a whole, as can be seen on God's green earth. The north and east of Navajoe is Indian Territory proper, and is used for ranching purposes by Texas cattlemen. This land can not be intruded on by settlers. The south and west, stretching away into a beautiful prairie, is Greer county, disputed territory. Greer is about ninety miles long and fifty miles wide, and contains over five thousand people. There is timber in Greer for fuel and posts for two years, and plenty of wood of the river, which will come into use when the Oklahoma bill passes, which must be soon.

People coming into Greer do not pay anything whatever for land, but settle down on 160 acres and go to work. The land has been sectionized by both the United States and Texas, so that the settler is sure that he is on a quarter-section, and is not afraid but what he can get his homestead under either of the powers. If any one is afraid of the title they can buy in adjoining counties. Navajoe is the gate to the new territory to be opened up, and has vacant homesteads for thousands of people in its vicinity now. And when the other side of the river is opened for settlement, when Cleveland's strong arm shall have burst that ring that has been robbing poor Indian, and it has become a thing of the past, classed with the whisky ring, salary grabbers, credit mobiliers, etc.; when the people of the north and east come to see us and see the pioneer's relic, the dug-out, with his new house in front, his farm under cultivation, his stock on native grass in February, the coal mines in operation, the mountains giving up their hoarded wealth of precious metals; when they climb the mountain peak and gaze over that country that would dazzle an artist, they will say those

fellows had a hard time getting this country, but it is worth it and ten times more. Navajoe has four grocery stores and one drug store and a wagon yard, hotel, school house and Masonic hall. Buckskin Joe owns the hotel and wagon yard, and issues The Emigrant Guide monthly.

The Town Company will donate every alternate lot to the colonists that build in Navajoe before December 1st, 1888, unless the odd numbered lots are all given away before that time.

Greer County.

The disputed territory between Texas and the United States, is a body of land ninety miles long and fifty miles wide, lying between the north and south Forks of the Red river in the southwest corner of the Indian Territory. The soil is a rich, sandy loam, adapted to corn, cotton and small grain, and is well watered, with sufficient timber for fire wood and fence posts for the swarms of settlers that are now pouring into that country. Over four thousand settlers took homesteads in Greer county last year, between July and December. The county had been organized the year before, but scarcely any one lived there but cattlemen till July 4, 1887, when Captain J. S. Works (Buckskin Joe), who was the leader of the Texas Oklahoma colony of over four hundred families, selected Navajoe Mountain in East Greer for a colony home. The Texas officers encouraged the movement, and in October started to make a survey of Greer county and sell the lands. To this Buckskin Joe and his colony objected and petitioned the officers to let them take 160-acre homesteads by the United States survey. This the Texas officers refused. The settlers then appealed to President Cleveland and Commissioner Sparks to prevent Texas from selling Greer lands. President Cleveland issued his proclamation warning Texas to not sell the land. Meantime the settlers rushed into Greer by the thousands. The colony system was merged into the Texas boom in January, and Vernon and Fort Worth and the Santa Fe railroad and Kansas City combined to assist Buckskin Joe, and excursion parties left Kansas City for Navajoe April 4th, May 9th and June 6th. When the excursion dates were filled, a new route from Kansas City to Greer by way of the Panhandle was established. Contracts for board and transportation made for the colonists at all stopping points and combining Greer, Hemphill and Wheeler counties in the Colony route and benefits.

CAPT. JOS. S. WORKS, (BUCKSKIN JOE)
Of Navajoe, Greer County, I. T., Founder and Manager of the Texas-Oklahoma Colony, Numbering over 400 Families.

Excursion, MONDAY, SEPT. 3, 188

Under the management of the

TEXAS-OKLAHOMA ∴ COLONY

SPECIAL CHARTERED CAR

Will leave the Union Depot, Kansas City, Mo., on Sept. 3, 1888, between 9 and 10 o'clock p. m., arriving at Canadian, Texas, Sept. 4th at 6 p. m., the railroad destination. The next day the party will be supplied with wagons and start on an overland trip to Greer county, distant over 100 miles. On the first night out, the party will stay at Mobeetie, near Ft. Elliott. The party will have a chance to see the Soldiers and Indian Scouts, on the frontier, as well as to visit Mobeetie, one of the oldest towns in the Panhandle. Leaving Mobeetie, the party will travel through Collingsworth county and enter Greer county on the west side, then traveling east through the entire county to Navajoe, the colony town and home. The entire trip from Canadian to Navajoe, with the exception of Mobeetie and the village of Mangum, will be through a sparsely settled country, inviting the emigrant to Take a Home.

This, probably, is the only excursion that will be run to the Panhandle this year and will be the cheapest trip ever taken to Greer, from the North, being fully eight dollars less than the April, May and June excursions to Navajoe. The fare from Kansas City to Navajoe and return, will be less than twenty dollars, (including 130 miles by wagon). Board will be 25 cents per meal at hotel. But 10 days at least will be spent camping out, where each one boards himself, at cost, each one should bring blankets and cup; cooking utensils will be furnished by the teamsters. Each one should bring provisions, for railroad trips it is the cheapest and pleasantest way. The excursion will travel over the Southern Kansas R. R.; part of the great Santa Fe route. All parties should report at the Santa Fe ticket office, 1050 Union ave, opposite Union Depot, Kansas City, not later than 8 o'clock p. m. Monday, Sept. 3d. This excursion is inaugurated as an advertisement of the Texas-Oklahoma Colony, which is being circulated throughout the North, and by its cheap rates, its printed details before starting, contracts for hotels and teams, etc. Diversified route, giving the prospector his choice from buying a railroad town lot in Texas, to a free lot in Oklahoma. From buying the land in sight in Texas to a free home with a squatter's right only, in Greer. A trip under the management of an experienced guide, who knows where the vacant homes are, contrasted by home seekers who do not, and go out to hunt them without a knowledge of what is ahead of them, will forever answer the question, what good does it do to join the Colony? The manager of the Colony will accompany the excursion from Kansas City to Navajoe, and all parties who intend to go, should notify him by letter, so that arrangements can be made to accommodate all.

Address till September 3d.

J. S. WORKS,
PHILLIPS HOUSE, KANSAS CITY, MO.

Navajoe, 1888. Front page of *The Emigrant Guide* for August, 1888. *(Courtesy Oklahoma Historical Society)*

Navajoe, *ca.* 1888. Home of Buckskin Joe. *(Courtesy Oklahoma Historical Society)*

Navajoe, *ca.* 1895. City Hotel was originally built by Buckskin Joe. It was later torn down and moved to Cordell. *(Courtesy Western History Collections, University of Oklahoma)*

wagon to replenish his stock of supplies before heading north to Kansas. Often a band of Kiowa or Comanche Indians would pitch their tepees near the north edge of the town while spending their "grass money." In the 1890s a mining boom in the Navajoe Mountains, a part of the Wichita Mountains, brought more people to the town. Navajoe was also the social center of a large but sparsely settled area.

After the opening of the Cheyenne and Arapaho Reservation and the lottery for land in the Comanche-Kiowa-Apache Reservation, several new towns were started. Mangum became the county seat of Old Greer County. The railroad extending westward from Lawton in the Comanche country was built about seven miles south of Navajoe at a new town called Headrick. People gradually moved to other places, and Navajoe disappeared. Only the cemetery now remains. Dr. E. E. Dale, a noted historian who lived in Navajoe when he was a boy, wrote:

"Here lie the bodies of more than one man who died with his boots on before the blazing six gun of an opponent and others who died peacefully in bed. Here also lie all that is mortal of little children, and of the tired pioneer women who came west with their husbands seeking a home on the prairie only to find in its bosom that rest which they had so seldom known in life."

Nicksville

COUNTY:	*Sequoyah*
LOCATION:	*(a) Sec. 34, T 13 N, R 23 E*
	(b) 6½ miles north, 3½ miles west of Sallisaw; 4 miles north, 7 miles east of Vian
MAP:	*Page 217*
POST OFFICE:	*April 25, 1828–October 2, 1829*

Navajoe, 1975. Cemetery is all that remains to indicate the former townsite.

Nicksville, *ca*. 1828. An impression, based upon written descriptions, of how the town may have appeared shortly after its abandonment. *(Courtesy Mildred R. Spence)*

Nicksville, predecessor of Dwight Mission, was located about midway between Fort Smith and Fort Gibson on the military road between the two places. When Lovely County, Arkansas, was organized in 1827, the Arkansas legislature appointed a commission to select a site for the county seat. They chose Nicksville, which at that time was a group of log cabins surrounding a large trading post. The town was established by Lt. Col. John Nicks, later a general, who was sutler at Fort Gibson. One of the first post offices in present-day Oklahoma was located here. A treaty in 1828 decided that Lovely County was a part of the Cherokee Nation instead of the state of Arkansas. Accordingly, Lovely County, along with the designation of Nicksville as county seat, was abolished. Shortly thereafter most of the cabins were abandoned.

At that time, as a result of the treaty in 1828, Dwight Mission, located in Arkansas, was seeking a new site so that it could continue to serve the Cherokee Indians. A report to the Mission Board described Nicksville as "a beautiful location, high land, healthy with good water, near the creek and above high water." Dwight Mission then moved to the Nicksville location and used the structures already in existence for its school and mission work.

Dwight Mission today occupies some of the site on which Nicksville stood. All of the original buildings, of course, are gone.

Non

COUNTY: *Hughes*
LOCATION: *(a) Sec. 34, T 4 N, R 10 E*
(b) 20½ miles south, 8½ miles east of Holdenville
MAP: *Page 220*
POST OFFICE: *October 22, 1901–October 31, 1954*

Non is located in the hills of east central Oklahoma. The village was originally named Cannon, but when a post office was applied for there was already one by that name, so the first syllable was dropped and the post office and town became Non.

Before World War I, Non had a blacksmith shop, four general stores, a grocery store, a lumber mill, a cotton gin, a school, and a church. There was also a doctor. The population probably never exceeded one hundred persons. Non was a Saturday town. It has been reported that on Saturdays "the streets were crowded with wagons. Folks were so thick you could hardly part your way through. Then they got to traveling—the highway got good."

Non is now an isolated community about one mile east of U.S. Highway 75. The post office and school are closed, and stores and other businesses have moved away. One church continues to have meetings each Sunday, and five homes remain in the vicinity. The Non cemetery, a well-kept one, to some extent records the life and death of the village.

Non, 1974. Cemetery is one-half mile west of the townsite.

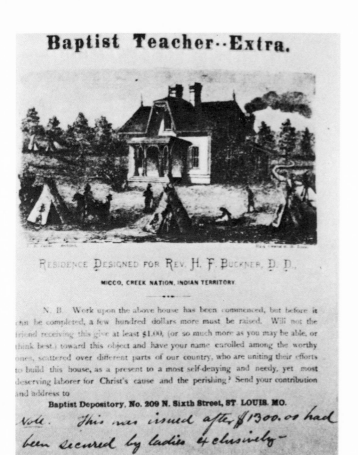

Baptist Teacher--Extra.

RESIDENCE DESIGNED FOR REV. H. F. BUCKNER, D. D.,
MICCO, CREEK NATION, INDIAN TERRITORY.

N. B. Work upon the above house has been commenced, but before it can be completed, a few hundred dollars more must be raised. Will not the friend receiving this give at least $1.00, (or so much more as you may be able, or think best,) toward this object and have your name enrolled among the worthy ones, scattered over different parts of our country, who are uniting their efforts to build this house, as a present to a most self-denying and needy, yet most deserving laborer for Christ's cause and the perishing? Send your contribution and address to

Baptist Depository, No. 209 N. Sixth Street, ST. LOUIS. MO.

Note. This was issued after $1300.00 had been secured by ladies exclusively—

North Fork Town, *ca.* 1855. Card mailed to persons living in the area soliciting funds to complete the building of the home for the Baptist minister. *(Courtesy Oklahoma Historical Society)*

North Fork Town

(MICCO)

COUNTY: *McIntosh*
LOCATION: *(a) Secs. 5/6, T 9 N, R 17 E*
              (b) 3 miles east of Eufaula
MAP: *Page 217*
POST OFFICE: *Micco, August 4, 1853–March 30, 1886*

North Fork Town was considered the crossroads point of the Creek Nation. It was in this vicinity that Spanish expeditions in the 1600s crossed the Canadian rivers in their search for precious metals. French trappers had trails along the Canadian and North Canadian during the 1700s when the fur trade flourished. Soon after the purchase of the Louisiana Territory by the United States, a trail used earlier by the Osage Indians but later known as the Texas Trail was followed between towns in Missouri and Texas. In this area North Fork Town developed and the Creek Trail of Tears ended.

In 1823 a trading post was started near the location, but it lasted for only a few months. As the Creeks moved into the fertile valleys of the area, beginning about 1830, permanent stores and blacksmith shops were established, and several homes, mostly log cabins, were built. In 1839 Josiah Gregg, noted for his development of the Santa Fe Trail, laid out the Gregg Trail from Webbers Falls through North Fork Town to Edwards' Post and westward. In the 1840s the Texas Trail past the town was much used to move cattle northward. In 1849 migrants on the way to western gold fields followed Marcy's California Road past North Fork Town. Grant Foreman, in the article "Ghost Towns and Old Roads" (*Daily Oklahoman*, February 14, 1937, p. 12D), wrote:

Long teams of four to six spans of oxen under the blows and imprecations of their drivers, strained and struggled to pull loaded wagons through the deep mud of springtime. They were part of the trek of hopeful California emigrants on the way through Indian Territory in 1849. Arrived at North Fork Town, many of them eagerly embraced the opportunity to exchange their heavy wagons with the Creek Indians for ponies on which they loaded their most essential belongings. These Indians thus became the owners of more good wagons than they had ever dreamed of possessing.

In 1849 the Methodists built a large school, called Asbury Mission, near North Fork Town. The main building was a large, three-story brick structure 110 feet long by 34 feet wide. It also had a basement. The school opened in 1850 when nearly one hundred students enrolled. The school was of such importance that it became the cultural center of community life. The post office, named Micco, was established in 1853. The school was later destroyed by fire.

During the Civil War, North Fork Town served as a supply base for the Confederate army, especially during the more northern operations. The battle of Honey Springs was fought about eighteen miles north of the town.

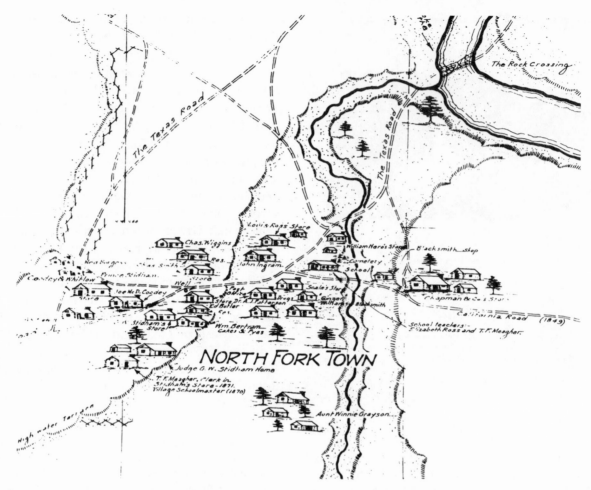

The Rock Crossing

Louis Ross's Store

Chas. Wiggins

William Hare's Store   Blacksmith shop

Cemetery
School

John Ingram.

The Texas Road

Store

Well.

Joe McD. Coodey   Post
Office   Scale's Sto.

Ginger   blacksmith

Drugs
Dr. A.J.Patterson
Ed Butler

Chapman & Co's Store

California Road   (1849)

Wm.Bertram
Cakes & Pyes

School teachers:
Elizabeth Ross and T.F.Meagher.

Stidham's
Store

Coodey & Whitlow
Store   Prince Stidham.

NORTH FORK TOWN

Judge G.W.Stidham Home

High water Territory

T.F.Meagher, Clerk in.
Stidham's Store - 1871.
Village Schoolmaster (1870)

Aunt Winnie Grayson.

North Fork Town, *ca.* 1871. Sketch map of the area by Thomas Meagher. *(Courtesy Indian Archives)*

In 1871–72, when the Missouri, Kansas and Texas Railroad was building through the Indian Nations from Kansas to Texas, tracks were laid about two miles west of North Fork Town. Several merchants raised a fund of five hundred dollars and gave it to the railroad to build a depot at the place that has become Eufaula. As a result, most of the business people moved to the new town, and North Fork Town ceased to exist as a business center.

The site of North Fork Town is now covered by the waters of Lake Eufaula. The few homes remaining in the area at the time the lake was formed and the old cemetery were moved. Today North Fork Town is remembered chiefly as a historical crossroads.

Old Agency Village
(THE RED STORE)

COUNTY: *Comanche*
LOCATION: *(a) Sec. 20, T 2 N, R 11 W*
            (b) 2 miles north, 1 mile east of the central business district of Lawton
MAP: *Page 218*

Old Agency Village, also known as The Red Store, was a subagency primarily for the Comanches, but other Indians could and did come to the village at various times. The place had three general stores or trading posts, a blacksmith shop where coffins were also made, a church that was used as a school when needed, the subagency office, and a few places where

Old Agency Village, *ca.* 1897. Payday for several groups of Indians. Note the tepees at the upper right. *(Courtesy Steve Wilson)*

Old Agency Village, *ca.* 1878. Post Trader's Store near Fort Sill. *(Courtesy Steve Wilson)*

people lived. Some homes were in the back of store buildings, one or two frame houses were built, and an arbor and tent combination was occupied by a Mexican group. When the Indians came for payment or supplies they lived in their tepees. The settlement had about fifty inhabitants other than the migratory Indians. "There were few laws and conventions, and life was lazy, restful and quite uneventful."

The two busiest times each year were when the Indians camped nearby to receive their "grass payment." Soldiers from Fort Sill would escort the agent who was to make the payment to Rush Springs or Marlow, the nearest railsites, to bring back the silver with which the payment was made. The pay period usually lasted one week or ten days. The Indians, after receiving their money, would pay the traders for the goods they had purchased on credit and then spend any that remained in a short time. Quanah Parker and Geronimo were the two most noted chiefs who brought groups to The Red Store. At certain times each year the government issued cattle to the Indians—one beef to every two families. The Indians might butcher the beef then or take it with them. On the day the animal was killed, they would turn the animal loose and run it for a while "to make it tender."

When Lawton was established in 1901 the Old Agency Village closed. All the original buildings have been torn down or moved. The site is now in the northeastern part of Lawton.

Orr, 1975. Remains of a building, some foundations, and playground equipment in the former schoolyard.

Orr, 1975. This sidewalk leading to nothing marks the north side of the former town square. A large general store, a barber shop, and a blacksmith shop used to be located in this area.

Orr

COUNTY:	*Love*
LOCATION:	*(a) Sec. 17, T 6 S, R 3 W*
	(b) 6½ miles north, 24 miles west of Marietta; 10 miles south, 3½ miles east of Ringling
MAP:	*Page 219*
POST OFFICE:	*July 21, 1892–November 29, 1957*

Orr, founded in the early 1890s, developed as an agricultural service center. Growth in population and services was continuous until about 1915, when approximately five hundred persons lived in the town and some fifteen to twenty commercial establishments served the townspeople and farmers living in the adjacent area.

The business district fronted on a square with stores or shops located on all four sides. No side, however, was completely built up. Most of the buildings were one-story frame structures, some being almost flat with the ground and others having higher foundations and front-porch loading docks. The largest stores, in both area occupied and total sales, were the general stores, which handled everything from drugs to groceries and from clothing to farm machines. The bank, a rock structure, and a "movie" were on the south side of the square. Churches, a school system, and a telephone exchange were organized shortly after Orr was established. A feed mill, cotton gins, and blacksmith shops were also in operation. In 1913 the town had two hotels and three doctors.

Orr began to decline about the time of World War I. Many young men who went into the service did not return. Cotton "wore out" the sandy soil, and formerly cultivated fields were returned to pasture. Few jobs were available during the depression years of the 1930s. State highways bypassed the town some three miles to the west and six miles to the south, and county roads leading to the area were and still are poor. In 1949 the high school was closed, and in 1963 the few remaining grade school students were transferred to other school districts.

The town square can still be located, but no business buildings remain. One small school building and the foundation of another, the storm cellar, and some playground equipment are on the school site. The cement sidewalk that led from the school to the square can be followed for a part of its way. One small church remains active.

Park Hill

COUNTY:	*Cherokee*
LOCATION:	*(a) Secs. 15/22, T 16 N, R 22 E*
	(b) 2½ miles south of Tahlequah
MAP:	*Page 217*
POST OFFICE:	*May 18, 1838–May 6, 1847; April 22, 1892–*
NEWSPAPER:	*Cherokee Advocate*
RAILROAD:	*Ozark and Cherokee Central Railway (Frisco), abandoned 1942*

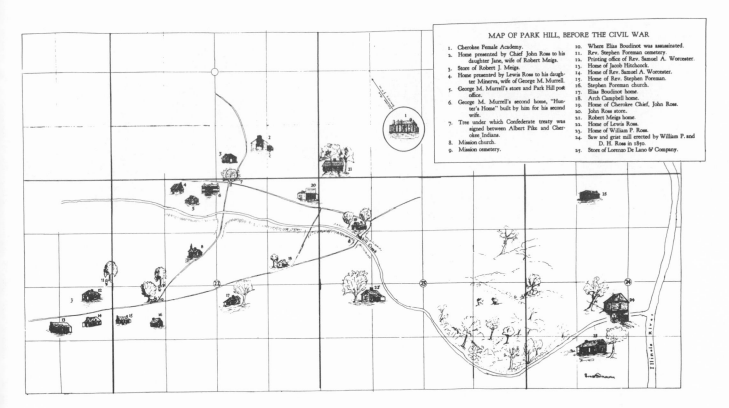

MAP OF PARK HILL, BEFORE THE CIVIL WAR

1. Cherokee Female Academy.
2. Home presented by Chief John Ross to his daughter Jane, wife of Robert Meigs.
3. Store of Robert J. Meigs.
4. Home presented by Lewis Ross to his daughter Minerva, wife of George M. Murrell.
5. George M. Murrell's store and Park Hill post office.
6. George M. Murrell's second home, "Hunter's Home" built by him for his second wife.
7. Tree under which Confederate treaty was signed between Albert Pike and Cherokee Indians.
8. Mission church.
9. Mission cemetery.
10. Where Elias Boudinot was assassinated.
11. Rev. Stephen Foreman cemetery.
12. Printing office of Rev. Samuel A. Worcester.
13. Home of Jacob Hitchcock.
14. Home of Rev. Samuel A. Worcester.
15. Home of Rev. Stephen Foreman.
16. Stephen Foreman church.
17. Elias Boudinot home.
18. Arch Campbell home.
19. Home of Cherokee Chief, John Ross.
20. John Ross store.
21. Robert Meigs home.
22. Home of Lewis Ross.
23. Home of William P. Ross.
24. Saw and grist mill erected by William P. and D. H. Ross in 1850.
25. Store of Lorenzo De Lano & Company.

From Grant Foreman, *Advancing the Frontier, 1830–1860*, Norman, University of Oklahoma Press, 1933.

Park Hill may well be the most historic of Oklahoma's ghost towns. The first two paragraphs in Carolyn Thomas Foreman's book *Park Hill* tell its story:

Park Hill is a name that spells romance in the Cherokee annals of Indian Territory. In the history of this small town is incorporated a large measure of the progress of the Cherokee Nation; the enlightenment brought to the region by the New England missionaries in religious and secular affairs; the establishment of the printing presses there and the subsequent production of millions of pages of the New Testament, hymn books, law and text books, and yearly almanacs, not only for the Cherokees, but also for the Choctaw Indians, made the town a center of culture.

Romance bloomed there, and grim tragedy shows its horrid face in the village; it was swept time and again by war, when women and children were obliged to hide in the woods from the ruthless bushwhackers bent on robbery and destruction.

Park Hill had its beginning with the establishment of a school and mission on the site in 1836. In 1837 the Rev. Samuel A. Worcester selected Park Hill as a permanent location for his printing press. The location, "an elevated and healthful one," was believed to be near the center of the Cherokee Nation. In 1839 Chief John Ross and his brother Lewis established homes in the vicinity. In 1847 it was announced that the Cherokee Female Seminary would be built in Park Hill. The building was "two stories, eighty feet square; the main body eighty by forty with two wings each forty feet with a passage of eighteen feet between them." The building was completed in 1849. Park Hill was not a compact village; it was spread over about three sections of land. As shown on the map, this pre–Civil War village had three stores, a saw and gristmill, the printing office, and a church in addition to the Female Academy. It should also be noted that the Cherokee leaders living in the area built large and beautiful homes such as Rose Cottage, the home of Chief John Ross, and Hunter's Home, the residence of George M. Murrell.

The Civil War was a period of destruction for Park Hill. Chief Ross tried to place his nation in a neutral position but did not succeed. Upon

Park Hill, 1852. The sawmill and gristmill erected by William P. and D. H. Ross in 1850. It was located near the confluence of Park Hill Creek with the Illinois River. *(Drawing by R. H. Mohler now hanging in Murrell House)*

Park Hill, *ca.* 1860. Rose Cottage, home of Chief John Ross. *(Courtesy Oklahoma Historical Society)*

the withdrawal of Federal troops from Fort Gibson, Chief Ross, the missionaries and teachers, most of the prominent citizens, and hundreds of Cherokees living in the area fled north and east to safer parts of the Union. Although Park Hill was never the scene of a battle, it was raided many times by bushwhackers and a few times by Confederate forces led by Stand Watie. A letter written by Dr. Torry declared that one living there would have seen "the destruction of the printing office . . . ruin of the beautiful brick church and the scattering of its membership. Everything at Park Hill, church, printing office and bindery, the station with all its buildings, was swept with the besom of destruction. . . ." A letter from Stand Watie to his wife stated: "I had the old council house set on fire and burnt down, also John Ross's home." Such was done even though the destruction was of no military value. The seminary was not destroyed, but was used by various groups.

Park Hill never recovered from the Civil War. After the people returned, a new schoolroom was added to the remains of the old school. Activities continued in it until 1886, when the school building burned. A new school was built about one mile north of the old location. In 1871 the Cherokee Female Seminary reopened, and it continued to operate until 1887, when it, too, was destroyed by fire. After the fire "all that was left of the pride of the Cherokee Nation were blackened columns." Later in the year the

site was sold, and the new seminary was built in Tahlequah. In 1888 a part of the town was destroyed by a tornado. During the early 1890s the post office, which had been closed since 1847, was reopened, and in 1902 the tracks of the Ozark and Cherokee Central Railroad were extended from Fayetteville, Arkansas, through Park Hill to Tahlequah and Muskogee. Although a few new stores located in the village, its new life did not long endure. The railroad was abandoned in 1942.

The Park Hill area today is the scene of many new activities and homes almost totally unre-

Park Hill, *ca.* 1860. Chief John Ross and his second wife, nee Mary Bryan Stapler. *(Courtesy Oklahoma Historical Society)*

Park Hill, 1975. Three columns of the Cherokee Female Seminary that remained standing after the fire of 1887.

Park Hill, *ca.* 1868. Church and school. The back room was added after the Civil War. *(Courtesy Oklahoma Historical Society)*

lated to the historic village. The columns of the seminary still stand in the Tsa-La-Gi area (a living re-creation of an ancient Cherokee community). Hunter's Home, now called the Murrell House, has been restored and refurnished and is under the control of the Oklahoma Tourism and Recreation Department. The Ross Cemetery and the Mission Cemetery are also places that attract many tourists.

Park Hill, 1887. Remains of Cherokee Seminary after the fire in 1886. *(Courtesy Western History Collections, University of Oklahoma)*

Park Hill, 1975. Gravestone of Rev. Samuel A. Worcester. *(Courtesy Western History Collections, University of Oklahoma)*

Park Hill, 1975. Hunter's Home, residence of George M. Murrell. It is now known as the Murrell House. *(Courtesy Oklahoma Department of Tourism and Recreation)*

Parkersburg

COUNTY: *Custer*
LOCATION: *(a) Sec. 29, T 12 N, R 17 W (b) 6 miles south, 4 miles west of Arapaho; 1½ miles south, 3 miles west of Clinton*
MAP: *Page 215*
POST OFFICE: *April 24, 1901–April 30, 1906*
RAILROAD: *Choctaw, Gulf and Oklahoma Railroad (Rock Island)*

Parkersburg was noted as the "cow town" of western Oklahoma. It served a large ranching area and in several ways typified the movie idea of a wild and wooly western frontier town. The townsite was designated in 1901 by the Choctaw, Gulf and Oklahoma Railroad, which started building westward from Weatherford to Amarillo. For some reason the town did not start building until late 1902.

In 1903 Parkersburg attained its greatest importance. Some seven hundred people resided in the town, which had two banks, two lumberyards, a cotton gin, an elevator, a large wagon yard, several stores, thirteen saloons, and almost as many gambling houses. At one time there were an estimated fifty business buildings, all one-story frame except the hardware store,

Parkersburg, *ca.* 1905. Students and teacher, School District No. 38. *(Courtesy* Clinton Daily News)

Parkersburg, 1904. Depot being loaded onto a flatcar for movement to Canute.

which had two stories. The railroad also built an attractive depot.

Typical of stories about Parkersburg is the one about the deputy sheriff who served the town. It seems that a judgment was rendered against the railroad for a small amount, but the railroad refused to pay. One day at train time the deputy took a log chain to the depot. When the passenger train pulled in, he attached the chain through spokes in the wheels. The train could not move until the railroad paid off the judgment.

The life of Parkersburg was short, and the town died as rapidly as it was born. Clinton was founded in 1903 only three miles to the east. About 1904 approximately one hundred buildings in Parkersburg were razed or moved to Clinton. The depot was loaded on a flatcar and moved westward to Canute. The one church in the town was moved south to a rural area.

Parkersburg lived for only five years. The old townsite is now partly in cultivation, partly in pasture.

Paw Paw

COUNTY: *Sequoyah*
LOCATION: *(a) Secs. 23/24, T 10 N, R 26 E*
(b) 9 miles south, 15½ miles east of Sallisaw; 5 miles south, 4½ miles east of Muldrow
MAP: *Page 217*
POST OFFICE: *December 26, 1882–May 31, 1915*

Paw Paw was an early river port a few miles upstream from Fort Smith on the Arkansas River. In 1901 the village had one large general store with a post office in a two-story building, a gristmill, a blacksmith shop, and a cotton gin. There were also a doctor and an undertaker. The second floor of the store building was used for meetings of various kinds. A church was located nearby, and the high school was about one mile from the village.

Approximately fifty people lived in Paw Paw, and over four hundred lived within a radius of five miles. Cotton, corn, and potatoes were the chief crops grown. They were brought to Paw Paw, where the river steamer picked up bales of cotton and 150-pound sacks of potatoes for the market in Fort Smith. People wanting to go to Fort Smith usually crossed the Arkansas River by ferry and then drove the five miles to the city.

The Paw Paw area is still a highly productive one. The village, however, is gone. The chief crops now are spinach, alfalfa, corn, and soybeans. In spite of the new Arkansas River Navigation System, no riverboats stop. All products are sent to market in trucks. The church is the only remaining reminder of the village; the rest of the land is in agricultural production.

Phroso, 1975. School, outbuildings, and a storm cave remain but are in dilapidated condition.

Phroso

COUNTY: *Major*
LOCATION: *(a) Sec. 21, T 21 N, R 15 W*
(b) 1 mile north, 19 miles west of Fairview
MAP: *Page 215*
POST OFFICE: *September 19, 1900–May 29, 1937*

Phroso is somewhat typical of numerous hamlets that developed in the dryer and rougher western part of the Cherokee Outlet. Soon after the Outlet was opened for settlement, a small store was started. The area had no roads, and transportation, either on horseback or in a horse- or ox-drawn vehicle, was slow. The store prospered and expanded as those living in the vicinity traded there because of the difficulty of getting to a larger place. Accordingly, other businesses were attracted. Soon a blacksmith shop had located nearby, and in 1900 a post office was located at the site. By 1905 a second blacksmith, a doctor who also started a drugstore, a shoe and boot maker, and a livestock dealer made their headquarters in Phroso. A few farmers built homes near the hamlet. A school was organized and a church started. In 1908 Phroso had a population of about sixty persons.

With the changing economic conditions and the technological advances since the late 1920s, plus the movement of population from rural to urban areas, hamlets like Phroso have disappeared. Much of the land formerly in crops has reverted to pasture. There is no longer a need for the store or the garage that eventually replaced the blacksmith shop. All that now remain are the unused school, its outbuildings, and a storm cave.

Picher, 1975. Foundations and remaining zinc mining structures are scattered throughout the incorporated limits of the city.

Picher

COUTY:	*Ottawa*
LOCATION:	*(a) Secs. 16/17/20/21, T 29 N, R 23 E*
	(b) 8 miles north, 2 miles east of Miami
MAP:	*Page 217*
POST OFFICE:	*June 2, 1916–*
NEWSPAPERS:	*Chat Pile; King Jack; Tri-State Tribune*
RAILROAD:	*Northeast Oklahoma Railroad*

Picher, in spite of its present population of a little over two thousand, must be considered a mining ghost town. During the period of the first big boom, about 1917–19, population of the city was estimated to be about 22,500, with some estimates in excess of 25,000. For the period of 1915 to about 1930 Picher was the center of the largest zinc mining area in the world, and during most of those years more than 50 percent of the world's zinc was mined in Ottawa County. "Jack" was the term applied to the zinc-lead ores mined in the Tri-State District, and Picher was known as "the town that jack built."

The finding of ore in the Picher area was something of an accident. Test holes were being dug around Commerce, but no ore was found. While the rig was being returned to Webb City, Missouri, it broke down near the present site of Picher. During repairs a test hole was drilled, and ore was struck at 270 feet, leading to the Picher strike in 1914. The first families moved into Picher in 1915 when the Whitebird Mill was established. For about three years there was little activity. During World War I the Germans took over the Belgian zinc smelters, creating a shortage of zinc in the Allied countries. Zinc

Picher, 1975. Fenced former business core of the city. Main Street ran north-south and Second Street east-west through this area.

prices leaped ahead, and the boom was on.

All land in the Picher area was either owned or leased by the Picher Company. Although the company laid out a townsite and people could secure land for building purposes, the company reserved the right to take over all surface areas on a thirty-day notice. The townsite was quickly filled with tents until clapboard shacks replaced them. People came from all parts of the nation. Everybody was geared to "make a fast buck."

In 1917 the railroad built into the town. In 1918 Picher citizens decided to incorporate as a city to try to bring law and order to the town and to improve the public welfare. The company donated four hundred dollars, and a citizen provided a lot "to be used in keeping up a high state of morals in the city." A jail was to be erected on the lot. The streets were frequently knee deep in mud. The first ordinance dealt with public peace, health, and safety. The council secured electric power for the city. Bonds were passed for the installation of waterworks and a sewage system. There was, however, defaulting on the bonds, which delayed the water system until 1920.

After the war the demand for zinc decreased. As in most boom towns, population declined rapidly, being about ten thousand in 1920. During the 1930s the depression had a disastrous effect on Picher. The town had few advantages to offer a prospective investor. Clear deeds to property were unobtainable. Giant chat piles existed within the city limits and covered areas once dense with homes. In spite of the thirty-day notice, however, some people did build good homes, and several good business buildings were constructed.

During the 1940s, World War II provided a minor boom in the zinc industries. The federal government subsidized the zinc producers, and the industry regained some of its former importance. After the war the subsidies stopped, and the mining companies were again in trouble. Most of the ore had been mined, so there was little that could be done. Those who had flocked to Picher during World War II departed just as rapidly, leaving the town in great disrepair.

In February, 1950, some two hundred residents were given a thirty-day notice to vacate their homes and businesses. The wholesale eviction notice came because of the imminent

danger of a cave-in. Nearly the entire town is undermined. The chert and limestone in which the mines were cut is strong enough to allow large rooms to be hollowed out, with pillars of the native rock left to support the roof. Inspectors found that two pillars beneath the main business district were showing signs of cracking, and stress was becoming critical. The 145-foot-thick subterranean roof was in danger of collapsing. This mine had not been worked for thirty years. The section to be vacated was two blocks wide and almost three blocks long. A total of twelve business buildings, including the bank, a thirty-eight-unit apartment and thirty-five residences were affected. A high cyclone fence was erected around the area and all buildings removed. "An already sick town had its heart torn out." During the 1960s, one area did cave in during the night. Some homes slid toward the middle of the depression.

The remains of Picher are anything but beautiful. On entering the town from any direction one passes mute testimony of its prolific and hectic past. Not only do giant slag heaps meet the eye, but some old tipples also remain in the area between. The rusting metal, rotting timbers, and broken windows lend a depressing atmosphere of decadence. Weeds and shrubs

Picher, 1975. Remains of the Connell Hotel and adjacent buildings on Connell Street (U.S. Highway 69). (Building torn down in 1976)

Picher, 1975. Empty business buildings on Main between Third and Fourth streets.

Picher, 1931. Aerial view of the largest lead and zinc mining center in the world. *Courtesy Western History Collections, University of Oklahoma)*

fill the fenced area of the previous business core. Walls of old buildings form piles of brick and stone where they have fallen. Large numbers of dilapidated homes are scattered throughout the city limits. Of the approximately sixty business buildings standing, about 70 percent are vacant. No mines are in operation.

The Eagle-Picher Company currently sells land to those who desire to buy. Low-income government housing has been built in the southeastern part of the town. Picher is now a bedroom community for people working in Miami, Joplin, and other nearby cities. The mining center that was Picher is no more.

Pine Valley

COUNTY: *LeFlore*
LOCATION: *(a) Sec. 11, T 2 N, R 24 E*
(b) 25 miles south, 6½ miles west of Poteau; 6 miles south, 16 miles east of Talihina
MAP: *Page 220*
POST OFFICE: *December 16, 1926–August 15, 1942*
RAILROAD: *Oklahoma and Rich Mountain Railroad, abandoned 1941*

Pine Valley, 1932. Main Street. On the left were the grocery store, hardware store, and drugstore, and on the right the hotel and theatre-church. *(Courtesy W. A. Cupp, Jr.)*

Pine Valley, founded in 1926, was really born full-grown. It was a town built, owned, and managed by the Pine Valley Lumber Company. Thousands of dollars were spent in surveying, platting lots and streets, establishing locations for businesses, building complete grade school and high school facilities, and erecting one of the largest sawmills and lumber finishing plants in Oklahoma. Lumber was sawed, planed, cured, graded, and shipped to all parts of the nation. The town had a large commissary, barber shop, hotel with seventy-two rooms, post office, and picture show which doubled as a church on Sunday. Approximately 100 houses were built in the Negro quarter for black workmen, who made up one-fourth of the labor force, and about 280 houses were constructed for white workmen. Most of the black workers came from Louisiana; the whites were largely from Oklahoma and Arkansas. A company-owned railroad, the Oklahoma and Rich Mountain, ran from Pine Valley to Page, where it connected with the Kansas City Southern. During the period of greatest activity, 1928–40, the population of Pine Valley averaged about fifteen hundred persons. The mills employed an average of eight hundred men and women.

The town apparently was well organized and well governed. All residents worked for the Pine Valley Lumber Company. Married workers had houses; single workers could live at the hotel. Goods sold in the commissary—groceries, clothing, drugs, hardware, and so on—were cheaper than those sold in neighboring communities, but workers did not have to buy at the commissary. Interdenominational church services were held each Sunday. During the summer, following services, basket dinners along a

Pine Valley, 1926. Hotel built by the lumber company had seventy-two rooms. *(Courtesy W. A. Cupp, Jr.)*

Pine Valley, 1974. All that remains of the sawmill town are foundations and a few concrete structures.

nearby creek bank were common. Company doctors served the community. Although the company office was robbed twice by outsiders, there appears to have been very little friction in the town.

The Pine Valley Lumber Company closed its mill in 1942 because most of the accessible trees of desired size had been cut. By 1953 the railroad and all buildings, except the office structure, had been dismantled and removed. Several concrete foundations still exist, the grade for the railroad can be seen in some places, and a few scars on the mountain sides indicate where tree slides existed.

Piney, 1975. Remains of the village store–post office.

Piney

COUNTY: *Adair*
LOCATION: *(a) Sec. 4, T 16 N, R 26 E*
(b) 5 miles north, 5 miles east of Stilwell; 7 miles south, 1 mile east of Westville
MAP: *Page 217*
POST OFFICE: *November 24, 1913–August 20, 1921*

Piney, settled in 1824, was the first capital of the Western Cherokees in what is now Oklahoma. At the time the village was established, the location was considered a part of Arkansas, since the western boundary of that state was not finalized until 1828. Although the capital was transferred from Piney to Tahlonteeskee in 1828 when most of the Cherokees migrated from Arkansas, the village continued to exist until about 1940.

The first important legislation enacted at Piney was the following:

By act of the Council at Piney on Piney Creek, Arkansas, Cherokee Nation, September 11, 1824, it is provided that the Executive Department of the Cherokee Government shall consist of three persons, that is: First Chief, Second Chief, and Third or Minor Chief, which Chiefs shall serve for a term of four years from the date of their appointment and the First and Second Chief shall each receive a salary of $100 per year, and the Third or Minor Chief a salary of $60 per year.

In 1824 there was sometimes conflict between the Cherokees and neighboring Plains tribes. Also, some early Cherokee settlers considered the Piney area unhealthy. Thus, there had developed a belief that one or two chiefs might die or be killed within a few days of each other, so the legislation provided for three.

Duncan O'Bryant, a missionary Baptist preacher, came to Piney soon after the settlement was started. It is believed that he was the first missionary in the Cherokee Nation. O'Bryant died in 1834, and his grave, marked by a granite stone, stands a short distance north of the old store.

Piney was never a large village; it reached its greatest extent about 1916. The post office was in one corner of the store. There was also a gristmill and a blacksmith shop. The old school is now used as a community building. The Piney community is somewhat isolated. Its roads, however, are blacktop or gravel. It is in a forested area in the Boston Mountain part of the Ozark Plateau. The country is beautiful, and the people are friendly; Piney is a worthwhile place to visit.

Piney, 1975. Gravestone of Duncan O'Bryant.

Pleasant Valley
(CAMPBELL)

COUNTY: *Logan*
LOCATION: *(a) Sec. 33, T 18 N, R 1 W*
               (b) 7 miles north, 7 miles east of
               Guthrie
MAP: *Page 216*
POST OFFICE: *February 29, 1904–May 31, 1947*
NEWSPAPER: *Banner Breezes*
RAILROAD: *Eastern Oklahoma Railway (San-*
               ta Fe), abandoned 1959

Pleasant Valley, first known as Campbell, had its start in 1899 in that part of northeastern Logan County known as Cowboy Flat. On January 29, 1900, a post office with the name of Anna was opened in Campbell, but the name was changed to Pleasant Valley on February 29, 1904. Prior to the opening of the Unassigned Lands in 1889, Cowboy Flat was used as grazing land for thousands of cattle. Many cowboys who worked with those herds "soonered" in the area before the run. They helped each other in holding claims, and in numerous cases they dumped cornerstones in the river.

In 1900 the Eastern Oklahoma Railroad built a line from Guthrie eastward to Cushing via Pleasant Valley. M. C. Rouse, an old-timer still living in the vicinity, states: "True to custom of frontier towns, one of the first buildings was a saloon. Chief clientele consisted of Irish workmen on the railroad. Business buildings of that time had the front end extended up as high as the gable. On the front of it was painted a man riding a two-hump camel, indicating the name of the town. The man wore a derby hat, and a deck of cards protruded from his pocket." With the coming of the railroad Pleasant Valley became the important center of Cowboy Flat. Eventually there were two passenger trains each way each day plus a freight each way. Many of the first homes built were small one-room affairs, and some were half-dugouts.

Pleasant Valley had its greatest period of prosperity between 1910 and 1930. A bank existed from 1909 to 1934. Agricultural land was productive enough to support two elevators, a gristmill, a cotton gin, and a feed mill. A small flour mill operated for five or six years about 1920. The two, and sometimes three, general stores bought eggs, butter, and cream in exchange for groceries, clothing, and farm equipment. A hardware store, blacksmith shops which changed to garages and filling stations, and a fifteen-room hotel also served the community.

Cultural life in Pleasant Valley functioned around its churches and school. In the 1920s an annual township fair was held, during which

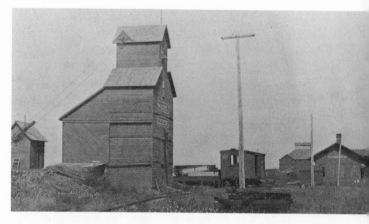

Pleasant Valley, *ca.* 1910. Elevators, the switchyard, and the depot. *(Courtesy M. C. Rouse)*

Pleasant Valley, 1908. Street Scene on Western Trail Avenue. *(Courtesy M. C. Rouse)*

Pleasant Valley, 1889. Rendezvous of the Dalton gang before the Coffeyville raid was located near the edge of town. *(Courtesy M. C. Rouse)*

there were horse races and other kinds of entertainment. For a few years there was a town band. A justice of the peace court was organized to settle local difficulties. One unique case was that in which a minister sued a bridegroom for nonpayment of a $2.50 marriage fee.

Pleasant Valley today is an isolated community served by neither railroad nor state high-way. The foundation of an old elevator is clearly visible, the walls of an old business building still stand, and a few small houses continue to be lived in. Some of the former streets remain open. Cowboy Flat continues to be good agricultural and grazing land. It is easy to understand why Pleasant Valley developed in such a location before modern transportation.

Port

COUNTY: *Washita*
LOCATION: *(a) Sec. 34, T 9 N, R 20 W*
             (b) 6 miles south, 18 miles west
             of Cordell
MAP: *Page 218*
POST OFFICE: *February 21, 1901–February 29,*
             1940

Port developed as an agricultural and school community. Founded shortly after the opening of the Cheyenne and Arapaho Reservation, the town was aided in its growth by the conflict existing between the neighboring villages of East Wood and West Wood. The settlers of East Wood moved the post office from West Wood to their village by force and renamed the place Wood. Meanwhile, a post office had been located at Port. Many West Wood settlers started trading and receiving their mail in Port. Within a few years Wood declined, and the post office was closed, thereby making Port the local trading center.

Before statehood Port had a population varying from 150 to 200. Businesses included a cotton gin, two general stores, a drugstore, a

Port, 1975. Abandoned store buildings. The area is now used as pasture and guarded by an electric fence.

blacksmith shop, a bank, two saloons, and an undertaker. The undertaker is remembered for the sign over his door, which read: COLD DRINKS AND COFFINS. By 1910 the business area had increased to include four additional general stores, a hotel, an elevator, and a telephone exchange, but the saloons were missing.

Port, 1924. The largest consolidated school in Oklahoma at that time. *(Courtesy* Sentinel Leader)

Port was always noted for its schools. During the first year a subscription school was taught in a dugout. The original school district, as established in 1893 included more than ten square miles. In 1922 several districts consolidated. Eventually the school district included almost ninety square miles, making it, during the 1930s, the largest district in area in Oklahoma. Sixteen school "trucks" operated over dirt and often unimproved roads, in all kinds of weather, to transport approximately six hundred students. Two large and modern school plants at different times provided the best facilities available. Decreasing population caused the school to close in 1966.

Port started declining as a trade center soon after the Orient railroad was built through Sentinel, about eight miles to the southeast, in 1908. Consolidation and mechanization of farms, the automobile, and improved roads caused the place to become a ghost town. Four abandoned homes and two unused store buildings remain. The area around the buildings is enclosed by an electric fence and is used for pasture. The school buildings, east of the town, after efforts to use them as a nursing home failed, remain unused but probably will be torn down. One large brick church, which appears to be in good condition, is used for hay storage.

Quay, ca. 1915. Main Street was not paved, causing many traffic problems during the rainy season. *(Courtesy Western History Collections, University of Oklahoma)*

Quay
(LAWSON)

COUNTY:	*Pawnee-Payne*
LOCATION:	*(a) Sec. 31, T 20 N, R 6 E*
	(b) 3 miles north, 19 miles east of Stillwater; 12 miles south, 5 miles east of Pawnee
MAP:	*Page 216*
POST OFFICE:	*Lawson, January 17, 1894–February 24, 1903; Quay, February 24, 1903–March 31, 1957*
NEWSPAPERS:	*Quay Transcript; Quay Times*
RAILROAD:	*Eastern Oklahoma Railway (Santa Fe)*

Quay, first known as Lawson, developed as a small railroad town when the Eastern Oklahoma Railway Company laid its lines from Newkirk to Pauls Valley between 1900 and 1904. It was a farming and livestock trade center in both Pawnee and Payne counties, the north side of Main Street being in Pawnee, the south side in Payne. At the time of statehood approximately one hundred persons lived in Quay. Two general stores, a grocery store, and a drugstore were the principal commercial activities. A bank, two small hotels, a restaurant, a blacksmith

Port, 1975. Large church located between the school and the town is no longer used.

shop, a livery stable, and a weekly newspaper also served the community. An elevator and a cotton gin were used by the local farmers. By 1913 a telephone exchange had been added, and the population had increased to about 150.

In 1914 oil was discovered in the town of Quay as well as in the surrounding area. Derricks competed with shacks, tents, shotgun houses, oil-field supply yards, and business buildings for space. Most business buildings were frame, and a few were two-story structures. Main Street became almost three-fourths of a mile in length. Boarding houses, rooming houses, hotels, and restaurants were numerous. So many migrants came to Quay seeking work that the town could not supply homes for the regular workers. Company-owned oil-field camps, one having about one hundred houses, were built near gasoline plants, supply yards, and similar places. Like other oil boom towns of the 1915–25 period, many gamblers, crooks of all types, and prostitutes came to Quay. Robbery was not uncommon, and several murders were committed. For a while law enforcement was a problem because of the county division of the town. Eventually the officers of both counties worked together. Population estimates when the boom was greatest state that at least five thousand persons lived in the town, with another five thousand in the surrounding oil producing area.

About 1918 oil production leveled off, and by 1922 it was declining. Two devastating fires destroyed sections of the town. The economic problems of the 1930s practically finished Quay. Today no stores remain. "Only a few scattered homes mark the site of the once noisy, fighting, dusty, ugly oil town of Quay."

Quay, *ca.* 1915. Typical oil-field rooming house or "hotel."

Quinlan

COUNTY: *Woodward*
LOCATION: *(a) Sec. 20, T 23 N, R 17 W*
(b) 1½ miles north, 19½ miles east of Woodward
MAP: *Page 215*
POST OFFICE: *April 29, 1901–*
NEWSPAPER: *Quinlan Mirror*
RAILROAD: *Southern Kansas Railway (Santa Fe)*

Quinlan developed as a supply base and shipping center for cattlemen after the railroad crossed the Cherokee Outlet in 1887. Before the opening of the Outlet for settlement in 1893, the area around Quinlan had been a part of one of the large leases where cattle were grazed before being shipped to market. After the opening of the Outlet many farmers settled in the vicinity and started growing wheat. Some of the land, however, was not well suited to this venture because of rough topography; thus, small ranches were formed by farm consolidation. Land that was suitable for growing wheat was used for that purpose. Quinlan, then, remained a cow town but added elevators to handle wheat shipments.

Being somewhat isolated, Quinlan developed a larger commercial core than was usual in frontier farming and ranching regions. In 1907 there were twelve stores in addition to a weekly newspaper, two hotels, two elevators, two livery stables, two lumberyards, a bank, a cotton gin, and a blacksmith shop. Before statehood two and often three saloons were open. Grain dealers and cattle buyers made Quinlan their headquarters. Two churches and a school were organized. The town had a population of approximately 325 persons.

Quinlan maintained itself until the late 1920s. Economic conditions caused many to move from the town. State Highway 15 bypassed the town about two miles to the south. No businesses, except two elevators, now remain open. The school is closed, one church is used part-time, the noted two-story hotel has been torn down, and many homes and buildings have burned, with very few being replaced. Much wheat land in the area has been returned to pasture. The once prosperous town is now almost deserted, but "trains still whistle at abandoned buildings as they hurry past."

Quinlan, 1909. Harrington Hotel, a popular meeting place for travelers in the area, especially drummers. *(Courtesy Western History Collections, University of Oklahoma)*

Quinlan, *ca.* 1903. Central Avenue looking east toward the railroad. *(Courtesy Western History Collections, University of Oklahoma)*

Quinlan, 1963. Central Avenue looking east toward the railroad. *(Courtesy David Sengenberger)*

Quinlan, 1975. The trains still whistle when they pass the principal remains of a once busy town. *(Courtesy Western History Collections, University of Oklahoma)*

Reed, *ca.* 1914. Rural mail deliveries were made by both mail hacks and motorcycles. *(Courtesy Western History Collections, University of Oklahoma)*

Reed

COUNTY: *Greer*
LOCATION: *(a) Sec. 13, T 5 N, R 24 W*
               (b) 1 mile north, 11 miles west
               of Mangum
MAP: *Page 218*
POST OFFICE: *September 16, 1892–*

Reed developed in one of the first parts of Old Greer County to be settled. Surrounded by fertile and relatively level land, Reed became the trade center of a productive agricultural area. The town was platted but never incorporated. Many of the first settlers of the area came from Texas, most believing they were only moving to another part of that state.

By 1900 Reed had its blacksmith shop, general store, local doctor, and cotton gin. In 1902 the town started building a school plant. By 1910 approximately 150 people lived in Reed, and its

business activities had increased to include three blacksmith shops and a lumber and coal yard. The cotton gin had been enlarged. Two doctors served the community. By 1915 the one-room "school building had been added to so many times that it was similar to a rambling country house." The school district then voted bonds to build a modern three-story brick building. Reed continued to grow until the late 1920s. Population increased to about three hundred, filling stations and garages largely replaced blacksmith shops, and a second cotton gin had been added. The town had installed a municipal water system.

In 1975 Reed had a population of thirty people. A grocery store, a cotton gin, and a service station remain open. The post office, one of the few in Oklahoma that still cancels stamps by hand, continues to serve the area. Most of the school plant no longer exists. The

Reed, 1973. Unused store buildings on the south side of State Highway 9.

town water system has been replaced by a rural system. Several empty store buildings stand on both sides of State Highway 9, but one old blacksmith shop continues to display its name. The long-time residents of Reed say that the depression years and the Dust Bowl, consolidation of farms, paving of highways, and the preference of many of the ranchers and farmers to live in Mangum caused the downfall of the town.

Reed, 1975. Remains of a blacksmith shop.

Reno City

COUNTY: *Canadian*
LOCATION: *(a) Sec. 28, T 13 N, R 7 W*
             (b) 2 miles north of central busi-
             ness district of El Reno
MAP: *Page 216*
POST OFFICE: *June 15, 1889–October 30, 1899*
NEWSPAPERS: *Reno County Press; Reno City*
             Eagle; Reno Capital

Reno City was located on the north side of the North Canadian River just north of the city of El Reno. Established at the time of the opening of the Unassigned Lands in 1889, Reno City was for a brief period the third largest town in Oklahoma Territory, having a population of between fifteen hundred and two thousand persons. The *First Directory of Oklahoma Territory*, published in 1890, listed fifteen stores in addition to two barber shops, two teamsters, two livery stables, four blacksmith shops, a bakery, a flour and feed mill, and a hotel. The town also had a doctor, a dentist, and an undertaker. At one time three newspapers were published in Reno City.

The life and death of Reno City were tied to the development of railroads through the territory. The Choctaw, Gulf and Oklahoma Railroad (Rock Island), building westward from Oklahoma City, asked the citizens of Reno City to pay a bonus of forty thousand dollars or divide their real estate holdings in order to secure trackage through their town. The residents of Reno City believed the railroad was bluffing and could not afford to pass up their town. Such, however, was not the case, for the railroad continued to lay tracks south of the North Canadian River and established El Reno. During these same years, 1889–90, the Chicago, Kansas and Nebraska Railroad (Rock Island) was extending its tracks south from the Kansas border toward Minco. Again, instead of routing through Reno City, the railroad decided to lay tracks through a deep ravine west of present-day Concho Indian School and extend due south across level land to the North Canadian River. It then bridged the river west of Reno City and turned east to the new railroad town of El Reno. With this decision the dreams of a metropolis being built at Reno City began to fade.

For a brief period the rivalry between Reno

Reno City, 1898. Pupils and teacher of the school. *(Courtesy Canadian County Historical Society)*

City and El Reno continued. However, when the hopes of Reno City to secure a railroad ended, the town started moving southward across the North Canadian River. Residents loaded their household goods, even their buildings, on wagons or crude rollers for movement. The principal obstacle to such moves was the unbridged and shallow river. The three-story hotel building had some difficulties and was for a few days stranded on the river bed. With true pioneer spirit, it operated continuously until it was removed to higher and more stable ground.

The townsite of Reno City is now largely in agricultural production. A foundation or two may remain, but all the original buildings have long since been removed or torn down.

Ron

COUNTY:	*Harmon*
LOCATION:	*(a) Sec. 29, T 4 N, R 25 W*
	(b) 8 miles north, 3½ miles east of Hollis
MAP:	*Page 218*

Ron never had a railroad, bus station, post office, or newspaper, but it was an important place for those living in the community. At its pinnacle Ron had a consolidated school, a cotton gin with three barracks buildings nearby, a grocery store, a church, and eight houses.

In the late 1930s, when large numbers of people were moving from the area, four school districts consolidated so that the local community could have a school system with grades one through twelve. The school system used the split term. School would begin about August 1 and continue until time for cotton harvest. Classes would then dismiss for about six weeks so students could help pick cotton. The first school year was 1939–40, the last 1963–64. Half the houses in Ron belonged to the school district and were used as homes for the staff.

Cotton was the chief crop. In order to secure laborers, mostly migrant Spanish-Americans, for work in the fields and at the gin, it was necessary to supply a place for the families to live. The barracks were brought to the community and divided into "one-room apartments." Except during the cotton picking and ginning season the buildings were usually vacant.

Ron, 1973. Abandoned school and cotton gin.

Ron, 1975. Barracks formerly used to house families of cotton pickers, Each door indicates an "apartment."

The Ron school system no longer exists, but the walls of the concrete building still stand. The cotton gin has been abandoned and the barracks moved to Hollis. The store and the church are closed. Farms have been condolidated, the cotton picker has replaced the field hands, and good roads have made the nearby larger communities accessible.

parlor, a hotel, and other businesses were opened. Within a year a bank was established, and two churches and a school system were organized.

The life of Rosedale depended to some extent upon the railroad. At best the Oklahoma Central was a high-risk venture. It extended from Lehigh to Chickasha via Ada, Rosedale, Purcell, and other small towns between those places. One official of the railroad said: "no

Rosedale

COUNTY: *McClain*
LOCATION: *(a) Sec. 10, T 5 N, R 1 E*
               (b) 6½ miles south, 10 miles east
               of Purcell
MAP: *Page 219*
POST OFFICE: *August 25, 1908–January 6, 1961*
RAILROAD: *Oklahoma Central Railway (San-*
               ta Fe), abandoned 1934

Rosedale was established in April, 1908, when a townsite of ninety acres was opened to home builders. During the first six months of its existence there was an influx of more than three hundred people, a majority of whom built homes. Since the soil in the area was very productive, the Oklahoma Central Railroad immediately constructed a depot in the town. Also during Rosedale's first half-year, two gristmills, two cotton gins, and a sawmill were put into operation. In addition, four general stores, two restaurants, a meat market, an ice cream

Rosedale, *ca.* 1916. Large general store. Gasoline for automobiles was kept boxed and locked. *(Courtesy McClain County Museum)*

Rosedale, 1975. Buildings still standing are in fair condition, but all stores have gone out of business.

Rosedale, *ca.* 1940. Larger stores were in brick buildings. Fire has burned out the store on the left. *(Courtesy Western History Collections, University of Oklahoma)*

sane man would ever think of building a railroad where the O. C. was located if he ever intended to operate it. The territory was already covered by good railroads and there was no chance to earn enough to pay operating expenses." The railroad went into receivership in June, 1908. In July, 1914, the Santa Fe gained control of the line. Bridges over the Canadian River were twice washed out. As highways through the area were developed, fewer goods were shipped into and out of Rosedale. In 1934 that part of the line through Rosedale was abandoned.

During the 1930s Rosedale declined rapidly and was never able to make a recovery. The bank closed and moved to Byars. State Highway 59 was built through the town, giving easy access to Purcell, Pauls Valley, and other cities. During the 1940s fire destroyed some of the older business buildings. So many people had moved from the community by the 1960s that the high school was closed. The grade school closed in 1971. A few empty store buildings and an unused school plant remain standing. Most of the remaining homes are occupied, but as two of the older women remarked, "Very few young people now live in town, and none are returning."

Russell, 1975. Last store is selling out all goods at a 25 percent discount.

stage, brought contestants and audiences from as far away as Elk City and Wichita Falls. These shows continued for about eight years, and it has been estimated that crowds of fifteen hundred were not uncommon. In the early 1940s the town had lighted softball diamonds, and often several games were going at the same time.

With the advent of World War II and the general movement of population from the area, Russell declined rapidly. Stores closed, the school was consolidated with other districts, farms were enlarged and mechanized, and the post office was closed for a second time. The last store sold its stock of goods and locked its doors in 1975. The cotton gin, being rebuilt after a fire, will continue to operate. About ten houses are occupied by farmers or older persons who have lived in the community several years.

Russell

COUNTY:	*Greer*
LOCATION:	*(a) Sec. 36, T 4 N, R 24 W*
	(b) 7 miles south, 9 miles west of Mangum
MAP:	*Page 218*
POST OFFICE:	*January 29, 1901–July 31, 1915; November 1, 1934–November 15, 1955*
NEWSPAPER:	*Russell Reporter*

Russell, a somewhat isolated village in Old Greer County, came into existence about 1900. A small general store in which the post office was located and a blacksmith shop served a rural area that extended for ten to fifteen miles around this core. In 1915 the post office was closed, since the area could be served better by rural carriers.

Russell continued as the local supply center. By 1925 the town had four grocery stores, a drugstore, a general store, a cafe, three garages, and a cotton gin. It also had a movie theatre which, during the summer, showed pictures outside. (This show may well have been the first drive-in movie in Oklahoma.) A consolidated school with seven teachers and more than three hundred students served a large area. In 1934, following the destruction of the post office at Blake by fire, a post office was reopened at Russell. In the early 1930s amateur shows, produced on Saturday nights on a lighted outdoor

Sacred Heart

(SACRED HEART MISSION)

COUNTY:	*Pottawatomie*
LOCATION:	*(a) Sec. 7, T 6 N, R 5 E*
	(b) 22½ miles south, 7 miles east of Shawnee; 1½ miles north, 6 miles east of Asher
MAP:	*Page 219*
POST OFFICE:	*Sacred Heart Mission, January 30, 1879–May 24, 1888; Sacred Heart, May 24, 1888–August 31, 1954*
NEWSPAPERS:	*Indian Advocate*

The birth, life, and demise of Sacred Heart village are so intertwined with the founding and closing of Sacred Heart Mission that the story of both must be told together.

In 1876 Father Isidore Robot, a member of the Order of St. Benedict, while on a missionary journey visited the area then recently settled by the Pottawatomie Indians. He was invited to stay with them and to organize a school and church. The site selected for the school and mission was a well-known landmark called Bald Hill. A branch of an old military road from Fort Smith to western forts crossed at the base of the

Sacred Heart, 1910. Abbey as rebuilt after the fire of 1901. *(Courtesy Father Joseph Murphy)*

Sacred Heart, 1940. Convent of the Immaculate Heart of Mary.

Sacred Heart, 1975. Grave of Abbott Isidore Robot, First Prefect Apostolic of Indian Territory, 1876–86.

placed at what was considered the highest point (about the middle of the road just north of the present church). Before 1900 the campus included the church, St. Mary's Academy and Mother House (girls' school), St. Benedict's Industrial School for Boys, and Sacred Heart Abbey Monastery. The monastery also housed the equipment and classrooms of Sacred Heart College. Thus, in less than a quarter of a century a school system from first grade through junior college had been perfected. On January 15, 1901, fire destroyed all the principal buildings and most of those of lesser importance. The March, 1901, issue of the *Indian Advocate* commented:

Desolation is spread over the blessed spot where Sacred Heart, Oklahoma once stood. The schools are dismissed, and the community is partly dispersed. A few Fathers and brothers are "roughing it" in log cabins—out buildings. The visitor, after a tiresome journey over the hills and valleys, across the interminable forests of the Territory, was agreeably surprised by the pleasing majestic sight of the Abbey buildings. Fraternal hospitality was tendered to him according to the traditions of the Benedictine Order. Today he finds but a heap of ashes and sad debris. The bells that for many years entertained life in the neighboring country, resound no more—they are melted. The sweet strains of music, that rejoiced many hearts, have ceased—for the books are burned and the artists have gone away.

By the mid-1880s a general store was started about where the remains of Sacred Heart village stand today. A few homes were located nearby, and the post office was shifted from the mission to the store. For a brief period the new community was known as Georgetown. The post office, however, retained the name of Sacred Heart, so the name Georgetown was abandoned. By 1900 the community had two general stores, a drugstore, a cotton gin, a blacksmith shop, and three doctors. A small hotel was in operation, and a protestant church had been built at the north edge of the village.

After the fire it was decided not to rebuild the abbey and college. (In 1912 Shawnee businessmen gave a section of land northwest of that city for the future St. Gregory's College.) The school for girls was rebuilt and continued in operation until after World War II. By that time enrollment had greatly decreased, and most of the students were adequately served by the public schools. The building was eventually torn

hill. Because there was a supply of good water and an abundance of grass nearby, the site was a favorite camping ground for freighters.

With the help of the Indians a log house suitable for both church and school was built. Small log cabins for living quarters were also constructed. Recognizing the need for a school for girls, the Convent of the Immaculate Heart of Mary was erected a short distance from the mission. Nuns, first from New Orleans and later from Illinois, came to conduct the school. In due time an abbey, a large church, and other buildings were completed. A large cross was

Sacred Heart, 1975. Bakery and two-story log cabin which was the first home of Father Robot. The buildings were restored in the 1960s.

down. The church was rebuilt about a quarter of a mile east of the original site on Bald Hill.

The village was not immediately affected by the fire. Hopes were high that the railroad building from Shawnee to Ada would come through Sacred Heart; instead, the tracks were laid three miles east through Konawa. During the 1925–35 years a store and a few homes were added, for the village had visions of an oil boom. Even though both the village and the mission were located in a part of the Greater Seminole Area, no oil was found in their vicinity. Because of the geology of the land, only one well was attempted.

Old foundations and outlines of abbey and school buildings remain. A two-story log hut, said to be part of the first structure built, still stands. It became the shoe shop in which the cobbler worked on the first floor and lived on the second floor. A medium-sized rock building, used as the bakery, also remains. The cemetery in which the early fathers and lay brothers were buried is on the same grounds, just east of where the school buildings were. East of the present church is a more recent cemetery, but directly across the road from it is an old weed-covered cemetery used by the Indian residents of the area many years ago.

The remains of store buildings stand on both sides of what was the main street of Sacred Heart village. A few homes, built along the section line east from the village, are in use. The rock school building, used by the public school district, remains. The large Catholic church on Bald Hill now reflects the memory of Sacred Heart—mission and village.

Sans Bois

COUNTY: *Haskell*
LOCATION: *(a) Sec. 26, T 8 N, R 20 E*
             (b) 8½ miles south, 2 miles west
             of Stigler; 1 mile north, 5 miles
             east of Kinta
MAP: *Page 220*
POST OFFICE: *September 1, 1879–October 31,*
             1916

Sans Bois, as described by Janice Holt Giles in her book *The Kinta Years*, "was barely a village. There was a general store, at least for a while after we moved to Kinta. There was a church, a cemetery, a school and the ruins of a Choctaw girls' academy—Sans Bois Academy." The village at that time, 1910, was no longer a place of importance for trade since the Fort Smith and Western Railroad had laid its tracks two miles to the south in 1902 and the town of Kinta had developed.

Sans Bois was at one time a very important place in the political life of the Choctaw Nation. Much of the land around the village was owned by members of the McCurtain family, and it was in Sans Bois that Green McCurtain, the last elected chief of the Choctaw Nation, lived. His

Sans Bois, 1975. Gravestone of Chief Green McCurtain and the McCurtain family burial plot.

Sans Bois, ca. 1905. Home of Chief Green McCurtain of the Choctaws. *(Courtesy Oklahoma Historical Society)*

influence in the lives and activities of the Choctaw people was tremendous. To this small settlement came the leaders of the various Choctaw districts as well as the prominent men of the other Indian Nations and the representatives of the government of the United States. At various times McCurtain had served his people as school trustee, representative, senator, district attorney, national treasurer of the Choctaw Nation, and, at the time of his death, December 27, 1910, Principal Chief.

No part of the village now remains. The cemetery, located about one-half mile north of where Sans Bois once stood, has many prominent Choctaw men and women buried in it. Across the road to the west of the cemetery stand the remaining ruins of the old jail and courthouse of Sans Bois County in the Moshulatubbee District of the Choctaw Nation.

Santa Fe

COUNTY: *Stephens*
LOCATION: *(a) Sec. 2, T 2 S, R 5 W*
               (b) 6 miles south, 16 miles east of Duncan; 3 miles south, 1 mile west of Velma
MAP: *Page 219*
POST OFFICE: *March 19, 1921–October 15, 1943*

Santa Fe, like many Oklahoma towns, was born when oil was discovered. Such a place is the result of the dreams and hopes, or the get-rich-quick schemes, of one or more individuals. The plans for Santa Fe, however, were honorable, but because of the oil boom they could not be carried out as planned. A plat for the town was drawn and recorded on February 21, 1921.

Santa Fe, 1973. Site where school plant was located. The inset shows the building in 1940s. *(Courtesy Flodelle Hooten Gates)*

When the owners went to the site a few days later to prepare for the formal opening, they "discovered that sooners were occupying some of the lots, that squatters dwelt in tents and shacks around the border, and that 300 persons were already living in the town." Plans for the formal opening were abandoned.

Santa Fe was literally carved out of a blackjack thicket. Trees, two feet in circumference at the base, were cut out of Main Street. About the only parts of town not covered with trees were the cleared streets. Several town lots were sold to investors and speculators, but a number of businessmen and prospective home builders also purchased land. Absentee ownership made "squatting" easy. As with most oil boom towns of the early 1920s, the first businesses started were lumberyards, machine shops, and oil-field supply houses. A hotel, a rooming house or two, and good "eating places" were essential for the unmarried workers or those who had left their families at home. Santa Fe had these plus the other necessary stores and offices. Gaslights were installed along Main Street. A rock building for a bank was constructed but never used, since the charter was never approved. A post office was opened, and a school and churches were started. Some oil wells had been drilled and were pumping inside the incorporated limits. Flodelle H. Gates, in *Santa Fe, OK* describes the town as follows: "At first sight, Santa Fe was a smelly, noisy, dirty mess! Tents, shanties, wagons, houses, children, oil rigs, mules, dogs, horses and equipment littered the field and blackjack thicket that was Santa Fe. There was little evidence that this was, in fact, a platted town."

Santa Fe had its greatest growth during the first four years of its life. After 1925 the shallow oil field settled into a period of somewhat constant production followed by a period of continuing decline. The 1950 census recorded a population of eight persons. Since that date the incorporation has been cancelled. The area that was Santa Fe still carries some of the marks of the once booming community. Some streets can be followed, the foundation of the school remains, a few old derricks stand, and litter shows where some homes or businesses were located, but the blackjacks are making an effort to return the site to the way it looked in the days before oil was found there.

170
s

Selman, 1974. The unused school plant that is now falling into ruin.

Selman

COUNTY: *Harper*
LOCATION: *(a) Sec. 20, T 27 N, R 21 W*
(b) 2 miles south, 7½ miles east of Buffalo
MAP: *Page 215*
POST OFFICE: *August 24, 1923–*
NEWSPAPER: *Harper County Journal*
RAILROAD: *Buffalo and Northwestern Rail-road (Santa Fe)*

Selman, 1974. Remains of the bank building.

Selman, established in 1920 after the Santa Fe extended its tracks from Waynoka to Buffalo, was one of the last agricultural towns in Oklahoma to be founded. Land for the town was donated by J. O. Selman, who owned a large ranch. Several buildings were moved in soon after the first auction sale of town lots. One grain company had completed its elevator and scales before the first sale and was ready for business when the town started. During its first year the new town acquired six business establishments, including a bank.

Charleston, a village about two miles northeast of Selman, moved almost en masse to the new location. The post office at Charleston was among the first institutions to change location. Its name, however, was not changed to Selman until 1923. The last Charleston business to move was a blacksmith shop.

Selman grew rapidly during its first five years. In 1925 the town had three general stores, three elevators, two garages, three cream stations, a grocery store, a variety store, a filling station, a lumberyard, a hotel, a cafe, a drugstore, a blacksmith shop, a barber shop, a telephone exchange, a bank, and a weekly newspaper. Two and sometimes three doctors served the community. There were two active churches, and an accredited school system had been developed. During this five-year period the population growth was from zero to about 350 persons. During the last half of the 1920s business and population remained stable, the principal change being the building of a new school plant.

Disaster struck suddenly in the mid-1930s. First, the bank closed. Other business closings soon followed. The economic depression plus the dust storms resulted in the consolidation of farms, the return of wheat farms to grazing lands, and the movement of people from the area. A few merchants tried to "hang on" but had little success. Since 1940, efforts to save Selman have failed. An enlarged and modern school plant was built in 1959, but nine years later enrollment had declined so much that the school was closed and the students were transferred to Buffalo. When U.S. Highway 64 was built, it passed three miles north of the town, resulting in greater isolation.

The remains of Selman indicate that it was obviously a place of some consequence, with a good school building, now in ruins, and abandoned business places. Some houses are inhabited, and an elevator is functional, the post office continues to exist, and the train makes irregular runs through the town, but the real Selman is now largely a memory.

Shamrock

COUNTY: *Creek*
LOCATION: *(a) Sec. 33, T 17 N, R 7 E*
(b) 6 miles south, 26 miles west of Sapulpa; 5½ miles south, 1½ miles east of Drumright
MAP: *Page 216*
POST OFFICE: *July 9, 1910–*
NEWSPAPERS: *Shamrock Brogue; Shamrock Blarney; Shamrock Democrat*
RAILROAD: *Sapulpa and Oil Fields Railroad (Frisco), abandoned 1957*

Shamrock, 1914. Gas well fire that burned out of control for sixty days. *(Courtesy Western History Collections, University of Oklahoma)*

Shamrock in 1913 was a country hamlet with two general stores, a restaurant, and a population of thirty-five people. Two years later, as the Cushing Oil Field was developing, the townsite was shifted to the southern edge of the field and became a full-fledged boom town with a population in excess of ten thousand persons. Not only did the town grow, but several oil-field camps, with such names as Dropright, Gasright, Alright, Downright, Damright, and Justright, also were located in the vicinity.

Shamrock took on an Irish tone when the new location was surveyed and platted. The main street was named Tipperary Road, and other streets were given such names as Cork, Dublin, Ireland, St. Patrick, and Killarney. Many buildings were painted green. An important acquisition by the town was a Blarney stone. The first newspaper was the *Shamrock Brogue*. In the first issue of the *Brogue* it was stated that Shamrock was "the only town in the United States where green stamps only can be sold by postmaster." A later rival of the *Brogue* was called the *Blarney*.

Like all such oil boom towns, Shamrock had its saloons, gambling halls, and tough individuals. The story is told that the Big Six gambling hall had a one-legged fiddle player who was known to take off his wooden leg and use it as a club to restore order when the occasion demanded. In one pool hall Ruby Darby, a noted oil-field entertainer, performed. She would get "on top of a pool table so everyone could see her dance." Some pool halls closed at midnight so that men could sleep on and under the tables. A former mayor of Shamrock recalled that he had seen Tom Slick and Harry Sinclair, both outstanding early-day oil-field developers, race a little buckskin team up and down Tipperary Road. "They'd have a few drinks and then see who could go the fastest." Probably the last "big excitement" in Shamrock was in 1932, when Charles A. "Pretty Boy" Floyd robbed the bank.

Shamrock began declining in the mid-1920s. Oil-field workers moved on to new boom towns where more work was assured and pay was higher. As in all other such places, stores, pool halls, "hotels," and various shops began to close. Nearby oil-field camps were sometimes deserted, and often the houses were moved to new locations. Business buildings, left unkept, soon began to decay and were vandalized. By 1930 the population of Shamrock had decreased to about seven hundred persons.

With the construction of State Highway 16 near the western edge of the town, the remaining three or four businesses moved from the old store area. About ten stone buildings, all in the process of falling down, plus wide sidewalks extending both east-west and north-south, show the magnitude of the former business section. Fewer than two hundred people now live in

Shamrock. As one old-timer, a woman, recently commented, "Instead of loud screeching music and pistol fire, you can hear the soft rustle of the cottonwood trees and the childish laughter of the few youngsters here as they play where mud-caked boots use to tromp." Her husband put it this way: "Shamrock may have been Big Bad Bill in its day, but it's certainly Sweet William now."

Silver City

COUNTY: *Grady*
LOCATION: *(a) Sec. 22, T 10 N, R 6 W*
             (b) 19 miles north, 8 miles east
             of Chickasha; 3 miles north of
             Tuttle
MAP: *Page 219*
POST OFFICE: *May 29, 1883–June 17, 1890*

Silver City, located just south of the Canadian River where it was crossed by the Chisholm Trail, was an important stopping point for cattlemen on their way to northern markets. Just when the village had its beginning is obscure. It is known, however, that a Mexican family living nearby sold quirts to cowboys before 1880. The Canadian may have caused the village to be located at its particular site. In the vicinity were three small creeks with good water, and the land between the creeks furnished a grazing area when the river was in flood. Even when the

Shamrock, 1975. All buildings of the old business district along Tipperary Road have been vacated.

Shamrock, ca. 1920. Auto Livery served either as a taxi or as a delivery service. *(Courtesy Western History Collections, University of Oklahoma)*

SILVER CITY 1889

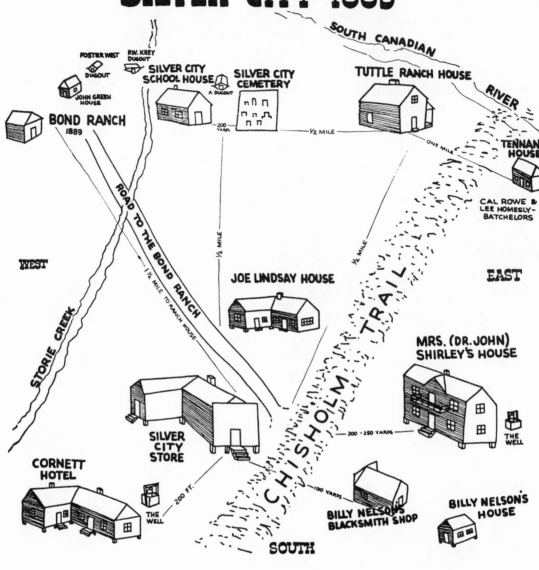

Silver City, 1889

water in the Canadian was low, quicksand could present a problem. Cattle, once they had started across, had to be kept moving. Most trail bosses preferred to hold the cattle on the south bank if the crossing could not be completed in daylight. With the opening of the Unassigned Lands, the Cheyenne and Arapaho Reservation, and the Cherokee Outlet for settlement, the Chisholm Trail ceased to exist.

In 1890, when the Rock Island extended its tracks south of the river, there was a general movement from Silver City to the new town of Minco. One of the noted pioneers of Silver City was Meta Chestnut, who had organized a subscription school. She also moved to Minco, where she started Minco Academy, which later became El Meta Bond College.

The only existing reminder of Silver City is the cemetery. All land formerly occupied by the village and trail is now in agricultural use.

TOP: Silver City, 1889. Silver City Store and Post Office. *(Courtesy Oklahoma Historical Society)*

CENTER: Silver City, *ca.* 1900. The original Bond ranch house. It was aptly known as Happy Hollow. *(Courtesy Norma Jean Gambill)*

LEFT: Silver City, 1975. Cemetery in which some of the early settlers of Silver City, including the Bonds, have been buried. *(Courtesy Norma Jean Gambill)*

Silver Lake, 1870. Home of John ("Old John") Sarcoxie, a Delaware Indian. *(Courtesy Elmer J. Sark)*

Silver Lake

COUNTY: *Washington*
LOCATION: *(a) Sec. 31, T 26 N, R 13 E*
               (b) 3 miles south of Bartlesville
MAP: *Page 217*

Silver Lake was named for the lake around which it developed. In 1866 the Delaware Indians living in Kansas bought a lake and some land adjacent to it from the Cherokees. Captain John "Old John" Sarcoxie, a Delaware, moved to the area in 1868 and built a large home at the northeast end of the lake. That house, recognized as the showplace of Silver Lake until it burned in 1907, became the center of religious and cultural life of the area. A church was also built on the shore of the lake, and Chief Journeycake preached there twice each month. A trading post was established on the east side of the lake, with a large storage barn just across the trail from the store. Indian hunting parties bartered buffalo hides for various supplies. Mail and necessary goods came by wagon from Coffeyville, Kansas.

In 1871 the Osage Indians purchased their reservation from the Cherokees. Believing that Silver Lake was west of the 96th meridian, which was to be the boundary between Osage and Cherokee lands, the Osage Agency was established at that place. An agency headquarters building, a school, a blacksmith shop, a commissary, and a payhouse for the disbursal of annuities were built, largely of logs, on the east side of the lake. In 1872 it was discovered that Silver Lake was east of the 96th meridian. The Osage Agency was then moved westward to Pawhuska.

From 1873 to about 1900 a small trading post or two operated in the area. Between the early 1900s and about 1935 the lake and some of the land adjoining it were used for recreational activities. The area today is an almost forgotten place of beauty, with tall stands of pecan, oak, and hackberry trees.

Skullyville

(SCULLYVILLE)

COUNTY: *LeFlore*
LOCATION: *(a) Sec. 17, T 9 , R 26 E*
(b) 14 miles north, 2½ miles east of Poteau; 1 mile north, 2½ miles east of Spiro
MAP: *Page 220*
POST OFFICE: *Choctaw Agency, June 26, 1833–August 16, 1860; Scullyville, August 16, 1860–December 14, 1860; Choctaw Agency, December 14, 1860–October 10, 1871; Oak Lodge, December 22, 1871–March 31, 1917*

The site for Skullyville was selected in 1831 when Major Francis W. Armstrong, an Indian Agent, was instructed to "establish an agency in the new country in the vicinity of Fort Smith, Arkansas." The site chosen was about fourteen miles southwest of Fort Smith and five miles from the Swallow Rock boat landing on the Arkansas River. The town was established in 1832 when the Choctaw Indians began arriving from Alabama and Mississippi. Skullyville was to serve as a center where annuities due the Choctaws were to be paid. The name is derived from the Choctaw word *iskuli*, meaning "money."

The site selected was an attractive and healthful location with a number of perennial springs. The agency building was erected on a hill near one of the largest springs. It was built with a stone foundation and with hewn logs, none of which were less than twelve inches in diameter when cut. The main building had three large rooms, a wide hallway, and a full-length porch. The Choctaws built log houses chinked with small pieces of wood and plastered with mud. The roofs were made of river oak shingles. The houses were strong, warm in winter, and durable. (Several stood for more than a hundred years.)

The government activities attracted commercial interests to the town. Stores with extensive stocks from eastern markets were established by licensed traders. Gold was the chief medium of exchange, but the traders bartered for Indian blankets, handicrafts, and pelts and furs. Frequently livestock was taken in exchange. Payments to the Indians were in gold coins shipped by boat in wooden kegs. It has been related that these kegs "were often left in the yard or on the front porch of the Agency, day and night without guard."

Skullyville also became a political and educational center. About 1845 the Methodist Church established two mission boarding schools. New Hope School for Girls was located one mile east of the town, and the Fort Coffee Academy for Boys was near the Arkansas River. Both schools progressed until the Civil War, when they were closed. New Hope School opened again in 1871 but closed permanently in 1896. In 1857 a convention for Choctaws was held in Skullyville. There the Skullyville Constitution

Skullyville, 1974. Monument in Skullyville Cemetery.

Skullyville, 1835. Original Choctaw Agency. *(Courtesy Oklahoma Historical Society)*

Skullyville, 1855. New Hope School. *(Courtesy Oklahoma Historical Society)*

was written and adopted; it united the different factions of the Choctaws and established a stable government for the Choctaw Nation.

Skullyville served as an early gateway to the west for both Indian and white migrants. In 1838 a large number of Chickasaw Indians passed through the town on their way to new western homes. About 1848 a few Seminole groups used the Fort Smith–Boggy Depot road which passed through Skullyville. Large numbers of forty-niners used the same road on their way to California. The Butterfield Overland Mail Route, established in 1858, made Skullyville the first stage stop out of Fort Smith.

The town grew in importance until the Civil War. During the last part of the conflict Skullyville was an outpost for the Confederates. The Union forces captured the town and destroyed many of the buildings and homes. The place never fully recovered from the ravages of war. It did, however, continue as a stage stop for a number of years. The post office at Skullyville was listed as Choctaw Agency when it was established in 1833, but it changed to Scullyville in 1860 and was then renamed Oak Lodge in 1871. The Oak Lodge post office was closed in 1917. When the Kansas City Southern Railroad was built through the area, it passed to the west of Oak Lodge, and Skullyville–Oak Lodge became a ghost town.

About all that is left of Skullyville is its cemetery, but it is well worth a visit. The site of nearby Fort Coffee should also be of interest. Several new homes have recently been built in the area as the density of population in this part of Oklahoma increases.

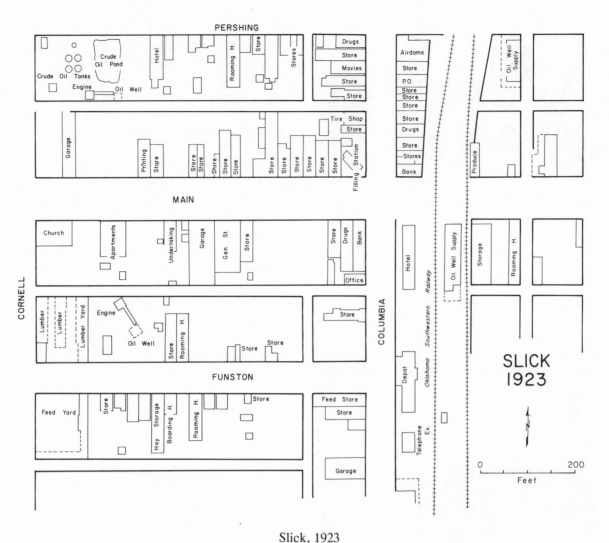

Slick, 1923

Slick

COUNTY: *Creek*
LOCATION: *(a) Sec. 17, T 15 N, R 10 E*
(b) 15 miles south, 8 miles west of Sapulpa; 4 miles south, 7 miles east of Bristow
MAP: *Page 216*
POST OFFICE: *April 28, 1920–*
NEWSPAPER: *Slick Spectator and Times*
RAILROAD: *Oklahoma Southwestern Railway, abandoned 1930*

Slick was named for Tom B. Slick who was known among the oil men as "Mad Tom Slick,"

"Dry Hole Slick," and "King of the Wildcatters." He was the discoverer of the Cushing Oil Field and numerous other oil pools. The town of Slick had its beginning in 1919 when Tom Slick brought in the discovery well. Within a short time tents and hastily constructed shacks became stores, cafes, pool halls, and various kinds of businesses. Soon many oil wells were being drilled, and there was a demand for oil-field roughnecks, roustabouts, and other workers. At the end of three months the town had an estimated population of five thousand. Many were drifters, but most were the boom town element that went along with every such oil development.

During the early 1920s, after the limits of the oil field had been determined, the town became

Slick, 1975. The former depot now serves as the First Baptist Church.

mill served farmers of the area. In 1920 the Oklahoma-Southwestern Railway Company laid its tracks from Bristow to Slick and then in 1921 extended the line to Nuyaka. A large depot was built to handle the crowds that flocked to Slick to "get rich from the gushing black gold." Roads and streets were mud or dust, depending on the weather.

The Slick boom did not last long. By 1930 population had decreased to fewer than five hundred, some stores had been destroyed by fire, and others had closed for lack of business. The railroad was abandoned in 1930.

Currently Slick has one store and a filling station. All railroad tracks have been removed. The once busy depot now serves as the First Baptist Church. Unused sidewalks, with grass and weeds growing in the cracks, hang over the edge of the streets. Most of the inhabitants are older people who have always lived in the area.

a production and shipping center. Slick had a business district about one-half mile in length. There were two banks, three hotels, several rooming houses, two oil-field supply firms, and numerous other stores. A cotton gin and grist-

Slick, 1925. Tom B. Slick, "King of the Wildcatters," oil-field developer. *(Courtesy Oklahoma Historical Society)*

Sod Town

COUNTY: *Beaver*
LOCATION: *(a) Sec. 22, T 1 N, R 26 E, Cimarron Meridian*
(b) 19 miles south, 15 miles east of Beaver
MAP: *Page 214*

Sod Town was unique among the early settlements of the Panhandle. It was the first town to be built in the eastern part of No Man's Land, and all of the buildings were constructed of blue creek sod. The village has been described as "standing irregularly and nakedly on the prairie." It had one store, a blacksmith shop, two saloons with pool halls, a restaurant, and a shack that served as a school. Doors and windowsills were unpainted and often broken, refuse littered the space between buildings, and building interiors were little more than dark, bad-smelling rooms.

The town was noted for the characters—horse theives and badmen—who loafed around the saloons. Most of the Chitwood gang, notorious horse thieves who lived nearby and frequented

Sod Town, *ca.* 1885. A sketch of the "Outlaw Town" by Halley Roberts. *(From* History of Beaver County*)*

Sod Town, *ca.* 1885. Large sod house much like the one at the right in the drawing. Note the sod roof as well as walls. *(Courtesy Western History Collections, University of Oklahoma)*

the saloons, were eventually hanged by vigilantes. In general, however, the thieves would not steal from neighbors who treated them in a friendly manner. Harry Parker, who as a pioneer youngster attended school in Sod Town, stated: "I do not recall the name of my first teacher in No Man's Land, but I do remember that two or three of the older students carried six-shooters to school. They would remove them and hang them on the wall by their hats."

Sod Town, spawned in poverty and crime, has passed into oblivion. The land where the town stood has been cultivated for a number of years, but the ruins of old sod buildings have left ridges that can still be seen from the road east of it.

Sod Town, *ca.* 1885. Sod house with a curved roof. Rocks were placed on top to hold the roof in place.

Strong City

COUNTY:	*Roger Mills*
LOCATION:	*(a) Secs. 24/25, T 14 N, R 23 W*
	(b) 4½ miles north, 4 miles east of Cheyenne
MAP:	*Page 215*
POST OFFICE:	*September 26, 1912–*
NEWSPAPERS:	*Strong City News; Strong City Herald; Strong City Progress; Strong City Press*
RAILROAD:	*Clinton and Oklahoma Western Railway (Santa Fe)*

In 1908 the Clinton and Oklahoma Western Railway Company, commonly called the "Cow," was organized with the objective of building a railroad from Clinton to Guymon. Plans called for the line to reach a point in Roger Mills County by 1912. Thus, in 1911 a group of businessmen who knew the Cow plans platted and incorporated the new town of Strong City in an area known as the "Snaky Bend" of the Washita River. Place in the townsite was reserved for a railway station, a rail yard, and a wye. The town immediately enjoyed a sudden boom and a thriving business, for it had a large trade territory.

By 1913 Strong City, with a population of about six hundred, was the largest town in Roger Mills County and one of the largest towns

Strong City, 1911. Part of a poster advertising the sale of lots in the new town. *(Courtesy Oklahoma Historical Society)*

Strong City, *ca.* 1915, The "Calf" making a return trip from Strong City to Cheyenne by backing all the way. *(From* Once Every Five Years *by Klina E. Casady)*

in western Oklahoma. In 1912 the Cotton Exchange Bank moved from Cheyenne, the designated county seat of Roger Mills County, to the new town. Also, the First State Bank was organized by people living in Strong City. In addition to the two banks, the town had two grocery stores, three general stores, three lumberyards, two drugstores, two grain and coal companies, two restaurants, and two dry-goods stores as well as furniture, clothing, and other stores. There were also a hotel, an active weekly newspaper, and four doctors. So alive was the community that there was considerable talk about asking for a vote regarding the moving of the county seat from Cheyenne to Strong City. When the original plat of the town was drawn, a rocky knoll near the center of the community was reserved as a location for the courthouse when and if Strong City should become the county seat. It was also announced that the Cow would not build any closer to Cheyenne.

Strong City, 1965. Tracks at the former rail terminal are often covered with sand and are seldom used. *(Courtesy Western History Collections, University of Oklahoma)*

Strong City, 1975. Remains of the first house, a log cabin later covered by boards, built in the new town.

Strong City, 1975. A lone brick wall and parts of the sidewalk are all that remain of the business district.

In spite of adversity, the people of Cheyenne did not give up. To add to the problems of Cheyenne, fire had destroyed most of the business buildings on the north side of Main Street. The town then voted bonds to put in a water system. One of the believers in Cheyenne started started rebuilding three of the burned buildings. He, along with others, decided Cheyenne must acquire a railroad. Accordingly, the Cheyenne Short Line Railroad was organized. Ten prosperous farmers and businessmen signed a note for a large sum of money, donations were given by others, and the city fathers decided to contribute the water bond money to the amount needed by letting the courts decide the legality of the proposition later. The route of the Cheyenne Short Line, called the "Calf," followed the Washita River, as "no bridges of any size were required and only light grading was necessary." Ties were the cheapest obtainable, said to be of cottonwood, and the rail was very light, fifty pounds to the yard. Rolling stock consisted of a flatcar, a boxcar, and a small eight-wheel engine. The boxcar was fitted to haul passengers and mail. Because the line had no wye, the train ran forward to Strong City and reverse to Cheyenne. *The Railroads of Oklahoma*, by Preston George and Sylvan R. Wood, states: "No right of way fences had been built and where the railroad had to cut through a pasture fence, a gate

was built across the track. It is said that no less than seven such gates had to be opened for passage of the train in the seven miles between Cheyenne and Strong City."

The Calf proved to be a success. Cheyenne regained its prestige and remained the county seat. In 1917 the Cheyenne Railroad was leased to the Clinton and Oklahoma Western Railway, and in 1928 the control of both was acquired by the Santa Fe. Strong City grew but little after 1915, but did continue to hold its own until the depression period of the 1930s. A water system was added, an accredited high school system was developed, and State Highway 33 was extended through the town. In 1935 the banks of Strong City, which had consolidated previously, moved to Cheyenne along with some of the retail stores. Consolidation of farms, the change from crops to pasture, and World War II caused the continued outward movement of people.

Strong City currently is indeed a ghost town. The rusting water tower stands on the hill above the town, but the old water system is not used. The last school closed in 1956. Of the fifteen houses remaining, seven stand vacant. The former business district is lined by wide sidewalks bordered by a lone brick wall and the foundations of former buildings. One church is in use, and a small post office continues to serve the area.

Sugden, *ca.* 1900. A group gathered at the leading hotel. *(Courtesy Oklahoma Historical Society)*

Sugden

COUNTY:	*Jefferson*
LOCATION:	*(a) Sec. 31, T 5 S, R 7 W*
	(b) 5 miles south, 1 mile east of Waurika
MAP:	*Page 219*
POST OFFICE:	*November 14, 1893–November 30, 1955*
NEWSPAPERS:	*Sugden Leader; Sugden Signal*
RAILROAD:	*Chicago, Rock Island and Pacific Railway*

Sugden got its start in the early 1890s when a general store was opened on the "shady banks of Beaver Creek." The town was named to honor the Sugg Brothers who operated a large ranch in the vicinity. The site of Sugden was favorable for growth, for the soil in the area was fertile, a railroad had already been extended through that part of the Chickasaw Nation, no other town was nearby, and it was only two miles from Comanche Indian lands that were certain to be opened. Sugden, therefore, was destined to become a shipping center for corn, cotton, wheat, cattle, and hogs by rail and for freight wagons carrying general supplies to the new towns in the southern part of the just-opened Cheyenne and Arapaho Reservation.

By 1900 Sugden had grown to "a thriving little town" with a cotton gin, a gristmill, a hotel, a blacksmith shop, a lumberyard, two general stores, a drugstore, a bank, and two doctors. The *Sugden Leader* was the leading newspaper in the southwestern part of the Chickasaw Nation. A school had been organized and the churches were active in community affairs. During the fall Quanah Parker would bring his group of Comanche Indians to the area and camp around a nearby lake. Tepees could be seen in almost every direction. The Indians gathered and sold pecans. The Sugg Brothers furnished them with beef and gave them a few cattle to take along when they moved.

ABOVE: Sugden, 1975. Small and ill-kept church is the only one remaining on the former townsite.

RIGHT: Sugden, 1895. In this frontier town the large church was built as soon as possible. *(Courtesy Oklahoma Historical Society)*

Sugden, 1975. J. E. Sugg, pioneer rancher and town founder. *(Courtesy Chisholm Trail Historical Museum)*

At the time of the Oklahoma Constitutional Convention the citizens of Sugden tried to have their town named the county seat of Jefferson County. The town of Ryan, however, was selected. After statehood a three-way battle involving Sugden, Ryan, and the newer town of Waurika resulted in the county seat being moved to Waurika. With the loss of that political conflict Sugden began to lose population and has continued to do so through each decade since.

Only a few homes and a church remain. The road leading to Sugden has to cross Beaver Creek. During some years floods have isolated the community, as bridges are low and narrow and roads are in poor condition. The school is now closed. No store buildings remain, and several blocks are covered with weeds or brush except for the remains of a few foundations. Sugden is where "just another small town slipped away and quietness reigns supreme."

Sulphur Springs

COUNTY: *Murray*
LOCATION: *(a) Sec. 3, T 1 S, R 3 E*
(b) Adjacent to the southern incorporated limits of Sulphur
MAP: *Page 219*
POST OFFICE: *October 2, 1895; moved from Platt National Park area to Sulphur in 1902*

Sulphur Springs developed along the banks of Sulphur Creek (now known as Travertine Creek) and around Sulphur Springs Park (now called Pavilion Springs) several years before the formation of Platt National Park. When the Five Civilized Tribes were moved westward, the area was allotted to the Choctaws and Chickasaws. After the Civil War, when the two groups formed separate nations, the area became a part of the Chickasaw Nation. Because of the topography, variety of fauna and flora, and number of springs, the Indians frequently gathered in the area. As legend has it: ". . . and when tired sinews forced the chase to halt, the warriors gathered their dried venison and ripened corn, and with the old and young, trailed the footsteps of their ancestors to the peaceful valley of rippling waters, where the shade of many trees cooled the heat of the summer day, and the surrounding hills admitted not the biting winds of winter, there to rest and fish and talk of conquest. Then it was that the old men grew glad of heart again and the fretful papoose ceased their whining."

In the 1880s and 1890s white cattlemen leased land or acquired ownership by intermarriage. Whites as well as Indians began to gather around the numerous fresh and mineral springs to "drink and bathe in the life giving waters." As a result, the town of Sulphur Springs began to develop as a health and pleasure resort. By 1900 the town, located in the area later set aside as Platt National Park, had six hotels, two of which were large; several rooming houses; two bath houses; six medical doctors; and a dentist. There was also one "Magnetic Healer" in residence. Numerous business establishments and a bank served a permanent population of fifteen hundred plus thousands of visitors throughout the year. Several of the business buildings were more or less shacks, the section along Sulphur Creek being generally known as "shanty town." As there were no railroads into the town, stage lines made daily scheduled trips to Davis for passengers.

The Chickasaw leaders, realizing what was happening to their medicinal springs and wanting to preserve the area for future generations, began to make contacts to get the area preserved. In 1902, to prevent the possibility of losing the area altogether, the Chickasaws ceded the area of the park to the United States govern-

Sulphur Springs, 1901. "Shanty Row," located between Beach Avenue and Sulphur Creek. *(Courtesy* Sulphur Times-Democrat*)*

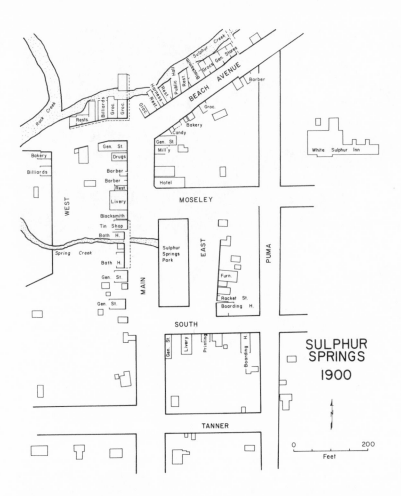

SULPHUR
SPRINGS
1900

0   200
Feet

Sulphur Springs, 1900

Sulphur Springs, *ca.* 1900. Paddlewheel boat used for tour trips on Sulphur Creek (Travertine Creek). *(Courtesy Oklahoma Historical Society)*

Sulphur Springs, 1901. Group gathered about the springs in Sulphur Springs Park, now Pavilion Springs. *(Courtesy Sulphur Times-Democrat)*

Sulphur Springs, *ca.* 1900. Harper Hotel. *(Courtesy L. L. Shirley)*

Sulphur Springs, 1975. Pavilion Springs, previously known as Sulphur Springs Park.

ment so that the springs could be used "by all men for perpetuity." The original act of July 1, 1902, set aside only the 640 acres surrounding the springs and Sulphur Creek. In 1904 another 208 acres were added. The land was purchased from the Chickasaws, and the park was named for Senator Orville H. Platt of Connecticut, a long-time member of the Bureau of Indian Affairs.

Following the establishment of Platt National Park, the town of Sulphur Springs had to move. Reports indicate that it became "a town on wheels" almost overnight. Some residents moved to land later added to the park and had to make a second move. Residences, cafes, dance pavilions, grocery stores, post office, and hotels were moved to lots in the new town location—present-day Sulphur.

Platt National Park (in 1976 the name was changed to Chickasaw National Recreational Area) now occupies all the land on which Sulphur Springs stood. Pavilion Springs, the center of the old Sulphur Springs Park, still flows. Using its location as a starting point, one can walk where streets formerly existed but will need to imagine the buildings that lined them, as none exist today. A visit to the park will prove to be a very worthwhile experience.

Sumner, 1930. The high school basketball court and dressing room for boys.

rail connections with north-south trains at Perry and Tulsa. The principal east-west highway in that part of Oklahoma traversed the business district.

With the closing of the bank in 1928, the consolidation of farms and the development of ranches, the construction of U.S. Highway 64 two miles to the south, and the general economic conditions during the 1930s, Sumner declined rapidly. In 1964 the high school closed. No businesses remain, but cement sidewalks indicate where old business buildings stood. Two small churches continue to meet on a part-time basis. About ten people now live within the incorporated limits of the old town.

Sumner

COUNTY: *Noble*
LOCATION: *(a) Sec. 8, T 21 N, R 2 E*
            (b) 2 miles north, 9 miles east of Perry; 1½ miles north, 6 miles west of Morrison
MAP: *Page 216*
POST OFFICE: *May 23, 1894–July 27, 1957*
RAILROAD: *Arkansas Valley and Western Railway (Frisco)*

Sumner was established at the time of the run opening the Cherokee Outlet in 1893. It has been estimated that two hundred persons came to the village during the first day of its existence, but within a week the population had decreased to less than one hundred. Developing as a service center for an agricultural area, Sumner was given a boost when the Frisco laid its tracks from Tulsa to Enid through the village in 1902. Soon thereafter an elevator and a cotton gin were built.

Sumner had its period of greatest importance about 1920. Two general stores, two elevators, a hotel, a bank, a garage, a filling station, a drugstore, and a blacksmith shop served the community. One doctor lived in Sumner. Three churches were active, and a consolidated school system was organized. The second floor of one rock business building served as a lodge hall and as a place to hold dances. Four passenger trains a day—two east, two west—gave good

Tahlonteeskee

COUNTY: *Sequoyah*
LOCATION: *(a) Sec. 10, T 12 N, R 21 E*
            (b) 4 miles north, 16½ miles west of Sallisaw; 1 mile south, 2 miles east of Gore
MAP: *Page 217*

Tahlonteeskee, located on Deep Creek, a tribu-

Tahlonteeskee, 1974. Replica of Court House.

tary of the Illinois River, was selected as the capital of the Cherokee Nation when those Cherokees living in Arkansas moved almost en masse from that state to Indian Territory in 1828–29. This Council Ground of the Western Cherokees was so named in honor of Chief Tahlonteeskee (Tolontusky, Toloouske, Tallontuskee, or Tollunteeskee), who migrated to the west in 1809 at the head of three hundred Cherokees, including seventy warriors. The Tahlonteeskee Council House, Court House, and Council Grounds were used by the Western Cherokees (Old Settlers) until after the "Act of Union" with the newly arrived Eastern Cherokees in 1839. After the adoption of the new constitution, all government business was carried on at Tahlequah. The new site, however, was not formally declared the capital of the Cherokee Nation until 1843.

The State of Oklahoma has constructed replicas of the Tahlonteeskee Court House and Council House a short distance east of Gore on U.S. Highway 64. The reconstructions are quite near the original site. One can easily visualize the beauty of the early setting in the adjacent hills.

Talala, 1900. Cattle in dipping vat. *(Courtesy Buck Dawson)*

Tahlonteeskee, 1974. Replica of Council House.

Talala

COUNTY:	*Rogers*
LOCATION:	*(a) Sec. 27, T 24 N, R 15 E*
	(b) 14 miles north, 5 miles west of Claremore
MAP:	*Page 217*
POST OFFICE:	*June 23, 1890–*
NEWSPAPERS:	*Talala Topic; Talala Gazette; Talala Gazette-Times; Talala Tribune; Talala Journal*
RAILROAD:	*Kansas and Arkansas Valley Railroad (Missouri Pacific)*

Talala came into existence about the time the Kansas and Arkansas Valley Railroad completed its tracks from Wagoner to Coffeyville, Kansas, in 1889. Located in a fertile agricultural area, the town developed as an agricultural shipping center. From about 1905 to 1915 Talala was one of the principal cattle shipping points on the

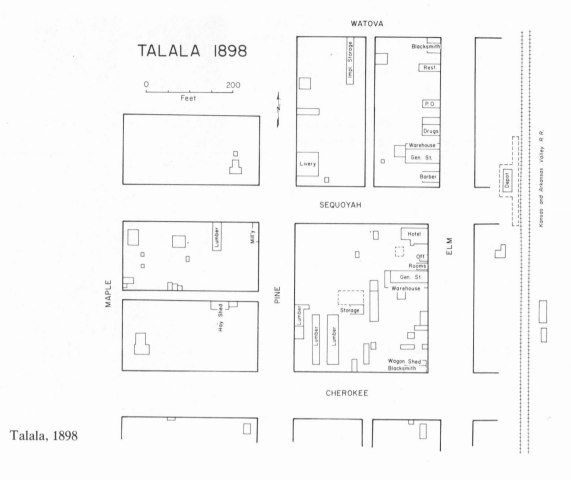

TALALA 1898

0   200
Feet

WATOVA

Impl. Storage

Livery

Blacksmith

Rest.

P.O.

Drugs

Warehouse

Gen. St.

Barber

Depot

Kansas and Arkansas Valley R.R.

SEQUOYAH

Lumber

Mill'y

Hay Shed

MAPLE

PINE

Hotel

Off.

Rooms

Gen. St.

Warehouse

Storage

Lumber

Lumber

Lumber

Wagon Shed

Blacksmith

ELM

CHEROKEE

Talala, 1898

Kansas and Arkansas Valley line. Cattle were shipped in and out from the Osage lands on the west to Chouteau on the east. Large stockyards and shipping pens as well as dipping vats were built. As many as ninety-eight cars of cattle were unloaded in a month, and thousands of head were shipped out yearly. Much hay was also grown and shipped from the area. The importance of agriculture to the town is indicated by the fact that about 1915 there were three hay dealers, two farm implement dealers, five livestock dealers, a poultry house, a hide dealer, two feed mills, a gristmill, and a harness shop operating in Talala.

By 1915 the main business district along Elm Street extended three blocks north-south and a block or more westward along both Cherokee and Sequoyah streets. Among the businesses were three general stores, a hotel, a drugstore, a restaurant, a bank, a lumberyard, a furniture store, a meat market, a grocery store, and a

livery stable. As business expanded, many new homes were built. At various times coal mining and oil drilling had some influence on population growth. Coal was mined west of Talala, and a shallow oil field was discovered to the northeast. Schools, churches, and fraternal organizations were established early in the life of the town.

The decline of Talala started during the first part of the 1920s. The development of such cities as Tulsa, Bartlesville, Claremore, and Nowata pulled business away from the smaller town as faster transportation developed. When U.S. Highway 169 was completed, the decline became rapid. About 150 persons continue to live in Talala, but shopping for most essentials must be done elsewhere. A filling station and a drive-in restaurant are the only retail places open. A large feed mill still serves the farmers and ranchers. The schools are closed, and two small churches struggle to remain active.

Bank's Prosperity Means Business

When you want to know anything about the business of a town look up its banking facilities. Mr. O. A. Fisk, one of the most successful business men of the state, the president of the First State Bank, has his massive business shoulder to the wheel and is working hard for the city. The First State Bank, with resources of $42,843.31, and deposits of $31,908.58, speaks well for the prosperity of the town and country.

Talala, 1910. Advertisement of First State Bank. *(Courtesy Ed Dikeman)*

A Word About Talala

And the Rapidly Growing business in This Thriving City

Talala is a village with a population of about 500 people, located on the St. Louis, Iron Mountain & Southern railroad thirty-five miles from the North and sixty miles from the East boundaries of Oklahoma. Surrounded by a level and nearly all undeveloped prairie country, that will at once appeal to the farmer who is in search of a home at a nominally low price.

The village has a fine large $10,000 brick school house; 1 church; 1 bank; (building brick) name, (First State Bank of Talala) organized under the laws of Oklahoma, and its depositors are protected by the State of Oklahoma Depositors' Guaranty Fund.

For further information call on write FARRAR & PENDLETON, The Pioneer Real Estate Men, who have had a continuous residence in Talala for 18 years. Talala, Okla. Rogers county; they will cheerfully furnish you with any information you may ask.

Talala, 1908. A Word About Talala. *(Courtesy Talala Gazette)*

Talala, 1905. Talala stockyards with cattle ready for shipment. *(Courtesy Buck Dawson)*

Tamaha

COUNTY: *Haskell*
LOCATION: *(a) Sec. 28, T 11 N, R 22 E*
(b) 9 miles north, 7½ miles east
of Stigler
MAP: *Page 220*
POST OFFICE: *April 17, 1884–April 15, 1954*
NEWSPAPERS: *Tamaha Banner; New Era*

Tamaha, one of the oldest towns in the Choctaw Nation, developed as a river port and river crossing point long before the Civil War. Located on the south bank of the Arkansas River, it was the most important river port between Fort Smith and Fort Gibson. Steamboats plying the Arkansas carried both passengers and freight to and from the Tamaha landing. A ferry, which had neither power nor cable, was moved across the river with either poles or large sweeps and two-man oars. Should only one or two travelers want to cross, a skiff would be used. During the Civil War the steamboat *J. R. Williams*, carrying a cargo valued at $120,000 and bound for Fort Gibson, was sunk in the river by the Choctaw Confederate forces at Tamaha on June 15, 1864. The ship was never recovered. The last

steamboat touched at Tamaha landing in 1912. After that, during a flood the Arkansas River shifted its main channel approximately two miles to the north.

Tamaha was an agricultural trading post for the Choctaw Indians. After the Civil War, and especially toward the end of the nineteenth century, the growing of cotton and corn became important. A cotton gin and gristmill were located near the river bank and each year, chiefly during the ginning season, many bales of cotton were shipped to Fort Smith. Sacks of corn and bales of furs were also sent down the river. Most corn was ground for either food or feed and used by the growers. The people living in the area had little money to spend for the luxury of wheat flour.

In 1895 Tamaha, with a population of about fifty persons, had one store, with the post office occupying one corner, and a jail. By 1905 the population had increased to about five hundred persons. There were five general stores, a meat market, a drugstore, two blacksmith shops, and a bank. There were also a hotel, two churches, and a grade school. A cotton gin and two gristmills were in operation. Most buildings were frame, although several homes were built of

Tamaha, 1975. Before the 1912 flood the Arkansas River flowed adjacent to the bluffs. With the completion of Robert S. Kerr Reservoir, water again extends to the bluffs.

Tamaha, 1975. Remains of the city jail.

logs. In 1919 a fire destroyed all the stores on both sides of the two-block-long main street. Several of the businesses were rebuilt, one or two with concrete blocks. In the early 1920s the bank was robbed, and it never reopened. Again in 1926 the business section of the town burned, but this time there was almost no rebuilding. People were already moving from the area. The high school, which was started before 1920, closed in 1931; the grade school continued until 1964. The post office, which opened in 1884, was first located in a private home. Over the

years mail came to Tamaha via steamboat, horseback, buggy, mail hack, and automobile. The post office remained open for seventy years.

Tamaha is a place that merits a visit. The small, square jail built over three-quarters of a century ago still stands. The old boat landing again has water lapping in it since the Robert S. Kerr Reservoir has been created as a part of the Arkansas River Navigation System. The school plant remains in relatively good condition. One small store with a gasoline pump is open for business, and a larger store has been added because of the recreational development. Just east of town is one of the oldest and best-kept cemeteries in Oklahoma. The oldest identifiable stone is dated 1832. No railroads have ever been built in the Tamaha vicinity, and all roads leading to the town today are gravel.

Three Sands

COUNTY:	*Noble-Kay*
LOCATION:	*(a) Secs. 2/3, T 24 N, R 1 W*
	(b) 21 miles north of Perry
MAP:	*Page 216*
POST OFFICE:	*May 4, 1923–April 24, 1942*
RAILROAD:	*Atchison, Topeka and Santa Fe, abandoned 1942*

Three Sands was a booming, brawling, battling oil-field town that started development in June, 1921, when the first oil strike of the area was made. Almost overnight Three Sands became a jungle of derricks. By 1923 the boom was at its height, and the town had a population estimated at seventy-five hundred.

Three Sands got its name from the three levels of oil-producing sands into which early wells were drilled. They were the upper and lower Hoover sands, at depths of 1,800 to 2,200 feet, and the Tonkawa sand at 2,650 to 2,700 feet. The field extended slightly northeast-southwest for a length of about four miles and was about two miles in width. In many places the legs of

Tamaha, 1975. The irregular stone in the center may mark the oldest grave in the cemetery.

three derricks interlocked, with a well to each sand. During the early 1920s Oklahoma had no conservation laws, and the "rule of capture" applied. In 1923 over thirty-three million barrels of high-grade crude were produced, and in the following two years about sixty-one million barrels of oil, along with the natural gas produced, sold for over $250 million. The Wilcox sand, one of the important producers in Oklahoma, was reached in 1926 at a depth of over 4,000 feet. Again there was a wild flurry of drilling. At one time a flush production from more than five hundred wells made a total average production of over one hundred thousand barrels daily.

In this mass of derricks, oil storage tanks, and pipelines, Three Sands developed not as a con-

LEFT: Three Sands, *ca.* 1924. Shotgun houses. *(Courtesy Western History Collections, University of Oklahoma)*

BELOW: Three Sands, *ca.* 1925. Stores and derricks in one of the business areas. *(Courtesy Western History Collections, University of Oklahoma)*

Three Sands, *ca.* 1927. Several tanks of crude oil ignited. There is no way to put out such a fire. *(Courtesy Western History Collections, University of Oklahoma)*

solidated city but instead as a series of business districts and oil-field camps strung out along the principal roads. Most camp homes were "shotgun" houses built with one room directly behind the other, and usually with only two or three rooms. All such places were of "box and strip" or "board and batten" construction, with wide boards nailed vertically and narrow strips nailed over the cracks between the wide boards. The houses were often painted with the distinctive colors of the oil company on whose lease they were located.

During the height of the boom, grocery stores, dry-goods stores, movie houses, and other businesses flourished. Cafes and hamburger joints were especially numerous. One area along the road between Three Sands and Salt Fork River was called Smackover; it was said that every other store there was a saloon. One report stated: "As oil poured from the earth, money rolled in like the tide. With the rugged oil field workers came gamblers, bootleggers, prostitutes and fly-by-night promoters bent on quick fortunes." One newsman visiting Three Sands wrote: "It's a crowd. You don't make up your mind to walk in any certain direction, you let the crowd decide the direction and you do your best to keep your feet and go with it. Those in the crowd were mostly oil field workers who ignore sleep and persist in living when the odds are against them."

The boom began dying during the last months of 1926. As pressure dropped with decreasing gas in the oil sands, production decreased rapidly. However, the town which sprang up overnight died slowly. Stores began closing one at a time. The last grocery closed in 1951. Comar High School, at the south edge of the field, closed in the 1930s, and the Three Sands schools closed in 1946. The last of the large gasoline plants stopped operation in 1951. Cattle now graze around old foundations or the remains of old wells. Few reminders of the once sprawling boom town remain.

Three Sands, *ca.* 1926. A long-range view of the oil field taken from the top of a derrick. Note the density of the derricks. *(Courtesy Western History Collections, University of Oklahoma)*

Three Sands, 1975. Fifty years ago this area was the heart of Three Sands.

Three Sands, *ca.* 1927. The Exchange Drug Store, Oil Field Lunch, and the rooming house are typical oil-field structures of the early 1920s. *(Courtesy Western History Collections, University of Oklahoma)*

Tidmore, 1906. Miss Lou Grisso, teacher of the one-room school, and her pupils. *(Courtesy Mrs. John B. Towns)*

Tidmore

COUNTY: *Seminole*
LOCATION: *(a) Secs. 29/30, T 9 N, R 6 E*
(b) 5 miles north, 12 miles west of Wewoka; 2 miles west of central business district of Seminole
MAP: *Page 219*
POST OFFICE: *May 17, 1902–February 6, 1907*

Tidmore, a settlement in the Seminole Nation, developed in the early 1890s and was the service center for the Seminole Indians, Seminole freedmen, and whites living nearby. A few small stores, a bank, and a lumberyard were the principal business activities. A one-teacher school served the community. In 1891 the Seminole Nation approved the construction of Mekasukey Academy about two miles from the village. The materials to be used in building the structure were sent to a "Mr. Tidmore," probably the contractor constructing the school, who lived in the village. As a result, the settlement became known as Tidmore.

In 1895 the Choctaw, Oklahoma and Gulf Railroad (Rock Island) extended its tracks through the area but refused to build into Tidmore. The village was located on low-lying and often muddy land near Wewoka Creek, a site not desirable for rail location. A depot, called Seminole, was located two miles east of Tidmore; thus, the village of Tidmore gradually moved eastward to the railroad. The bank, a general store, and the lumberyard were the first to change location. No part of Tidmore now exists. Mekasukey Academy was closed in 1930, and later the building was torn down.

Tidmore, *ca.* 1910. Mekasukey Academy for Boys. *(Courtesy Oklahoma Historical Society)*

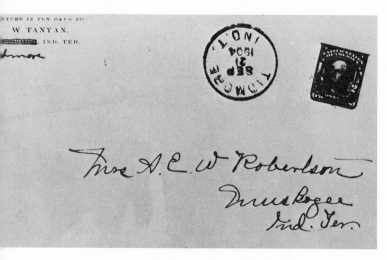

Tidmore, 1904. Tidmore postmark on a card addressed to Alice Robertson, a member of the U.S. Congress, 1921–23. *(Courtesy Mrs. John B. Towns)*

Tuskahoma, *ca.* 1895. Lumber and planing mill adjacent to the Frisco tracks. *(Courtesy Claude W. Curran)*

Tuskahoma
(TUSHKA HOMMA)

COUNTY: *Pushmataha*
LOCATION: *(a) Sec. 26, T 2 N, R 19 E*
(b) 26 miles north, 19½ miles east of Antlers; 2 miles north, 4 miles east of Clayton
MAP: *Page 220*
POST OFFICE: *February 27, 1884–*
NEWSPAPER: *Tuskahoma Item*
RAILROAD: *Fort Smith and Southern Railway (Frisco)*

Tuskahoma is the center of a historic community, "a community where the early historic feeling creeps upon a visitor." Tuskahoma, a Choctaw word meaning "red warrior," is near the meeting grounds and the final capitol building of the Choctaw Nation.

Located near the foot of the Kiamichi Mountain range and adjacent to the Kiamichi River, the site is indeed a beautiful one. As seen originally by the Choctaws, the mountains were densely forested with pines and oaks, the Kiamichi was a fairly clear free-flowing stream well stocked with fish, and wild animals of various kinds roamed the forests and grasslands of the area. No persons had previously inhabited the region permanently, although some Plains Indians may have hunted in the area for brief periods.

Tuskahoma was started by H. T. Jackson, who built the first store and house in the town as well as the first hotel. He was also the postmaster. The Fort Smith and Southern Railroad (Frisco) extended its tracks from Fort Smith, Arkansas, to Paris, Texas, in 1886, passing through Tuskahoma. Soon thereafter another hotel and a livery stable were built on the west side of the tracks.

In the late 1880s Tuskahoma became an important milling and shipping center for lumber. Across the Kiamichi River from the town several sawmills rough cut logs brought down from the slopes of the Kiamichi Mountains and Potato Hills. This rough-cut lumber was then hauled to the mill in town. The road crossed the river at a low-water ford, but in the rainy season during periods of high water there was considerable difficulty in crossing. All lumber brought into town was planed in the large Tuskahoma Planing Mill. Dressed or planed lumber was then conveyed to a large shed where flatcars entered to be loaded from both sides.

Among the provisions of the Treaty of Dancing Rabbit Creek was the promise to the Choctaws for funds to build a council house near the center of the new Choctaw Nation. The site selected was on a mound approximately one and one-half miles northwest of Tuskahoma. This new capital was named Nanih Waiya. It did not, however, become the permanent capital, as factional disputes caused the seat of government to be moved to various places. In 1883 money was appropriated for the building of the capitol which now stands near Tuskahoma. The building, a two-story structure with a mansard garret third story, was constructed of wood from the surrounding forests and red bricks made of native clay. The building, which cost thirty thousand dollars, had meeting rooms and offices for the legislative, judicial, and executive

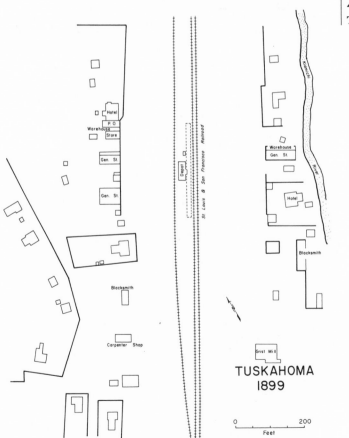

Tuskahoma, 1899

Tuskahoma, 1975. Choctaw Capitol and Arbor.

branches of government. It was believed to be the finest capitol structure in Indian Territory. The building served as the seat of government for the Choctaw Nation until tribal government ended in 1906. In 1938 the building was rededicated as a historical and educational institution. The Tuskahoma Female Academy was located about two miles north of the structure, and one of the principal old burying grounds is a short distance north of the building.

Tuskahoma had its greatest population, approximately three hundred persons, about 1915. At that time five general stores, a drugstore, a bank, a hotel, and a grocery store made up the commercial district. Churches were active, and a school system had been developed. After statehood, as the importance of the Choctaw government decreased, as the amount of prime timber for cutting lessened, and as highways and transportation improved, Tuskahoma declined.

Currently a small grocery store–filling station is the only business in town. Lumber is no longer cut, and the mill has long since been dismantled and moved. Old piles of sawdust, however, can still be found. A small grade school continues to operate, and two churches are active. Many of the people living in the town are older people. The capitol building and the old burying ground are tourist attractions, and their condition has been improved.

Violet Springs

COUNTY: *Pottawatomie*
LOCATION: *(a) Sec. 21, T 6 N, R 5 E*
(b) 24 miles south, 8 miles east of Shawnee; 1 mile north, 1 mile west of Konawa
MAP: *Page 219*
POST OFFICE: *April 6, 1899–September 29, 1906*

Violet Springs sounds like the name of a peace-loving community, but the town was just the opposite. Located less than one-half mile from the boundary of Oklahoma Territory with the Seminole Nation, Violet Springs was one of the "most wild and wooly" whiskey towns along that line. Founded in the early 1890s, the place flourished as a saloon town. Between 1895 and 1905 Violet Springs had five stores and eight saloons. Three doctors were "kept very busy much of the time," as there was a steady influx of Indians and "wild men" from the surrounding territory. One former resident reported that a killing was not at all uncommon, and as many as eight men had been killed in a single day. A cemetery was started across the road from the town. As late as 1927 one corner of the "city of the dead" was reserved for those who had met violent deaths in the turbulent life of the frontier town. A strong jail, one that outlived the town by several years, was in constant use when the place had a marshal.

During the 1895–1905 period the population of Violet Springs was about six hundred people. Farmers traded in the town, since it had a blacksmith shop, two cotton gins, a sawmill, and a saddle shop. The Masons, Modern Woodmen, Knights of Pythias, and IOOF were all active. A one-room school was built near Violet Springs, but there was never a church building. On a few occasions circuit riders held services in the schoolhouse.

In 1899 a fire destroyed every store building and a few homes in Violet Springs. Those merchants that rebuilt located two blocks north of the burned out area. In 1903 the Oklahoma City-Ada-Atoka Railroad routed its tracks east of the town when the townsite developers failed to meet its demands. The new town of Konawa, located on the railroad just inside the Seminole Nation, was founded in 1904. By 1907 most merchants had moved their stores to Konawa, and as "dry" statehood was approaching the saloon keepers either closed up shop or moved to another state.

All stores, residences, and other buildings of Violet Springs are now gone. The remains of the jail have been destroyed, and the entire area is now used for agricultural purposes. The cemetery, however, remains and is now used by former residents of the area and by those families now living in that vicinity. It is across the road from the larger Konawa cemetery.

White Bead

(WHITE BEAD HILL)

COUNTY: *Garvin*
LOCATION: *(a) Sec. 3, T 3 N, R 1 W*
(b) 1 mile north, 4 miles west of Pauls Valley
MAP: *Page 219*
POST OFFICE: *April 26, 1895–June 15, 1912*
RAILROAD: *Kiowa, Chickasha and Fort Smith Railway (Santa Fe)*

White Bead, first known as White Bead Hill, was an important stage stop on the government freight road from Caddo, a railroad station on the Katy, to Fort Sill. The first store was established in 1870. The village site was in the Washita River valley at the base of the hill. The valley provided a lowland route westward and was used extensively until railroads built across the western part of Oklahoma Territory. In 1902, after the Santa Fe had completed its tracks through Pauls Valley, a branch line was extended westward from Pauls Valley to Lindsay via White Bead. About 1900 White Bead had a population of approximately three hundred.

White Bead became an important education center in the Chickasaw Nation when the Methodists built Pierce Institute in the village. The school had five teachers. Subjects taught ranged from the elementary classes to Hebrew, trigonometry, and public speaking on the junior col-

White Bead, 1886. Pierce Institute. *(From* Garvin County History*)*

White Bead, 1895. IOOF Lodge Hall. *(From* Garvin County History*)*

White Bead, 1975. Washita River adjacent to the area where the town was located.

lege level. The ten-acre campus had a large, two-story building in which classes and church services were held. There was also a dormitory for boys and a six-room house for girls. Both Indian and white students were accepted. The school was at its peak from 1885 to 1888, when enrollment reached two hundred pupils. After 1888 the school rapidly decreased in size and influence, becoming a local school by 1890. In 1904 the large building was severely damaged during a windstorm. As much lumber as possible was salvaged and used in the building of a church.

Nothing of the original White Bead remains. The entire area is used for agricultural purposes.

Wildman

COUNTY: *Kiowa*
LOCATION: *(a) Secs. 22/26, T 4 N, R 17 W*
              (b) 15½ miles south, 7 miles east
              of Hobart; 3½ miles south, 3½
              miles east of Roosevelt
MAP: *Page 218*
POST OFFICE: *May 3, 1901–November 15, 1904*
NEWSPAPER: *Otter Creek Miner*

Wildman was just what its name indicates—"a wild west, hard shooting, tough mining town made up of grizzled miners and unscrupulous gamblers with a liberal seasoning of bandits." Some of the names of the more famous citizens of the "wild little village" were Scandalous John, Judge Fox (a former probate judge), H. Foster Bain (a government claim jumper), Carl Zerkle, "Nine Fingers," and Sam Bibe. It has been said that one of the first "diggings developed in Wildman was the graveyard." Only a few deaths from shootings were ever reported, but the Boothill Cemetery was a well-populated area.

Wildman was started in the fall of 1900 when the federal government opened the Wichita Mountain region to mineral exploration. Saloons and gambling houses dominated the business district, although the town also had two grocery stores, two hotels, a general store, a hardware store, a restaurant, a drugstore, and an assayer's office. The community always had at least one doctor. A two-room schoolhouse was built, but no church building ever existed. The school was used for the few religious meetings conducted by "sky pilots" who visited the town. The most unique building was the first post office. It was a boxcarlike structure on wheels, somewhat like a cook shack used for threshing crews, which could be moved when necessary. Visiting cowboys and gamblers frequently became involved in "shooting up" the town. When the old post office was abandoned,

Wildman, *ca.* 1902. Cyanide processing plant. The tramway led from the ore mill to Gold Bells Mine. *(Courtesy Steve Wilson)*

Wildman, 1973. Gold Bells Mine and the remains of the cyanide mill.

it was reported that there were no fewer than a dozen bullet holes in the structure.

Traces of gold, silver, and other minerals were found in the extremely hard granite. Numerous shafts and tunnels were dug, especially in the vicinity of Nest Egg Mountain. Large amounts of money were spent by both prospectors and financiers in the sinking of shafts and the building of smelters. Eventually, however, it became clear that it was almost impossible to smelt the hard granite. A railroad that wanted to build through Wildman was prevented from doing so because certain miners "planned to build their own railroad when they hit pay dirt."

The only current evidence that Wildman ever existed is the remains of a few concrete foundations and parts of an old smelter. All commercial buildings and homes, even the foundations, have been removed, and the land has been returned to agricultural use.

Wirt
(RAGTOWN)

COUNTY:	*Carter*
LOCATION:	*(a) Sec. 5, T 4 S, R 3 W*
	(b) 4 miles north, 23 miles west of Ardmore; 2 miles west of the central business district of Healdton (now within the incorporated limits of Healdton)
MAP:	*Page 219*
POST OFFICE:	*December 12, 1914–December 30, 1972*

Wirt, first known as Ragtown, was named in honor of Wirt Franklin, one of the discoverers of the Carter County oil pool. The town was founded in 1913 shortly after the discovery well near Healdton came in. One of the largest oil producers in the field was near Wirt. It came in with an initial production of five thousand barrels per day.

Wirt had stores along both sides of Main Street, including a bank and a movie theatre.

Wirt, *ca.* 1915. Traffic problems in a booming oil town. *(Courtesy Western History Collections, University of Oklahoma)*

Wirt, 1920. One of the many fires that burned parts of the town. *(Courtesy Healdton Chamber of Commerce)*

Wirt, 1920. Burned-out area after the Christmas fire. *(Courtesy Oklahoma Historical Society)*

Wirt, 1975. Only a few business buildings still stand, none in use.

Most of the remaining houses are typical of oil-field type homes of the 1915–25 period. Several continue in use. Numerous wells are still pumping. With a little imagination a visitor to the area can visualize Wirt as it really was—Ragtown.

The second stories of some buildings were noted brothels. The town was destroyed by fire four or five times (no one seems to know the exact number) but was always rebuilt. The buildings along Main Street were set far back from the curb with the idea that the flames could not reach across the street. Most homes were two- or three-room shotgun houses in which the residents simply existed. The houses have been described as a collection of shacks. Many inhabitants were squatters who lived in any vacant house, if such could be found, or pitched a tent in some little-used place.

Extreme lawlessness and moral turpitude flourished, and the town became known for its disregard for law and order. The killing or wounding of police officers was not uncommon. It was a town where "hard and quick fists, tough and thick skulls, and the ready use of revolvers was the rule and not the exception." Women as well as men were stabbed, shot, or found with their skulls crushed. The most prosperous of the commercial institutions was the undertaking parlor. Most of the time there was at least one corpse being prepared for burial, and there were times when several awaited the undertaker's care.

Present-day Wirt has been added into the incorporated limits of Healdton. No commercial activities remain in the old townsite, but one unused, cluttered store building still stands.

Woodford
(BYWATER)

COUNTY: *Carter*
LOCATION: *(a) Sec. 34, T 2 S, R 1 W*
            (b) 11½ miles north, 9 miles west
            of Ardmore
MAP: *Page 219*
POST OFFICE: *February 4, 1884–November 22,*
            1974

Woodford got its start when, in 1870, the Bywater brothers established their store and blacksmith shop on the south side of the Arbuckle Mountains. The site selected was near where the Whiskey Trail entered the mountains and a sulphur spring supplied large quantities of water. At first the village was known as Bywater, but when a post office was established the settlement was officially named Woodford in honor or the first postmaster.

Woodford, 1975. Weed-covered path of the Old Whiskey Trail into the Arbuckle Mountains.

Woodford, 1975. Last store and post office in the original townsite, both closed.

Before statehood the settlement was somewhat isolated and primitive. Section lines had not been completely surveyed. The road to Ardmore cut across grazing lands or fields southeastward as necessary; the roads to northern towns followed various mountain valleys and passes. Stores, homes, and other buildings were usually logs covered with sheet iron or rough lumber. Most houses had one room, although a few were two log rooms with a covered breezeway between them. A school was started at an early date.

Woodford attained its period of greatest importance about 1915. At that time the town had a population of approximately two hundred. Five stores, a blacksmith shop, a barber shop, and a hotel served the community. A telephone exchange had been installed. A cotton gin and a livestock dealer showed the importance of agriculture in the area. An asphalt mining company had its headquarters in the town. In the 1920s a consolidated school district was formed and a high school established.

Woodford, 1975. Sulphur Spring still flows. Recently a protective cover has been built about the spring.

As with other such communities, Woodford declined during the depression of the 1930s and World War II. The school plant has now been destroyed. State Highway 53 passes along the south edge of what remains of the town, but the post office and stores in the original business district are closed. The dirt road past the old store and beside the spring leads to Mountain Lake in the Arbuckles. Recently the spring has been cleaned, and it now flows freely. A roof has been built over it, and the sides of the pool are somewhat stabilized.

Woodville
(HARNEY)

COUNTY: *Marshall*
LOCATION: *(a) Sec. 26, T 7 S, R 6 E*
            (b) 11½ miles south, 7 miles east of Madill; 5 miles south, 5 miles east of Kingston
MAP: *Page 219*
POST OFFICE: *July 8, 1888; moved to site of new Woodville*
NEWSPAPERS: *Woodville Banner; Woodville Beacon; Woodville Star*
RAILROAD: *St. Louis, Oklahoma and Southern Railway (Frisco), abandoned 1942*

Woodville came into existence about 1880 when a small building was constructed to store supplies hauled from Denison, Texas, for people living in the area. Gradually, as the community was settled, stores and homes were built of lumber hauled from Texas towns in wagons pulled by oxen or horses. As there were no roads, it was not uncommon for wagons or buggies to cut across fields; thus, there were many trails leading to the growing village.

In 1900 the Frisco put its tracks about one mile north of Woodville. Soon thereafter the stores, blacksmith shop, and cotton gin as well as most homes were moved to the new location. Woodville then had its boom period—1901–10. Nine brick buildings were constructed. A bank building, with the first story built of stone quarried nearby and the second story of brick, was the showplace of the town. A sawmill, possibly the largest in Indian Territory at that time, supplied lumber for Woodville and other developing communities. A telephone system was installed. A three-story brick school was built in 1908 and was considered "tops" in educational facilities. The first automobile came to Woodville in 1907, but getting gasoline for the car was a problem. During the decade the population increased from less than one hundred to almost five hundred.

A public well was dug in the intersection of Broadway and Main Street. As reported in the *Madill Record*, September 11, 1952: "This well became an institution in Woodville. Since there was no other water system, nearly everyone got their water from the well. Nearly always someone could be seen either filling a bucket for his

Woodville, 1939. Public well at the intersection of Main Street and Broadway. *(Courtesy Oklahoma Publishing Company)*

home, getting a drink, or filling a large can to take back to the farm. It was common for farmers to come to Woodville in a wagon to get barrels of water. The well was constructed with wooden sides and a peaked roof. The well caused many problems when the construction of a highway from Madill to Denison was conceived. The people of Woodville wanted the highway to come through town but they didn't want the old landmark covered up. The highway was routed through the edge of town because of the well."

Woodville had to be abandoned in the early 1940s when Denison Dam was constructed and Lake Texoma was formed. The site of the old town is covered when the lake is at high-water level. Buildings were torn down. Some were rebuilt in New Woodville. Several homes and the cemetery were moved. About the only reminders of Old Woodville are the two islands a few yards offshore. They are the remains of the overpass of the Frisco. At low water some foundations and the old bank vault may be seen.

Yeldell

COUNTY:	*Jackson*
LOCATION:	*(a) Sec. 9, T 1 S, R 20 W*
	(b) 10 miles south, 1½ miles east
	of Altus
MAP:	*Page 218*
POST OFFICE:	*May 28, 1892–December 31, 1904*

Yeldell was established by three brothers in 1888. They purchased the land from the state of Texas and paid for it with land scrip. (In 1888 Texas considered all land south and west of the North Fork of Red River as part of that state.)

The purchased area was about ten miles northwest of Doan's Crossing on Red River. Cattlemen moving herds northward along the Great Western Trail from Doan's Crossing started early in the morning, as it was difficult to get cattle across the Red River—sometimes because of floodwaters, sometimes quicksand. The end of the day's drive was usually in the vicinity of Yeldell, since the large Nine Mile Spring was only about one mile from the trading post. Also, Yeldell was located on the Fort Supply Road, which extended from Doan's Crossing to Fort Supply.

Other people soon settled near the combination trading post and dwelling that the brothers had built. Shortly after the trading post was built, the brothers had a well dug to a depth of about twenty-five feet. It had a diameter of about five feet. Since the well was dug into sandstone rock in an old floodplain, there was always an adequate water supply even during the dry years. Another store, a blacksmith, and a doctor came to the new village. Yeldell became a division point on the Fort Supply stage route where horses were changed. When the demand arose, a small half-dugout schoolhouse was built a short distance north of the trading post. Sunday school and church meetings were held in the school. The village also had a very active Masonic Lodge.

About 1900 the town of Elmer was started some three miles to the west of Yeldell. At approximately the same time, two miles to the southeast, the crossroads village of Hess was established. In 1908 the Kansas City, Mexico and Orient Railroad extended its tracks south from Altus through Elmer into Texas. Soon thereafter most of the population of Yeldell moved to Elmer. Because trade was diverted, and the stage line and cattle trail had long since been abandoned, the trading post building was also moved to Elmer. Other buildings were torn down or moved.

No village now exists where Yeldell once stood. The old hand-dug well, however, furnishes much of the water now used by the large consolidated school that stands about where the trading post was located. The Masonic Lodge continues to live in Elmer, for in that town the lodge is known as the Yeldell Lodge.

Yewed

COUNTY: *Alfalfa*
LOCATION: *(a) Sec. 32, T 26 N, R 11 W*
(b) 4 miles south, 3 miles west of Cherokee
MAP: *Page 215*
POST OFFICE: *December 24, 1898–April 30, 1952*
NEWSPAPER: *The Hustler*
RAILROAD: *Kansas City, Mexico and Orient Railway (Santa Fe)*

Yewed was never an incorporated town, nor has it ever been recognized for any specific activity. The town, however, has become noted for the spelling of its name. Shortly after the victory of Admiral Dewey at Manila Bay in 1898, an application was made for a rural post office, and the name Dewey was suggested. The application was approved, but since there was another post office with the name of Dewey, the Post Office Department reversed the spelling. Thus, the rural post office of Yewed and, a short time later, the town of Yewed came into existence.

The town of Yewed was platted in 1902. Some lots were sold, but payment was deferred until after the Kansas City, Mexico and Orient Railroad had laid its tracks and built a depot. Probably no more than fifty persons ever lived in the town at the same time. The principal activities revolved around an elevator, a roller mill, and a grain dealer. There were also two stores, a blacksmith shop, and two churches. No school was ever built.

The elevator continues to operate, and the old post office building still stands. All other activities have ceased. Only two elderly ladies continue to live in Yewed.

Yewed, 1974. Remains of the post office building.

Maps

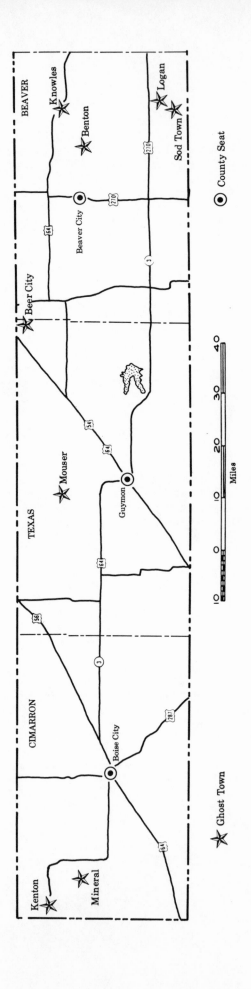

MAP 1. Panhandle

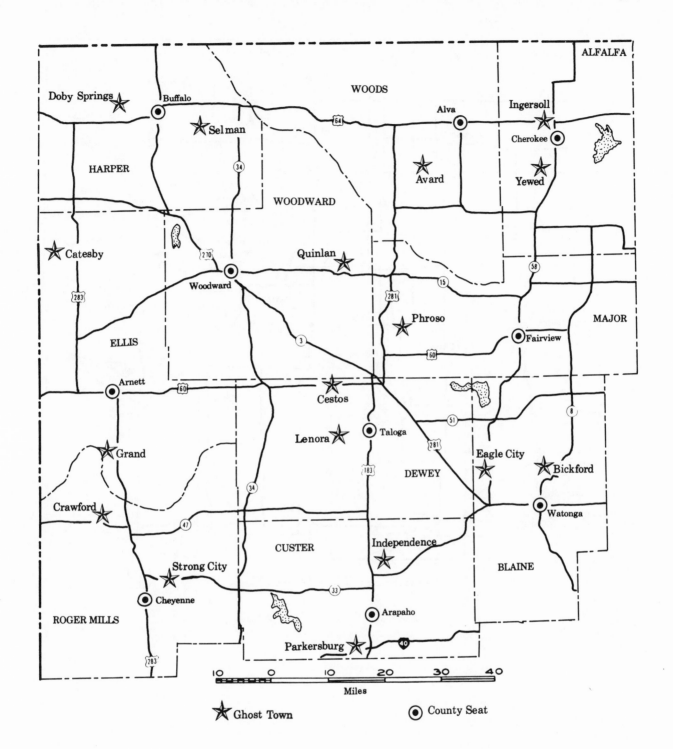

ALFALFA

WOODS

Doby Springs ★ ●Buffalo

★ Selman

Alva ●

Ingersoll ★

Cherokee ●

HARPER

34

WOODWARD

Avard ★

Yewed ★

Catesby ★

270

Quinlan ★

58

283

Woodward ●

15

MAJOR

281

ELLIS

3

Phroso ★

●Fairview

60

Arnett ●

60

Cestos ★

8

Grand ★

Lenora ★

●Taloga

51

Eagle City ★

Bickford ★

Crawford ★

34

DEWEY

183

281

●Watonga

47

Strong City ★

CUSTER

Independence ★

BLAINE

●Cheyenne

33

ROGER MILLS

Arapaho ●

283

Parkersburg ★

40

10   0   10   20   30   40

Miles

★ Ghost Town   ● County Seat

MAP 2. Northwestern

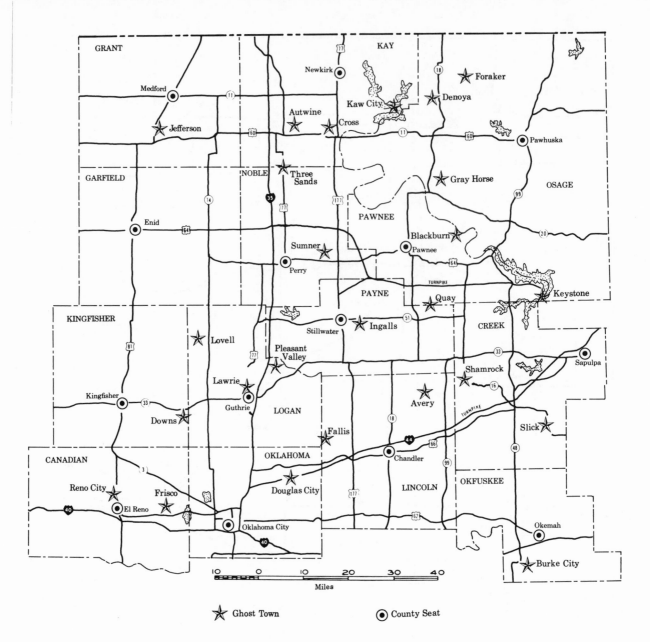

GRANT

Medford ⊙

✪ Jefferson

KAY

Newkirk ⊙

✪ Foraker

✪ Denoya

Kaw City

Autwine ✪

Cross

⊙ Pawhuska

GARFIELD

NOBLE

✪ Three
Sands

✪ Gray Horse

OSAGE

Enid ⊙

PAWNEE

Sumner ✪

Blackburn ✪

Perry ⊙

Pawnee ⊙

PAYNE

TURNPIKE

KINGFISHER

Quay ✪

Keystone ✪

Lovell ✪

Stillwater ⊙

Ingalls ✪

CREEK

Sapulpa ⊙

Pleasant
Valley ✪

Shamrock ✪

Lawrie ✪

Kingfisher ⊙

Guthrie ⊙

LOGAN

Avery ✪

Slick ✪

Downs ✪

Fallis ✪

CANADIAN

OKLAHOMA

Chandler ⊙

OKFUSKEE

Reno City ✪

Frisco ✪

El Reno ⊙

Douglas City ✪

LINCOLN

Oklahoma City ⊙

Okemah ⊙

✪ Burke City

10   0   10   20   30   40

Miles

✪ Ghost Town   ⊙ County Seat

MAP 3. North Central

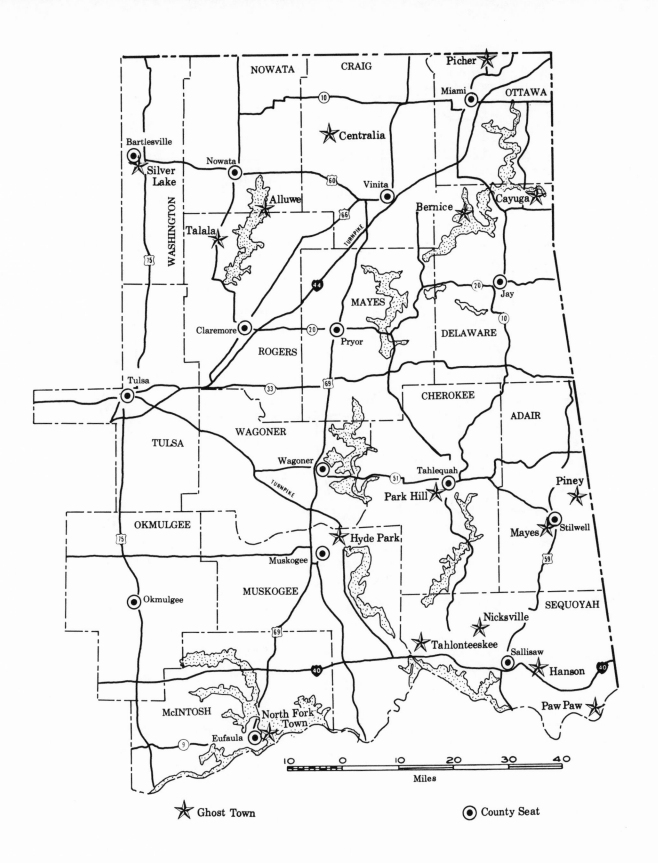

NOWATA CRAIG

Picher ★

Miami ⊙ OTTAWA

★ Centralia

Bartlesville ⊙
Silver ★
Lake

Nowata ⊙

WASHINGTON

60

Vinita ⊙

Bernice ★

Cayuga ★

★ Alluwe

66

★ Talala

TURNPIKE

44

20 Jay ⊙

MAYES

10

Claremore ⊙

20

Pryor ⊙

DELAWARE

ROGERS

75

Tulsa ⊙

33

69

CHEROKEE

ADAIR

WAGONER

TURNPIKE

Wagoner ⊙

51 Tahlequah ⊙

Piney ★

TULSA

Park Hill ★

Mayes ★ ⊙ Stilwell

OKMULGEE

75

★ Hyde Park

Muskogee ⊙

59

Okmulgee ⊙

SEQUOYAH

MUSKOGEE

Nicksville ★

69

★ Tahlonteeskee

Sallisaw ⊙

40

Hanson ★

40

McINTOSH

North Fork
Town ★

Paw Paw ★

Eufaula ⊙

9

10 0 10 20 30 40

Miles

★ Ghost Town   ⊙ County Seat

MAP 4. Northeastern

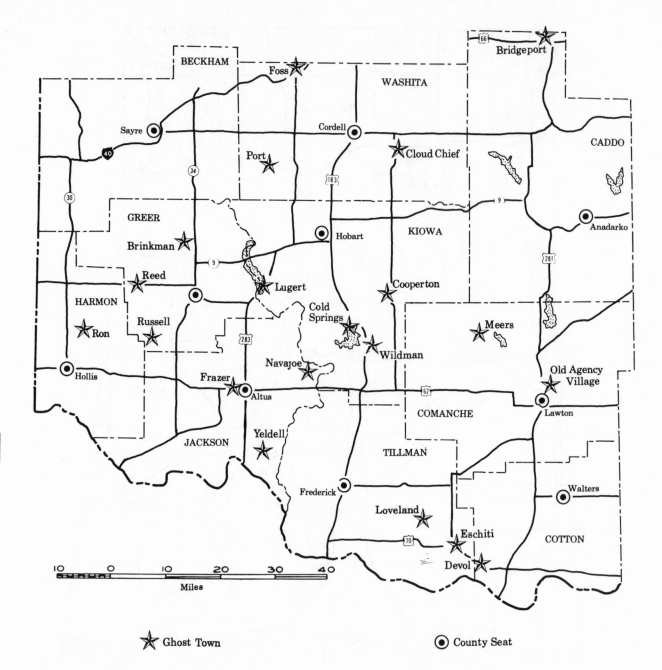

BECKHAM

Foss

WASHITA

Bridgeport

66

Sayre

40

30

Cordell

CADDO

34

Port

Cloud Chief

9

GREER

183

Anadarko

Brinkman

KIOWA

Hobart

9

281

Reed

Cooperton

Lugert

HARMON

Cold
Springs

Russell

Meers

Ron

283

Navajoe

Wildman

Hollis

Old Agency
Village

Frazer

Altus

62

COMANCHE

Lawton

JACKSON

Yeldell

TILLMAN

218
MAPS

Frederick

Walters

Loveland

Eschiti

COTTON

70

Devol

10   0   10   20   30   40

Miles

★ Ghost Town

◉ County Seat

MAP 5. Southwestern

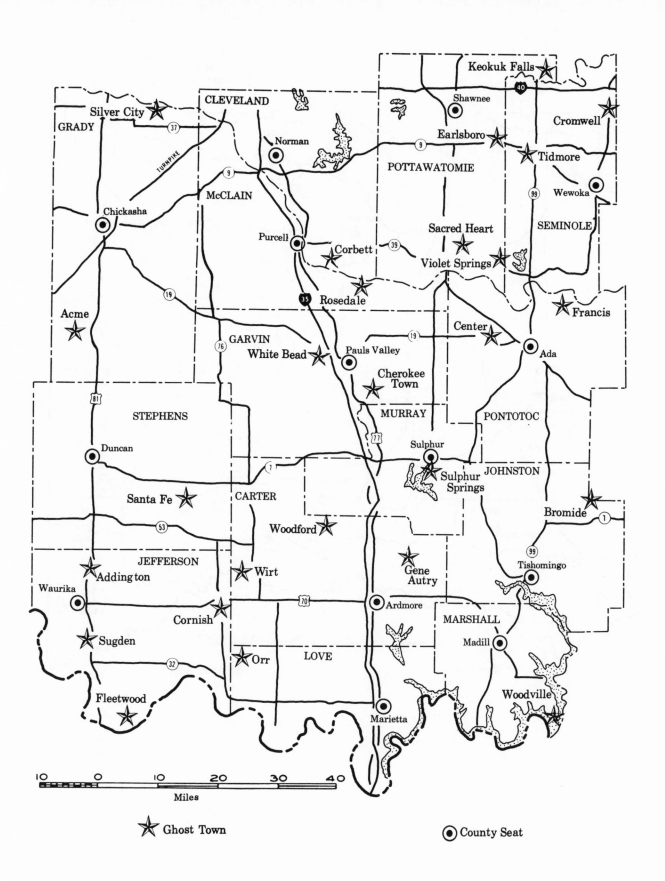

GRADY

Silver City

CLEVELAND

Keokuk Falls

Shawnee

40

Cromwell

Norman

Earlsboro

Tidmore

POTTAWATOMIE

9

37

TURNPIKE

McCLAIN

99

Wewoka

Chickasha

SEMINOLE

Purcell

Corbett

39

Sacred Heart

Violet Springs

Acme

35

Rosedale

Francis

19

GARVIN

White Bead

Pauls Valley

Center

Ada

76

Cherokee
Town

STEPHENS

MURRAY

PONTOTOC

81

Duncan

Sulphur

JOHNSTON

Santa Fe

CARTER

1

Sulphur
Springs

Bromide

53

Woodford

99

Tishomingo

JEFFERSON

Waurika

Addington

Wirt

Gene
Autry

70

Ardmore

MARSHALL

Madill

Cornish

Sugden

32

Orr

LOVE

Woodville

Fleetwood

Marietta

10   0   10   20   30   40

Miles

Ghost Town   County Seat

MAP 6. South Central

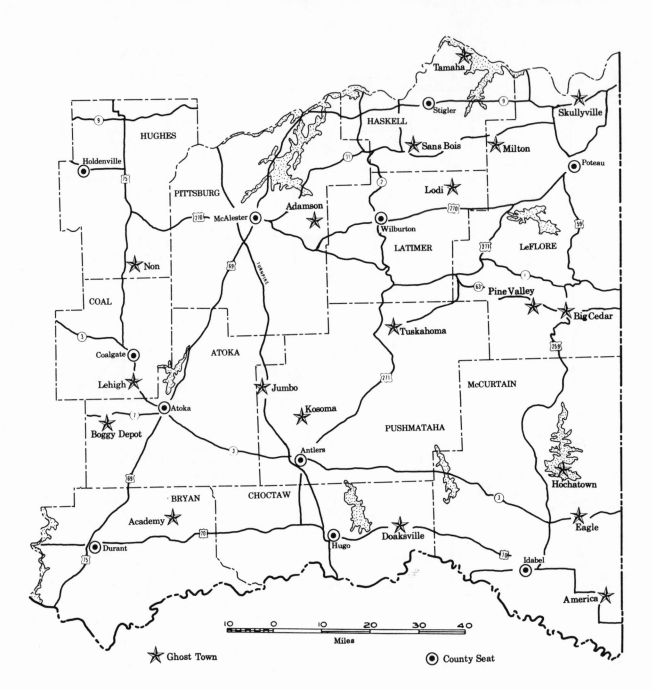

Tamaha

Stigler

HASKELL

Skullyville

HUGHES

Sans Bois

Milton

Holdenville

Poteau

PITTSBURG

Lodi

McAlester

Adamson

Wilburton

LATIMER

LeFLORE

Non

COAL

Pine Valley

Big Cedar

Tuskahoma

ATOKA

Coalgate

Lehigh

Jumbo

McCURTAIN

Atoka

Kosoma

Boggy Depot

PUSHMATAHA

Antlers

Hochatown

BRYAN

CHOCTAW

Academy

Eagle

Durant

Hugo

Doaksville

Idabel

America

10   0   10   20   30   40

Miles

★ Ghost Town   ◉ County Seat

MAP 7. Southeastern

Selected Bibliography

Books

Bailey, Minnie Elizabeth. *Reconstruction in Indian Territory, 1865–1877.* Ann Arbor, University Microfilms, Inc., 1968.

Barker, Ballard M., and William C. Jameson. *Platt National Park.* Norman, University of Oklahoma Press, 1975.

Benedict, John O. *Muskogee and Northeastern Oklahoma.* Chicago, The S. J. Clarke Publishing Co., 1922.

Bennett, Joanne R., and Patricia D. Cordell. *A Pictorial History of Bartlesville.* Bartlesville, Okla., The Washington County Historical Society, 1972.

Boecher, Lee. *Shortgrass Country.* Guthrie, Okla., Midwest Publishing Company, 1969.

Boone, Marijane. *Newkirk and Kay County.* Ponca City, Okla., Skinner and Sons, Printers, 1973.

Campbell, O. B. *Mission to the Cherokees.* Oklahoma City, Metro Press, 1973.

———. *Vinita, I.T.—The Story of a Frontier Town of the Cherokee Nation, 1871–1907.* Oklahoma City, Metro Press, 1972.

Carter, W. A. *McCurtain County and Southeast Oklahoma.* Fort Worth, Tribune Publishing Co., 1923.

Casady, Mrs. John. *A Romance of the Soil: Reclamation of Roger Mills County.* Oklahoma City, Colorgraphics, 1971.

Chambers, Homer S. *The Enduring Rock.* Blackwell, Okla., Blackwell Publications, Inc., 1954.

Chesser, Cecil. *Across the Lonely Years: The Story of Jackson County.* Altus, Okla., Altus Printing Co., 1971.

Chrisman, Harry E. *Fifty Years on the Owl Hoot Trail.* Chicago, Sage Books, 1969.

———. *Lost Trails of the Cimarron.* Denver, Sage Books, 1961.

Clark, Stanley. *The Oil Century.* Norman, University of Oklahoma Press, 1958.

Crumley, Russell W. *Roughneck: The Way of Life in the Oil Fields.* Evanston, Ill., Row, Peterson and Co., 1941.

Cunningham, Robert E. *Perry: Pride of the Prairies.* Stillwater, Okla., Frontier Printers, Inc., 1974.

Dale, Edward Everett. *Frontier Ways.* Austin, University of Texas Press, 1959.

Debo, Angie. *Oklahoma—Foot-loose and Fancy-free.* Norman, University of Oklahoma Press, 1949.

———. *The Road to Disappearance.* Norman, University of Oklahoma Press, 1941.

———. *The Rise and Fall of the Choctaw Republic.* Norman, University of Oklahoma Press, 1934.

Douglas, Rose (ed.). *Sage and Sod: Harper County, Oklahoma, 1885–1973.* Buffalo, Okla., Harper County Historical Society, 1974.

Forbes, Gerald. *Flush Production.* Norman, University of Oklahoma Press, 1942.

Foreman, Carolyn Thomas. *North Fork Town.* Muskogee, Okla., Hoffman Printing Co., n.d.

———. *Oklahoma Imprints.* Norman, University of Oklahoma Press, 1936.

Foreman, Grant. *Advancing the Frontier, 1830–1860.* Norman, University of Oklahoma Press, 1933.

———. *History of Oklahoma.* Norman, University of Oklahoma Press, 1942.

———. *Muskogee and Eastern Oklahoma.* Muskogee, Okla., Star Printery, n.d.

Fortson, John. *Pott County and What Has Come of It.* Shawnee, Okla., Pottawatomie County Historical Society, 1936.

Gard, Wayne. *The Chisholm Trail.* Norman, University of Oklahoma Press, 1954.

Gates, Flodelle Hooton. *Santa Fe, OK!* Fort Worth, Miran Publishers, 1974.

Gazetteer and Business Directory of Indian Territory, 1901. Buffalo, N.Y., McMasters Publishing Co., 1902.

George, Preston, and Sylvan R. Wood. *Railroads of Oklahoma—June 6, 1870–July 1, 1974.* Oklahoma City, Oklahoma Department of Highways, 1974.

Gibson, Arrell M. *The Chickasaws.* Norman, University of Oklahoma Press, 1971.

———. *Oklahoma—A History of Five Centuries.* Norman, Harlow Publishing Corp., 1965.

Giles, Janice Holt. *The Kinta Years.* Boston, Houghton Mifflin Co., 1973.

Gill, Ed. *Oklahoma in the 1920's.* Muskogee, Okla., Thomason Printing Co., 1974.

Gould, Charles N. *Covered Wagon Geologist.* Norman, University of Oklahoma Press, 1959.

———. *Geography of Oklahoma.* Ardmore, Okla., Bunn Brothers, 1909.

———. *Oklahoma Place Names.* Norman, University of Oklahoma Press, 1933.

———. *Travels Through Oklahoma.* Oklahoma City, Harlow Publishing Co., 1928.

Harris, Phil. *This Is Three Forks Country.* Muskogee, Okla., Hoffman Printing Co., 1965.

Henderson, Arn. *Document for an Anonymous Indian.* Norman, Point Riders Press, 1974.

History of Sequoyah County, 1829–1975. Sallisaw, Okla., Sequoyah County Historical Society, 1976.

Hofsommer, Donovan L. *Katy Northwest.* Boulder, Colo., Pruett Publishing Co., 1976.

Jackson, Berenice (ed). *A History of Beaver County.* Beaver City, Okla., Beaver County Historical Society, 1971.

Jayne, Velma T., and Stella C. Rockwell. *O County Faces and Places.* Enid, Okla., Harold Allen, Printer, 1968.

Johnson, Roy M. *Oklahoma South of the Canadian.* Chicago, The S. J. Clarke Publishing Co., Inc., 1925.

Little, William D., Jr. *Oklahoma Historical Markers in the Circulation Territory of the Ada Evening News.* Ada, Okla., News Publishing and Printing Co., n.d.

McGalliard, Mac. *Reporter's Notebook.* Ardmore, Okla., Sprekelmeyer Printing Co., 1973.

McGuire, Paul. *Osage County.* N.p., 1969.

McReynolds, Edwin C. *Oklahoma—A History of the Sooner State.* Norman, University of Oklahoma Press, 1954.

———. *The Seminoles.* Norman, University of Oklahoma Press, 1957.

Makoske, Lucy Jane. *Adair County—History and Legend.* Stilwell, Okla., Chamber of Commerce, 1974.

Mathews, John Joseph. *The Osages.* Norman, University of Oklahoma Press, 1961.

Medlock, Julius Lester. *When Swallows Fly Home.* Oklahoma City, Northwest Printing Company, 1962.

Miller, R. G. *See and Know Oklahoma.* Oklahoma City, Oklahoma Publishing Co., n.d.

Mooney, Charles W. *Doctor in Belle Star Country.* Oklahoma City, The Century Press, 1975.

———. *Localized History of Pottawatomie County, Oklahoma, to 1907.* Midwest City, Okla., Thunderbird Industries, 1971.

Morgan, E. Buford. *The Wichita Mountains: Ancient Oasis of the Prairies.* Waco, Texas, Texian Press, 1973.

Morris, John W. *Oklahoma Geography.* Oklahoma City, Harlow Publishing Corporation, 1965.

———(ed.). *Geography of Oklahoma.* Oklahoma City, Oklahoma Historical Society, 1977.

———, Charles R. Goins, and Edwin C. McReynolds. *Historical Atlas of Oklahoma.* 2d ed. Norman, University of Oklahoma Press, 1976.

Murphy, Joseph F. *Tenacious Monks.* Shawnee, Okla., Benedictine Color Press, 1974.

Oklahoma State Gazetteer and Business Directory, 1909. Memphis, Tenn., R. L. Polk and Co., 1909.

Osborn, Campbell. *Oklahoma Comes of Age.* Oklahoma City, The Campbell Publishers, 1965.

Peck, Henry L. *The Proud Heritage of LeFlore County.* Muskogee, Okla., Hoffman Printing Co., 1963.

Ragland, Hobert D. *The History of Rush Springs.* Rush Springs, Okla., Gazette Publishing Co., 1952.

Rhyne, Jennings J. *Social and Community Problems of Oklahoma.* Guthrie, Okla., Co-operative Publishing Co., 1929.

Rister, Carl Coke. *No Man's Land.* Norman, University of Oklahoma Press, 1948.

———. *Oil! Titan of the Southwest.* Norman, University of Oklahoma Press, 1949.

Roff, Charles L. *We Were Young Together.* New York, Vantage Press, 1973.

Rouse, M. C. *Cowboy Flat: From Cow Country to Combine.* N.p., n.d.

Ruth, Kent. *Oklahoma Travel Handbook.* Norman, University of Oklahoma Press, 1977.

———. *Window on the Past.* Oklahoma City, Oklahoma Publishing Co., 1974.

———(ed.). *Oklahoma—A Guide to the Sooner State.* Norman, University of Oklahoma Press, 1957.

Shirk, George H. *Oklahoma Place Names.* Norman, University of Oklahoma Press, 1974.

Smallwood, James (ed.). *And Gladly Teach.* Norman, University of Oklahoma Press, 1976.

Snider, L. C. *Geography of Oklahoma.* Norman, Oklahoma Geological Survey, 1917.

Spear, Tommie (ed.). *History of Sequoyah County, 1828–1975.* Sallisaw, Sequoyah County Historical Society, 1976.

Stanley, Ruth Houston. *Iowa Chapel Community.* N.p., 1975.

Stoner, Elbert. *The Spirit of '89.* Edmond, Okla., Old North Books, 1969.

Teal, Kaye M. *Black History in Oklahoma.* Oklahoma City, Oklahoma City Public Schools, 1971.

Thoburn, Joseph B. *Oklahoma: A History.* New York, Lewis Historical Publishing Co., Inc., 1929.

Wallace, Allie B. *Frontier Life in Oklahoma.* Washington, D.C., Public Affairs Press, 1964.

Wardell, Morris L. *Political History of the Cherokees.* Norman, University of Oklahoma Press, 1938.

Webb, Guy P. *History of Grant County, Oklahoma: 1811–1970.* North Newton, Kansas, Grant County Historical Society, 1971.

Wells, Laura Lou. *Young Cushing in Oklahoma Territory.* Stillwater, Okla., Frontier Printers, Inc., 1975.

Wilson, Steve. *Oklahoma Treasures and Treasure Tales.* Norman, University of Oklahoma Press, 1976.

Wornstaff, Marie M. *The History of Hinton.* Hinton, Okla., Wettengel Publishing Co., 1974.

Wyatt, Robert Lee, III. *Gateway to the Big Pasture—Devol.* Marceline, Mo., Walsworth Publishers, 1974.

———. *Grandfield—The Hub of the Big Pasture.* Marceline, Mo., Walsworth Publishers, 1974.

Journals

Each of the following journals has published articles about numerous towns and settlements of Oklahoma.

The Chronicles of Oklahoma. Published quarterly by the Oklahoma Historical Society, 2100 North Lincoln Boulevard, Oklahoma City.

Great Plains Journal. Published semiannually by the Institute of the Great Plains, Elmer Thomas Park, Lawton, Okla.

Oklahoma Today. Published quarterly by the Division of Tourism and Recreation, Will Rogers Memorial Building, Oklahoma City.

Prairie Lore. Published quarterly by the Southwestern Oklahoma Historical Society, 916½ B Avenue, Lawton, Okla.

Index

226

228